PENGU

THE PRINCESS AT THE WINDOW

Donna Laframboise has been writing a weekly opinion column for *The Toronto Star* since 1992. Her work has also appeared in *The Globe and Mail* and *Toronto Life*. She holds a degree in Women's Studies from the University of Toronto and is currently a member of the Board of Directors of the Canadian Civil Liberties Association.

DONNA LAFRAMBOISE

THE PRINCESS AT THE WINDOW

A *new gender morality*

Penguin Books

PENGUIN BOOKS
Published by the Penguin Group
Penguin Books Canada Ltd, 10 Alcorn Avenue, Toronto, Ontario, Canada M4V 3B2
Penguin Books Ltd, 27 Wrights Lane, London W8 5TZ, England
Penguin Books USA Inc., 375 Hudson Street, New York, New York 10014, U.S.A.
Penguin Books Australia Ltd, Ringwood, Victoria, Australia
Penguin Books (NZ) Ltd, 182-190 Wairau Road, Auckland 10, New Zealand

Penguin Books Ltd, Registered Offices: Harmondsworth, Middlesex, England

Published in Penguin Books, 1996

10 9 8 7 6 5 4 3 2 1

Copyright © Donna Laframboise, 1996

Manufactured in Canada

Canadian Cataloguing in Publication Data

Laframboise, Donna.
The princess at the window

ISBN 0-14-025690-3

1. Feminism—Canada. 2. Feminism—United States. I. Title.

HQ1453.L34 1996   305.42'0971   C95-932638-3

Excerpts from the following used by permission.
Hot and Bothered: Sex and Love in the '90s. Reprinted by permission of Wendy Dennis. Copyright © 1992 Wendy Dennis.
The Myth of Male Power: Why Men are the Disposable Sex. Reprinted by permission of Warren Farrell. Copyright © 1993 by Warren Farrell

The sudden assertion of human criteria within a dehumanizing framework of political manipulation can be like a flash of lightning illuminating a dark landscape. And truth is suddenly truth again, reason is reason, and honour honour.

–Vaclav Havel
"Letter to Alexander Dubcek"
August 9, 1969

for Alan, my husband and my best friend

Acknowledgments

My heartfelt thanks to all those who provided encouragement and assistance. To Toronto Star publisher John Honderich for taking a chance on a young, unknown writer four years ago. To Canadian Civil Liberties Association general counsel, Alan Borovoy, a hero from my teen years whom I never dreamed I'd get to have lunch with on a regular basis. To Robert Fulford for introducing me to my agent, Beverley Slopen, whose good cheer and firm manner keep me well grounded. To publisher Cynthia Good and all the other fabulous people at Penguin Canada, who've made my first book-publishing experience a true delight.

Princess might not have been written if it were not for the generosity of my mother-in-law, Louise Jolley, who permitted me to escape to her hideaway and never let me know how worried she was that I was there alone. A big 'thank you,' also, to my parents, Euclide and Katherine; to Connie Cassis, Janice Dean, John Dunlop, Anne Francis, Amy Friedman, Donna Gollan, Peter Israel, Greg Laframboise, Catherine Marjoribanks, Marguerite Martindale, Irene Ogrizek, Lisa Pomerant, Marjaleena Repo, Kevin Speicher, John Sweet, Helen Takala, Stephen Trumper and Rebecca Walsh for all your help. Professionally and personally, I've been blessed.

Contents

Introduction
1

PART ONE—*Whither the Women's Movement?*

1. Ann Landers and the Lunatic Fringe   15
2. He Says, She Says   49
3. Double Standards, '90s Style   87
4. Office Politics   128

PART TWO—*Flinging Open New Windows*

5. Enter: The Men's Movement   167
6. Men and Power   203
7. Our Secret Garden   240
8. Sex, Lies and Court Transcripts   277

Epilogue:
Approaching Tomorrow
313

Notes
325

Introduction

Once upon a time there was a princess with silken hair and bright, flashing eyes. She lived in a beautiful castle, surrounded by luxury. But an evil spell had been cast on her when she was a small child. One day, while she stood looking out her bedroom window, thick vines grew up from the floor and spread over her feet, rooting her to that one spot. From that day forward, the princess had to sleep sitting upright in a velvet-lined chair. She had to have her long, shimmering gowns and breakfasts of fruit and honey brought to her each morning.

The princess spent much of her time staring down at the bluebells and hollyhocks that grew beneath her window. Through silver opera glasses, she watched the songbirds flit from tree branch to tree branch and the squirrels chase each other through the royal hedges. By the time she was a young woman, the princess knew a great deal about the garden—and had come to believe the entire world was just like it.

When her brother told her that, to the south of the castle, a gurgling stream flowed down from the mountains and passed under a lavender bridge, the princess laughed. "We all know water comes in ponds," she said, pointing to the one below her window. "There's no such thing as a stream, so don't try to confuse me."

When her father told her that, to the west, the trees grew

dark and tall so it was always shade, and only a few white flowers managed to bloom near the cool earth, the princess scoffed. "Flowers appear in abundance," she said impatiently. "They're many-hued and gorgeous and lush. Just look out my window, Father. How can you say such a thing?"

When her mother told her that, near the eastern entrance to the castle, the frogs were bluish-green with voices as beautiful as nightingales, the princess grew angry. "I've spent years studying frogs, here at this ledge," she said. "I understand them better than you ever will. And I'm telling you, Mother," she declared coldly, her face turning ugly with rage, "that frogs are greyish-green and have rasping, loathsome voices."

The king and queen consulted far and wide about how to break the spell, but nothing helped free their daughter. Then, one afternoon, the sky darkened. The ground shook and the castle trembled as a whirling tornado swept through the kingdom. Arriving at the princess's room, the king and queen gasped. The vines that had imprisoned their child for so long were now withered and limp, but the room was empty.

From down another hallway, they heard the princess shrieking. "Oh dear, oh dear!" she shouted. "This isn't right. It isn't right, I say."

The whirling winds had set the princess down in front of a different window. But just as the king and queen arrived, a new set of vines pushed up through the floor and wound around their daughter's feet once again.

Later, having become used to her new view, the princess hugged her parents for the first time in many months. "How silly I've been," she said, looking out at the winding stream that gurgled beneath the lavender bridge, "to believe in such things as ponds. It's obvious that water comes from the mountains, that it flows and flows, going right by us without stopping."

The princess put her opera glasses to her eyes. "Never speak to me of ponds again," she said.

Like the princess, when our society embraces one idea, it has a tendency to repudiate totally another. Like the princess, we aren't very good at remembering the complexity of the world around us—at acknowledging that ponds *and* streams can exist at the same time. Instead, the pendulum of public opinion swings from one extreme to the next.

Not long ago, the traditional family was considered a necessary component of a healthy, stable society. Today, it's frequently portrayed as the root of all evil, as a place where violence and abuse flourish. Not long ago, sexual harassment wasn't even recognized as a problem in the workplace. Today, merely being *accused* of a minor offence can destroy a man's career. Not long ago, qualities and characteristics traditionally considered male were exalted over female ones. Today, it seems the most admirable traits are feminine, while anything masculine is now suspect.

Personally, I think of humanity as inhabiting an enormous castle with hundreds of windows, each of which reveals something important about our world. I invite you to accompany me to another floor of the castle, to brush away the cobwebs from the glass and to peer out through a different window at gender politics, at the common ground women and men still share.

I was born in 1963, three years before the National Organization for Women was founded in the United States and nine years before its counterpart, the National Action Committee on the Status of Women, was established in Canada. My mother was sixteen years old when she got married and eighteen when she gave birth to me, the first of her three children. She never finished high school and has spent her paid working life cooking, cleaning and waitressing. My father is an auto mechanic. Oil and grease have seasoned his hands and discoloured his fingernails. He works for a company that owns school buses and, on bitterly cold winter mornings when they worry about whether or not the engines will shudder into wakefulness, he still punches in extra early.

Even before I left my parents' home and their rural community, I was an activist. I wrote hotheaded articles for a local newspaper and was accused of being unpatriotic, anti-religious and a Communist. I sent elected officials letters protesting nuclear waste and formed an environmental group in my high school. I attended meetings in support of native land claims and, while native classmates travelled to the nation's capital for a demonstration, organized a local picket in support.

When I was in my early twenties and living in the big city, Gloria Steinem came to town to promote her first book, *Outrageous Acts and Everyday Rebellions*. Together with my now-sister-in-law, I lined up to see her, wishing I'd bought a few more copies in order to give away the precious autographed volumes as gifts. When it was our turn to approach the platform where she sat, I swallowed my nervousness long enough to tell her I thought she was "wonderful." She replied in her calm, measured way, "I think we're all wonderful." My high lasted for days.

Also around that time, I attended an information evening on midwifery—not because I had plans to become pregnant any time soon but because Michele Landsberg, one of Canada's most prominent feminists (whose feisty newspaper columns I greatly admired), was a guest speaker. After viewing the documentary film *Not a Love Story*, I became convinced pornography was harmful to women. I bought my mother a copy of *Our Bodies, Ourselves* and donated feminist books to public libraries.

I enrolled as an undergraduate at the University of Toronto and went on to complete a double major in English and women's studies. I took courses on women and the law, women in western political thought, women and religion, British women writers and so forth. The women's studies department gave out two awards. I received one of them, the Helen Gregory MacGill Prize, in my first year. Later, I graduated *magna cum laude*.

Consequently, I know a good deal about feminism, and about why this movement was and is so necessary. I know that Aristotle considered women inferior because they supposedly lacked qualities men possess, and that Thomas Aquinas viewed female persons as defective males. I know that women used to be prohibited from owning property, and that religious authorities routinely advised women to be ruled by their husbands. I know that Saudi Arabian women still are not permitted to drive and cannot travel outside the country without their spouses' permission. I know that women are brutally beaten, raped and murdered by violent males.

I'm one of those people who, on a regular basis, turned up at pro-choice events to support free-standing abortion clinics during the bitter struggles of the 1980s. I've been a union shop steward, a peace activist and an International Women's Day organizer. I currently sit on the board of directors of the Canadian Civil Liberties Association. I've long been a proponent of female self-defence training, and my articles on this topic have appeared in Canada's most prominent newspapers as well as in the *Canadian Woman Studies* journal.[1] When I got married, I kept my own name.

In short, my personal history attests to the fact that I am neither an anti-feminist, a racist nor a right-winger. Nor would it be accurate to describe me as "a good girl whose opinions are dutifully in line with prevailing prejudice." Nevertheless, I've been called such things recently, either directly or by implication, because some of the columns I now write for *The Toronto Star* (Canada's largest daily newspaper) have dared to criticize certain trends in the North American women's movement.

And frankly, I'm getting ticked off.

As a social activist my first allegiance has been to principles such as reason, fairness and justice. I haven't devoted time and energy to feminist causes simply so that a group I belong to could acquire privileges and benefits for itself; my aim has been to help make the world *in general* a better place. In other words, what's of immediate benefit to women and what's reasonable and fair aren't necessarily the same thing. Since males aged fifteen to forty commit most of the rapes in our society,[2] it might benefit women if all males of that age were herded onto army bases and forced to remain there during those years. But such a course of action would be both unreasonable and unjust. It would punish millions of innocent men. It would deny them basic freedoms and disrupt their lives in an unconscionable manner. No one who believes in fair play could support such a proposal, however strong a feminist she might be.

Which is why people who criticize the women's movement aren't automatically its enemies. There *are* individuals who'd like to return us to a world of rigid sex roles in which women remain barefoot and pregnant in the kitchen, but while pockets of such thinking continue to exist, large expanses of society have rejected such attitudes. For example, public opinion polls today tell us that young men are even more relaxed about having a female boss than older women are.[3] When we look back at all the thousands of years of human history, we have to admit that the few generations currently inhabiting the industrialized world have moved in the right direction on women's issues at breathtaking speed. The idea that women are men's equals has triumphed. Things are far from perfect, but the Bastille has been stormed and it has fallen—and remarkably few lives have been lost during the course of this fundamental, revolutionary change in social beliefs and attitudes.

Now it's important that we regain a sense of perspective and proportion. We have to remember that it's *justice* for which we've fought. When feminism gets tangled up in confused thinking, when it starts demanding measures that are unjust, we all have a moral duty to protest. The only way those who do so can be considered enemies is if the women's movement never was about justice in the first place but was instead merely an exercise in grab-all-you-can-get politics, or in the exchanging of one oppressive social order for another.

Feminism must be as open to criticism as any other philosophy in our culture. It must be judged by the same standards. We must be prepared to acknowledge that a lie is still a lie—even when it's told by feminists with good intentions.

In this book I argue that today's North American feminism is giving female equality a bad name, that it is extremist, self-obsessed, arrogant and intolerant. While such elements have always been present in feminism, as in other social movements, I argue that it is now impossible to distinguish these elements from the mainstream. I show how popular feminist spokespersons and the mainstream feminist press have embraced personalities with offensive, bigoted opinions, and how highly questionable ideas have been elevated to feminist dogma. Moreover, I demonstrate the alarming manner in which such views are permeating popular culture, influencing public policy and receiving official sanction from our social and political institutions.

It is precisely because such thinking is not confined to the pages of obscure journals, but is instead having a profound effect on ordinary people's lives, that feminism risks generating a backlash far worse than the one alleged to have occurred during the 1980s. Sooner or later, a society inundated with loony feminist notions is going to slam on the brakes. When that happens, the very idea of feminism, together with all its positive contributions, will become suspect. The general public will harden its heart and grow cynical. Its knee-jerk tendency will be to dismiss all feminist protest out of hand and to declare itself weary of complaints regarding female disadvantage, no matter how justified they might be. Since a social climate in which the notion of female equality has lost its respectability will likely be more dangerous to women than the current state of affairs, it behoves those of us who care about such matters to try to prevent this from occurring.

In its broadest sense feminism can be defined as a belief that women should have the same social, political and economic rights as men. But just as there are many kinds of Christians—pacifist Quakers, Jehovah's Witnesses and right-wing fundamentalists all call themselves by this name—there are also different kinds of feminists. This book is concerned with mainstream feminism, with the people who are recognized, by society at large, as legitimate feminist spokespersons. Sometimes I refer to these people as "establishment" feminists.

Over the past few years, a growing number of women have written books critical of mainstream feminism. Among them are Rene Denfeld, Amy Friedman, Camille Paglia, Daphne Patai and Noretta Koertge, Katie Roiphe and Christina Hoff Sommers. I refer to these women as "dissident" feminists. While I have my disagreements with a number of them, they have all influenced my thinking, and their voices have sustained me during dark moments of despair. Some of them have been accused of jumping on a bandwagon, of trying to attract attention to themselves, of attempting to cash in on a media backlash against feminism. But it should come as no surprise that women of different ages and in different parts of North America have been looking at the same trends in a movement we care about and have been arriving at similar conclusions. It should come as no surprise that a number of us have, independently of one another, spent the past few years gathering our research material, refining our arguments and then writing books such as this one. My own work has questioned feminist assumptions and practices since early 1991, before I'd heard of any of my above-mentioned sisters. And I have often felt like a voice in the wilderness.

But this is much more than a book about what's gone wrong with the women's movement. I believe it's possible to intercept the pendulum in mid-swing, before it reaches the outer limit and then slices through all of us on the rebound. In Part Two of this book, therefore, I argue that our old ways of looking at gender issues are no longer adequate. I argue that it's time to take the next logical step, to re-examine the assumptions that underlie our beliefs about men, women and sexual politics, and to give a fair hearing to the ideas percolating in the emerging men's movement.

Because once you become used to questioning prevailing social norms, something unexpected can happen. You can begin to observe that, while women often do have a difficult time, life isn't necessarily a walk in the park for men, either. While women's options have been restricted by society's expectations of us, men are also required to fit themselves into moulds that are confining and restrictive.

In North America, as late as the 1970s, many girls and women weren't permitted to wear trousers to school or work. These policies changed after they were challenged by feminism. Women, it was argued, weren't going to lose their femininity simply by wearing clothes society had arbitrarily designated as "masculine."[4] Now, a woman can get up in the morning and, depending on her mood, put on a floral print dress, a miniskirt, a hot-pink belt, a three-piece suit, pantihose, blue jeans, an oversized shirt with leggings, high heels or thigh-high boots. She can wear lots of make-up or no make-up. She can carry a purse or not. She can tie a large floppy hat on her head or wear a baseball cap backward. A woman can walk down the street dressed in any of the above and no one is going to suspect her of being homosexual, mentally unstable or a sex offender.

But how many of the options I've just listed are open to someone who happens to have been born male? The suit, the blue jeans and the baseball cap. Fewer than one-third. If the sexes were reversed in this instance, if society were telling women they were permitted only one option for every three men enjoyed, feminists would be raising the roof, and rightly so. This is, quite simply, a blatant case of sex discrimination. While it may appear at first glance to be a trivial one, it reveals our societal blindness. Not only is this a double standard few of us have even noticed, it's one that many of our fellow citizens might consider necessary. How many people do you know who would be comfortable allowing a small child to talk to a man wearing spiked heels and make-up at the bus stop, or would want their daughter to date him?

How is it that a society set up to benefit men at the expense of women (as feminism insists it has been) continues to restrict males to such a small number of clothing choices long after it gave up dictating such nonsense to women? How do we explain the fact that we compel male but not female children to internalize such a long list of clothing taboos? If the clothes we wear function, at least partly, as modes of personal expression, why does male personal expression continue to be so narrowly defined in a world men have deliberately designed for their own advantage?

On prom night in May 1993, an eighteen-year-old Knoxville, Iowa, student was arrested at his own high school for trespassing. His crime consisted of showing up in the red, sequined, spaghetti-strap dress his sister had worn to her prom the year before. According to the media, the school had been aware of the young man's plans a day in advance and had tried to discourage him. The decision to involve police, therefore, appears not to have been made in the heat of the moment by a flustered chaperone. Rather, it was a calculated case of calling in the heavy artillery to enforce a sexist social convention—a convention that dis-criminates against males.[5]

In October 1994, a teenager in Barrie, Ontario, was walking home from a dance club with his girlfriend when a group of harassing, taunting young men began to follow them. The couple ducked into a convenience store, hoping to shake them off, but the group was in hot pursuit. Shortly afterward, the sixteen-year-old male was viciously attacked. He was punched and kicked so severely that his jaw was broken in at least two places, necessitating surgery. Police officers (I spoke to them directly at the time) were able to discover only one reason for the attack. The victim was wearing a kilt.[6]

Men have it all, don't they? The world is their oyster. Everything has been set up to promote their freedom and convenience. Or maybe it's more complicated than that.

In recent decades, women have asserted our right to an increasing number of choices. We've demanded a share in all those things that had been considered off limits simply because of our sex. We've insisted that society stop viewing us as "female" and start treating us as "human," that it quit forcing us to conform to conventional notions of what women like, want or are. I agree, absolutely, with all of this. But sometimes feminism has seen only what it was inclined to see. Indeed, it appears that we've been so preoccupied with the "women are getting a bad deal" perspective that we have—inadvertently or otherwise—begun boarding up other windows in the castle, denying that they even exist.

Just because women's lives have been twisted and maimed by their sex role throughout history doesn't mean men's haven't as well. Both these things can be true at the same time. Nor is this a contest. It may be that women have borne the brunt of the injustice in the world. If you could tally up all the terrible things that have happened to women throughout history *because they were women* (such as infanticide, sexual assault and forced prostitution) and compare it with all the terrible things that have happened to men *because they were men* (such as being blown apart in rat-infested, mud-filled trenches during wartime), perhaps women would be the "winners," or, rather, the losers. As horrifying as such a finding would be to many feminists, it isn't overly relevant. *Human* suffering is the issue, here. Human suffering is what any moral person is opposed to. Which set of reproductive organs—or which race/religion/nationality/sexual orientation, etc.—is associated with the person experiencing the agony is, in the final analysis, beside the point.

It would appear that we feminists, who have declared ourselves experts on gender relations and sex-role stereotyping, have missed a few things. Despite the fact that men face more restrictive rules when it comes to clothing than do women, for example, we've overlooked it completely. We haven't incorporated it into our analysis of who has free choice and who hasn't. And if we've missed something so obvious, perhaps we should be asking ourselves what else we have failed to take into account. What other insights might expand our understanding of how sex roles affect all our lives?

Incidentally, I don't think we feminists should be too hard on ourselves. Many of our mistakes and excesses were understandable in a young movement full of energetic but inexperienced and politically naive people. But feminism isn't an infant any longer and it can no longer be excused for acting like one, for making incessant demands while remaining oblivious to the needs, rights and hurts of others who share the same planet.

I believe it's now time to make a small but significant perceptual shift: to release our minds from the category of "women's rights" and to start thinking, genuinely, about the broader notion of "gender issues"—about how the accident of being born male or female has, for too long, prohibited each of us from achieving our full potential and from affirming our truest selves.

If we want to move beyond our current state of gender hostility and finger-pointing, if we want to achieve a saner, more humane society, women and men need to acknowledge that the world is a complex place containing both ponds and streams, stout hollyhocks and delicate crocuses, frogs with melodic voices and with grating ones. We need to acknowledge that just because women have been forced to conform to dehumanizing stereotypes doesn't mean men haven't as well. That just because women suffer doesn't mean men don't too, albeit sometimes in different ways.

We need to reaffirm our commitment to truth, reason and justice. We need to arrive at a new understanding of our respective experiences.

PART ONE

Whither the Women's Movement?

Looking back over my life, which has now lasted sixty-six years, what I see is a succession of great mass events, boilings up of emotion, of wild partisan passion, that pass, but while they last it is not possible to do more than think: "These slogans, or these accusations, these claims, these trumpetings, quite soon they will seem to everyone ridiculous and even shameful."

–Doris Lessing[1]

CHAPTER ONE

Ann Landers and the Lunatic Fringe

In January 1995, newspaper advice columnist Ann Landers published a letter from a LONGTIME READER IN ST. LOUIS. After fifty-three years of marriage, ST. LOUIS's wife had died recently. His letter contained a list of things he wished he'd done more often while she was alive. In addition to encouraging her to play the piano, take walks with him and travel more frequently, the grieving widower wrote, "I should have told her I loved her every day, without fail, kissed her more often and brought home flowers for no special reason."

A month earlier, Ann had printed a query from SYD, asking whether it was appropriate to offer to contribute money toward the baby-sitter after inviting a woman who had children out on a date. Perplexed about what is and isn't proper behaviour in the confusing '90s, but wanting to do the right thing, SYD explained, "There are times when the sitter costs more than the dinner check. I'd like to chip

15

in and help the woman out."

On another occasion, CHINO VALLEY, ARIZ. told Ann that although her husband isn't as romantic as she would like, he is dearly cherished. "This wonderful guy got up at 5 a.m. last week and put new tires on my bike," wrote CHINO. "He does the dishes every night so I can rest up from my day, even though his might have been tougher. And he is a fabulous father to our three children."

In September 1994, PEGGY IN O'FALLON wrote about how she'd learned "honesty, respect, courage, faith, responsibility and kindness" from her father, who'd grown up in the Depression and had been forced to join the work force before completing grade eight. "I thank God every day for giving me such a fine role model," said PEGGY. "I am happily married to a man who is very much like my dad."

Readers of Ann's column also heard, on the same day, from STILL IN LOVE, who wrote: "After 29 years of marriage I realize that I am no longer Number 1 in my wife's life." LOVE said he felt he came somewhere after the houseplants, the pet cats and the couple's two adult children on his wife's list of priorities. His final paragraph read: "Actually, I don't believe it's necessary to be Number 1 every day. As long as I am on her list, I am satisfied."[2]

In these letters, males are flesh and blood. They are loving husbands and fathers. They are single men sensitive to the financial circumstances of their dates. They are also people who have made compromises with life that strike some of us as sad. This isn't the only view of men one gets in Ann Landers, of course. Here, as elsewhere, there is no shortage of alcoholic or philandering husbands, men who ignore their families during medical emergencies in order to play golf, thirty-nine-year-olds afraid to tell their parents they're living with someone and men who beat their wives and rape their acquaintances.[3] But the point is that that's not *all* they are.

In the world according to Ann Landers, men are diverse creatures. If the only thing you knew about human males was what you'd read in Ann's columns, it would be difficult to say anything about them as a group. While some of them behave badly, others conduct themselves admirably. While some are cowardly, others are honourable. While some are aggressive, others are passive. And while some are callous, others are self-sacrificing. In short, men, because they are first and foremost human beings, run the gamut.

So, too, do women. Many of Ann's correspondents praise women to the heavens: they are strangers who perform touching acts of random kindness, teachers who inspire children to look forward to school each day, loving mothers and people described as "fine, strong [and] lovely" by their ex's new spouse.

It's also abundantly clear that some women have plenty of negative qualities. They are grandmothers who emotionally manipulate those around them, causing marriage breakdowns while destroying "every vestige of joy" in their homes. They are mothers who neglect their children in favour of soap operas. They are housewives who cause their hard-working husbands unending grief with their irresponsible use of credit cards. They are people who secretly make duplicate keys and let themselves into their grown children's homes to snoop.[4]

In late 1994, Ann published a letter that accused her of fabricating a correspondence from a woman who'd been surprised by her daughter's seventeen-year-old boyfriend while skinny-dipping in the family pool. The woman reported that she was infatuated with the young man, who had kissed her and now wished to begin an affair. Ann insisted she hadn't made it up. "I've received stacks of letters from teenage girls who view their mothers as serious competition," she responded. "Moreover, some girls have stated frankly that their mothers are extremely aggressive and 'up to plenty.'"

A few months previously, a middle-aged man from GAINESVILLE, FLA. told Ann about his alcoholic wife of twenty years: "Her constant arguing has given me high blood pressure and headaches," he wrote. "I have heard her pray for me to die. She's told me many times that she hates me. Several weeks ago, I set up an appointment with a marriage counselor, but she canceled it."

There was also the May 1994 letter from SEEN TOO MUCH, the brother of a man married to an abusive wife. She "trashed my brother's car, shredded his clothes, threw bleach in his face and tried to run him over with her car," wrote TOO MUCH. "She swears she is going to kill him even if she has to hang for it." Although the couple had been separated for a year, the woman continued to stalk and attack her husband.[5]

Ann Landers, the thousands of people who write to her and the millions who read her column faithfully acknowledge that, as well as being sugar and spice and everything nice, the female half of the population has its darker side. Like men, the group of people we call "women" is made up of fabulous individuals as well as horrible ones.

It's not possible to reach a conclusion that's even remotely scientific from the anecdotes or opinions that appear in these columns, of course. We can't determine that more males are devoted family men than irresponsible ne'er-do-wells, or that most females are conscientious and caring rather than shallow and nasty. But the fact that Ann Landers has been a long-standing fixture in hundreds of respectable newspapers suggests that the issues she chooses to highlight strike a chord with a significant portion of the North American population, that ordinary people consider the world she reflects to be a reasonably authentic one.

In Ann's universe, men *and* women bring other people immense joy and cause them intense pain. But this diverse, complex view is quite different from the one being disseminated by mainstream North American feminism. Social movements always have their lunatic fringe, of course. The peace movement, civil rights campaigns, pro-life forces—they have all been known to attract people who make outrageous, fanatical statements and who sometimes are prepared to commit criminal acts in addition to violating laws of common decency. It isn't fair to judge a social movement by its few inevitable nutbars. But when the mainstream of the movement refuses to distance itself from extremist elements—when, in fact, it embraces them—then there's a problem.

On those occasions when people complain about the tone of feminism these days (in newspaper opinion columns, for example), the inevitable response goes something like this: There may be some feminists who are a little unhinged, who bash men, but that's not what feminism means to most people. Feminism, for most of us, is simply about fairness. In the words of one woman responding to a newspaper column, it's about "equal opportunity, equal respect and equal partnerships with men." We know, says this writer, "that the majority of men are honest and decent."[6]

This is the sort of feminism to which I also subscribe. But are these, in fact, the messages emanating from mainstream feminism in the 1990s? I invite you to turn to a book titled *The War Against Women*. Published in 1992, it was written by Marilyn French, who is described, on the cover, as a best-selling "author and feminist scholar." French's 1977 novel, *The Women's Room*, had an important impact on my own thinking and functioned as a consciousness-raiser for a generation of women.

Her thesis in *The War Against Women* is that men have been waging a centuries-long global attack on women. According to her, men have a "need to dominate women" and carry out a "purposeful policy" of oppression against them, up to and including murder.[7] She claims that "all male violence toward women is part of a concerted campaign," that controlling female reproduction "is a silent agenda in every level of male activity" and that men have a "deep, unacknowledged sexual hatred of women."[8]

Her book is full of statements such as: "Most films and television shows are produced by men for men. Their *main purposes* are to show white males triumphant, to teach gender roles, and to cater to *men's delight* in male predation and victimization of women [my italics]."[9]

Although French says her comments aren't directed against individual men and admits that any specific male may allow his "affectionate respect" for a woman to overcome his "drive to control her," that doesn't stop her from alleging that female oppression is maintained by ordinary men "with a fervor and dedication to duty that any secret police force might envy."[10] Arguing that it isn't necessary to physically assault women in order to keep them down, French provides a list of ten things she says the "*vast majority of men in the world do one or more of* [original italics]." Since this list apparently proves that men as a group are objectionable, I've paraphrased it here, rearranging the order somewhat to make it easier to analyze:

1. Not hiring women for well-paying jobs
2. Paying women less than men for doing the same or more work
3. Beating their spouse
4. Murdering their spouse
5. Raping women they know or women who are strangers
6. Sexually molesting female children
7. Failing to pay child support
8. Treating women "disrespectfully" at work

9. Treating women "disrespectfully" at home
10. Expecting spouses to be their servants[11]

To start with, while it's true that many men make decisions regarding the hiring and pay rates of female employees, *most* men do not. My father, for example, who has punched a time-clock throughout his working life, has never been in a position to commit the first two crimes that appear on this list. For every manager making such decisions, whether in a bank or a steel plant, there are many more employees who have no opportunity to do so.

What about the next four? Battering, murdering, raping and sexually molesting. Some men do commit these crimes, and any number of them is too many. But *most men* do not. Think of the males in your family, your neighbourhood, or at your workplace. If French wants to argue that the majority of men are guilty of these horrors, she's going to have to provide more convincing evidence than her own say-so, since most people's experience of the world tells us this is false. It's a mistake to accept as true a theory that bears no relation whatsoever to the world in which you live. People who want you to disregard the evidence in front of your nose should be required to meet a high standard of proof.

Point number seven: not supporting one's children. Once again, there's no question that some men financially abandon their offspring. We call them "deadbeat dads," a term that makes it clear society disapproves of such behaviour. But if French wants to claim that *most* of the men who father children refuse to support them, we need hard data—not data about how many divorced men are in arrears, but what percentage of *all* fathers this represents.

Points eight through ten, treating women disrespectfully at work or home and expecting spouses to act as servants, are a little trickier. How can we know whether most males have or have not behaved disrespectfully to someone belonging to half the human race, or whether they've ever treated their wives like servants? I've certainly behaved disrespectfully toward people who happen to be women, and have sometimes expected my husband to perform more than his fair share of the household chores while I've struggled to meet deadlines. I also wonder whether many of us could plead innocent to treating our mothers—to whom we surely owe as much consideration as our spouses—as servants from time to time? If French is talking about the kinds of minor offences that characterize everyday life, then, without a doubt, most men *as well as most women* are guilty of the last three transgressions on her list and therefore are appalling human beings.

If, however, she wants to argue that the majority of men blatantly domineer over the women in their lives, either at work or at home, that's another matter—and one even more difficult to verify. There certainly are jerks who believe their wives should be constantly jumping up to fetch them a cold beer, but if we think back to the Ann Landers letters, in a number of cases it was women who set the tone in the home. An abusive wife, a manipulative grandmother or a woman who considers her husband less important than her houseplants isn't being oppressed by the men around her. Even if we were to fall back on the argument that there are more abusive husbands than wives (the truth of which is a whole other matter and will be discussed later), that still fails to prove that *most* males treat women like garbage.

This raises another issue: French's repeated use of Third World examples to tar the men living in industrialized nations. My younger brother, who prepares the majority of the meals he and his fiancée eat at home, should not be lumped in with Kenyan men who, French tells us, "gamble, buy liquor, and rent prostitutes, while their families starve," or Afghani males who, she alleges, want to eliminate female education and paid work.[12]

From this perspective, and this perspective only, French is probably right: most men around the globe likely treat women terribly. After all, it's only recently that people living in certain parts of the world have begun questioning centuries-old ideas about male superiority. But if she needs to resort to mixing apples and oranges in order to condemn as hopeless misogynists most of the men her readers share their lives with, then her conclusion is tenuous.

While French admits women possess some power (in families, as well as when they help foster the inflated self-image of men), and although she devotes four sentences to acknowledging that women are also capable of cruelty and abuse (as compared with two hundred pages cataloguing male sins), she never permits these ideas to influence her opinions.[13] Instead, she consistently interprets male behaviour in the worst possible light. According to her, men never go to war to *protect* their families and communities, but because male culture has turned them into bloodthirsty monsters. Fathers don't fight for custody of their children in court because they've been involved with them from the delivery room onward and can't imagine waking up in the morning without them, but merely in order to cause trouble for their ex-wives.[14]

Women, on the other hand, have only the purest of motives in French's view. For example, she tells us that they mutilate the genitals of millions of African girls for altruism's sake, to "save them from being social outcasts." In her words, "women only seem to be in control of the practice [since] men will not marry an unmutilated girl."[15]

The War Against Women, then, tells us that men are violent and depraved, and that they use their power to victimize women. It holds men fully responsible for the fact that the world's a mess. When women misuse *their* power and behave barbarically, it says that's the fault of men too.

In democratic societies such as ours, people have the right not only to hold all sorts of opinions but to share them with large numbers of other people via newspapers, magazines, books, radio, television, film, computer networks and so forth. I believe that that right is essential to a healthy society. Therefore, when I say I seriously doubt French would have found a publisher for *The War Against Women* if she'd been making the same kinds of sweeping generalizations and employing similarly loaded language about any other identifiable group in our society, I'm not suggesting for a moment that her book deserves to be censored. Nevertheless, I think it's worth asking ourselves whether a respectable publisher would have gone near a manuscript that claimed that Jews, gays or the disabled mourn the deaths of their children less than other people do. (French says that when children die, mothers feel the loss more acutely than do fathers.[16])

The larger, more important issue, though, is this: how did mainstream feminism respond to *The War Against Women*? Did other feminists make an effort to dissociate themselves from a book that paints half the human race as violent brutes? Did the feminists we think of as being reasonable and moderate have a problem with statements that compare ordinary men to secret police? Did they feel any discomfort whatsoever with lines such as: "In personal and public life, in kitchen, bedroom and halls of parliament, men wage unremitting war against women"?[17]

The defender of feminism I quoted earlier said most feminists recognize that "the majority of men are honest and decent." French's book includes no such recognition, but that didn't prevent it from being embraced with open arms by mainstream feminism. The paperback copy of *The War Against Women* features an endorsement from Gloria Steinem on the front cover. According to Steinem, North America's most respected and influential feminist spokesperson, "If you can read only one book about what's wrong with this country, *The War Against Women* is it. Marilyn French writes about the state of the world as if women mattered—and (suddenly) we do." *Ms.* magazine (the publication most readily associated with mainstream feminism) described *The War Against Women* as an "impressive marshaling of facts" and a "powerful indictment of patriarchy." Indeed, its brief review was entirely positive. Eighteen months later, when *Ms.* sponsored a round-table discussion about women and pornography, French was one of four guest participants.[18] Evidently, the magazine editors didn't consider the anti-male rhetoric running through *The War Against Women* extreme enough to distance themselves from her.

Nor is the respectability that French enjoys in such circles an isolated phenomenon. When similar opinions are advanced by other fanatically minded individuals, such as law professor Catharine MacKinnon, they too receive a warm reception. Known for her denunciations of pornography, MacKinnon is a prolific writer who travels the continent delivering passionate speeches about how women are victimized by sexually explicit material. Her influence, not only within feminism but radiating outward to society at large, is significant. In the early 1990s, MacKinnon co-authored a brief whose arguments were later adopted by the Supreme Court of Canada, thus fundamentally altering legal notions about what kind of pornography is and is not acceptable within Canadian borders.[19] She says versions of anti-pornography legislation she helped draw up have been introduced in Germany, the Philippines and Sweden.[20] In October 1991, MacKinnon was the subject of a glowing cover story by the *New York Times Magazine*.[21] She has been interviewed by *Ladies' Home Journal* and invited to appear on television shows such as *Donahue* and *Today*. During the Anita Hill–Clarence Thomas hearings,

MacKinnon provided live analysis for NBC TV news. She has also participated in television panel discussions on topics such as date rape.[22]

In women's studies courses, MacKinnon's work routinely turns up as required reading.[23] This wouldn't be a problem if her ideas were being vigorously debated in such classes. But far too often, students are simply told this is what feminism is and what feminists believe.[24]

MacKinnon not only writes for Ms. magazine, she is frequently cited with approval in its pages.[25] Indeed, one 1991 article complained that MacKinnon's colleague Andrea Dworkin, with whom she drafted the anti-pornography legislation, is "sometimes" required to defend this legislation when speaking at U.S. colleges, the implication being that such ideas should be above debate.[26] Naomi Wolf's 1990 feminist best-seller, The Beauty Myth, cites MacKinnon,[27] and when the National Organization for Women was asked about its position on pornography recently, it too sent out a packet that included photocopies of MacKinnon's work.[28]

The fact that mainstream feminism has made no attempt to put distance between itself and MacKinnon is distressing, because the kinds of opinions she has been expressing for over a decade are ones few feminists who enjoy healthy, active sex lives are likely to be comfortable with.

MacKinnon has become famous for her insistence that, in a society where the sexes aren't equal, women are afraid of men or depend on them for economic survival and so aren't in a position to genuinely refuse to participate in sexual intercourse. This means, then, that women can never be viewed as having given consent of our own free will. In other words: all sex is rape. Anyone who thinks this is a distortion of MacKinnon's views is invited to turn to her 1989 book Toward a Feminist Theory of the State, in which she declares:

> Compare victims' reports of rape with women's
> reports of sex. They look a lot alike. Compare vic-
> tims' reports of rape with what pornography says
> sex is. They look a lot alike. In this light, the major
> distinction between intercourse (normal) and rape
> (abnormal) is that the normal happens so often
> that one cannot get anyone to see anything wrong
> with it.[29]

In her 1987 essay "Feminism, Marxism, Method, and the State," she writes:

> Instead of asking, what is the violation of rape,
> what if we ask, what is the non-violation of inter-
> course? To tell what is wrong with rape, explain
> what is right about sex…. Perhaps the wrong of
> rape has proven so difficult to articulate because
> the unquestionable starting point has been that
> rape is definable as distinct from intercourse, when
> for women it is difficult to distinguish them under
> conditions of male dominance.[30]

Elsewhere, she states: "when force is a normalized part of sex, when no is taken to mean yes, when fear and despair produce acquiescence and acquiescence is taken to mean consent, consent is not a meaningful concept."[31] A bit later she adds: "Consent means that whatever you are forced to do is attributed to your free will." MacKinnon suggests that "free speech," "sex" and "women being used" are interchangeable terms and that "sexual freedom" really means "the freedom to abuse." She says that, in our society, "sex is what women *have* to sell, sex is what we are, sex is what we are valued for, we are born sex, we die sex [original italics]."[32]

If MacKinnon were routinely qualifying these statements with phrases such as "in a sense" or "in some situations" or "from a certain point of view, you could say
that..." her opinions wouldn't be so disturbing. Indeed, she
might simply be thought of as an academic who gets carried
away with her own theories from time to time. But as a
lawyer, MacKinnon is well aware that the way things are
phrased is important. If what she really means is that sex is
a horrible experience for *some* women *some* of the time, she
should say so. But she doesn't.

MacKinnon considers the Miss America Pageant and
the most violent pornography to be clearly connected to
one another.[33] Despite there being no evidence that violence against women is any less prevalent in Islamic countries, where porn is strictly prohibited, MacKinnon is
nevertheless convinced that pornography causes sexual
assault and abuse and that it must be eliminated from
North American society.

Whether or not you happen to agree with her views
regarding pornography, there's no disputing the fact that
MacKinnon is on a crusade. And, like other evangelists,
she is an intense, emotionally persuasive and charismatic
speaker. She paints a world of moral absolutes in which
there is no middle ground, no room for ambiguity or
debate. Either you see things her way or you're helping to
promote violence against women. Either you sign on as
foot soldiers in her holy war or you are hopeless sinners
destined to everlasting perdition. (She describes feminists
who disagree with her as "collaborationist" individuals
who are "fronting for male supremacists."[34]) This is the
kind of thinking mainstream feminism is now associated
with. This is what the women's movement has come to in
the 1990s.

There's no question that thousands of women are sexually assaulted by male acquaintances and strangers each

year, but anyone who zeroes in on one kind of violence and then obsesses about it to the point at which it distorts or cancels out everything else deserves to be viewed with a healthy dose of scepticism. It's as though MacKinnon has taken an image of rape, magnified it to hundreds of times its original size and projected it onto a screen so large that for a while we forget that other screens even exist. In the process, the image has become so blurred, its edges so diffuse, that she herself now has trouble distinguishing acts of brutal violence from consensual love-making.

MacKinnon is looking out at the world through one window only. She insists that this window *is* reality, that everything can be reduced to violence against women. (Indeed, she vigorously rejects the notion that her views are simply a "point of view."[35]) Her July/August 1993 Ms. magazine cover story about rapes in the former Yugoslavia, for example, doesn't talk about the cities that are in rubble, the historical treasures that have been lost, the children who are having their psyches moulded by the destruction and cruelty all around them. It doesn't talk about civilians starving to death after being cut off from food and water, or about the thousands of promising young men and women who've died in this war and what a loss this is for all of humanity. Without acknowledging this larger context, MacKinnon zeroes in on the fact that one element of the practice known as "ethnic cleansing" being perpetrated in this conflict involves the systematic rape of some female prisoners and the videotaping of a portion of this violence.

As a result, it's difficult to escape the feeling that MacKinnon cares almost as much about the fact that the harrowing experiences these people have endured provide her with new ammunition as she does about the human beings themselves. I know that's an uncharitable thing to say, but what else are we to make of the highly inappropriate parallels she draws between the situation in that part of the world and pornography and prostitution elsewhere?

MacKinnon begins the second paragraph of her article with the following:

> In what is called peacetime, pornography is made
> from rape in studios, on sets, in private bedrooms,
> in basements, in alleys, in prison cells, and in
> brothels. It should be no surprise to find it being
> made in a "rape theater" in a Serbian-run concen-
> tration camp.... Still, it comes as a shock, a clarify-
> ing jolt.

A page later, she adds, "As it is in this war, prostitution is forced on women every day; what is a brothel but a captive setting for organized serial rape?"[36] To compare the brutal, blood-soaked gang rapes of these prisoners of war to porno-graphic videos produced in North America by film compa-nies employing consenting adults, or by amateurs using camcorders in the comfort of their own homes, is to trivial-ize the barbarity to which this first group of women has been subjected. To compare the campaign of ethnic cleans-ing occurring in Bosnia-Herzegovina to the experiences of women working in Nevada's government-licensed brothels, or even to those who turn tricks in the inner city to pay for their next drug fix, is an affront to the memories of the women who didn't survive such horrors in their devastated homeland.

The absence of qualifiers in the above quotes suggests that both MacKinnon and the editors at Ms. believed she was preaching to the converted. MacKinnon doesn't say that *some* of the videotaping that goes on in private bed-rooms is coerced. I'd have no problem acknowledging that that's true. She doesn't say that *in some parts of the world*— such as Thailand or the Philippines—girls and women are imprisoned in brothels against their will. Rather, she's implying that *all* pornography "is made from rape" and that *all* prostitutes are really having sex against their will.

Since MacKinnon considers even consensual sex in loving relationships rape, these assertions aren't too astonishing. But we should be very clear about what the position of Ms. is in the face of such fanaticism.

First of all, it's conceivable that a magazine might say: "Well, we know this writer has some strange ideas, but there's another side to her work that's much more soberminded. And this particular piece is so outstanding that we've decided to publish it even though we might damage our reputation by aligning ourselves with her." But that's not what occurred here. Rather, MacKinnon said the kinds of things in this article that she's known for saying, and Ms. did everything it could to help her spread the word—they put it on the cover.

In a different vein, it could be argued that it's not so much what Ms. publishes as what it declines to publish that's crucial; that the absence of articles that challenge MacKinnon's hyperbolic assertions is the real problem. Alternatively, it could be claimed that Ms. editors simply put MacKinnon's piece on the cover because they knew controversy attracts readers and sells copies.

While I'm sympathetic to both these perspectives, it's worth considering what the repercussions might be if a mainstream African-American magazine were to publish a cover story authored by black extremist Louis Farrakhan. While it would certainly be appropriate for such a magazine to report on Farrakhan and perhaps even to profile him, a disinterested observer could be forgiven for thinking that any publication that allowed him to *write* the cover story himself, and then presented it without a disclaimer, was, in fact, endorsing his racist and sexist views.

But to get back to MacKinnon's beliefs, if all sex is really rape, then it must follow that all (heterosexual) men are rapists. This is an even more outrageous notion than Marilyn French's contention that most men treat women badly. Yet MacKinnon's message, when it comes to men, is hard to mistake. According to her, pornography tells us that:

> ...what men want is: women bound, women bat-
> tered, women tortured, women humiliated, women
> degraded and defiled, women killed. Or, to be fair
> to the soft core, women sexually accessible, have-
> able, there for them, wanting to be taken and used,
> with perhaps just a little light bondage.[37]

Elsewhere, she writes that men "just want to hurt us, domi-
nate us and control us, and that is fucking us."[38] So much for the kind of feminism that believes "the majority of men are honest and decent."

Moreover, if all men are rapists, then all women are rape victims, even though many of us know we've never had sex against our will and are aware that, on numerous occasions, we were the ones to initiate it. According to MacKinnon, women are also rape victims when they choose to have sex for money, perform as exotic dancers or pose for sexually explicit photos and take part in pornographic films. MacKinnon says it doesn't matter that these women have signed release forms. She's decided that they wouldn't willingly do these things if they weren't being coerced by men or by society at large. She believes she knows better what a perfect stranger would really prefer to be doing.

In other words, women don't really have minds of our own. Our interpretations of our actions and lives aren't important. If MacKinnon were running the world, women would be considered legally incompetent, on the level of a child or a mentally disabled person, when we signed certain kinds of papers—papers that would be legally binding on men.[39]

Anyone tempted to go along with such reasoning should be aware that it opens up a can of worms. If we say that women are, as a group, routinely being coerced into having sex, becoming prostitutes, or posing for porn, what's preventing us from being coerced into other things as well? Who can say we're following our true inclinations when we mark our Xs at the ballot box? Or when we decide to seek an abortion? I'm willing to bet there are many pro-lifers who'd love to tell us that we aren't really in our right minds, that *they* know what's best for us. Feminism can't have it both ways. Either women are assumed to be in full possession of our faculties and capable of making our own decisions (until proven otherwise, on a case-by-case basis) or not.

The fact that MacKinnon enjoys such a cozy relationship with Ms., despite her intolerant, condescending views toward women with whom she differs *and* her extravagant male-bashing, indicates that the lunatic fringe has taken over mainstream feminism. Moderate, sensible feminists aren't found in one place while offensive, extreme thinkers are off in a corner somewhere else. Alarmingly, these two groups have now become indistinguishable.

But maybe we're jumping to conclusions too quickly. Maybe it's worth spending a few minutes flipping through other back issues of 1990s Ms. magazines to double-check whether the picture I've sketched is an accurate one. Surely not every article the magazine publishes displays such questionable opinions? Surely there are reasonable voices?

There's no question that the coverage of international women's news in Ms. is often solid, and it devotes considerably more space to letters to the editor than most publications, something I view as a plus. Regular contributions from the Boston Women's Health Collective, which produces the feminist classic *Our Bodies, Ourselves*, are high points, and I have no desire to criticize the fiction, poetry and artwork. But this is a magazine that readers send to U.S. Supreme Court justices in order to inform them about feminist issues.[40] Well-modulated, sensible articles should be the norm. Surely the women's movement is mature enough and rich enough in talent that we shouldn't have to feel as though we've stumbled into the twilight zone every time we open a copy of the magazine. Surely this is a *minimum* standard.

Debate is a good thing. The magazine wouldn't be doing its job if it weren't challenging people's assumptions on a regular basis. But there's a difference between being thought-provoking and being ridiculous—or even shameful. Moreover, precious little debate actually takes place within Ms., aside from the letters pages. Instead, the magazine spends much of its time spooning out large dollops of dogma, anti-male hostility and self-indulgent emotion.

In 1991, Ms. published a three-page article titled "Orchids in the Arctic: the Predicament of Women Who Love Men." Written by Kay Leigh Hagan, a former heterosexual turned lesbian, it seeks to give women who still sleep with men guidance about living life with "the oppressor." It tells us that by having sex with men we are being "intimately colonized," and that those of us who think we are married to or are the daughters of exceptional men are "in denial." The author says that if she keeps one rule in mind ("If he can hurt you, he will"), she finds her own "interactions with men improve considerably." She further recommends the use of condoms—not for reasons of safe sex, but so that there is always a physical barrier when we sleep with the enemy—and urges us to get a room of our own "with a door that locks."[41]

The January/February 1992 issue of Ms. had this message emblazoned on its cover in red and white lettering:

"RAGE + WOMEN = POWER." Strange, isn't it? Throughout recorded history, people have warned us about the destructive influence of anger. According to Horace, the ancient Roman poet, "Anger is a short madness." St. Augustine said that "Anger is a weed; hate is the tree." George Jean Nathan, the American critic who died in 1958, wrote that "No man can think clearly when his fists are clenched," and the Old Testament warns, "Be not hasty in thy spirit to be angry: for anger resteth in the bosom of fools."

Even in the *Star Wars* movie trilogy, a pop culture morality play, anger is a negative quality. The evil emperor, who tries to corrupt Luke Skywalker by turning him to the "dark side," urges the young man to surrender himself to anger. "Good, I can feel your anger," the emperor says. "Use your aggressive feelings, boy; let the hate flow through you." Luke's light-sabers are blue and green, colours associated with cool-headedness and reason. Darth Vader, on the other hand, who succumbed to the temptations of evil, has a red light-saber, a colour associated with passion and rage.

It says something about the arrogance of contemporary feminism that we think we can ignore with impunity the wisdom of the ages, that just because the feminist poet Adrienne Rich wrote about her "visionary anger" in 1973, somehow not only anger but rage are emotions we should be cultivating, that they are essential tools in our struggle to remake the world. To paraphrase Betty Friedan, although the wise men of history may have been wrong about women, they weren't wrong about everything. Human strengths and failings haven't changed much in the past couple thousand years.[42]

Don't get me wrong, I've got nothing against healthy measures of indignation from time to time, and I appreciate that women have often been expected to be meek and mild. Moreover, I know that psychoanalytic theory holds that expressing anger is healthy. But when anger or rage is

considered a legitimate *political* tool, when we no longer
value reason above passion, when we start insisting that
one of the seven deadly sins is really a virtue, we court disaster. We condemn ourselves to an endless cycle of injustice and still more anger. Because it is only when we are
able to put aside our feelings of rage, as legitimate as they
may sometimes be, that wars can end.

On other occasions, Ms. has told its readers that North
American women live in "a society saturated by violent
misogyny" and declared that it's a myth that rape is "perpetrated only by an aberrant fringe" of men.[43] It has advised
readers that "your husband, lover, son or brother may be a
terrorist in waiting" and announced in large type that "A
man beats a woman because he *can* do it. He calls it love
and so does everybody else [original italics]."[44] In one article, two male writers inform us that: "men who batter and
men who don't are not that different. Male violence is normal in our society and vast numbers of men participate.
Men batter because we have been trained to; because there
are few social sanctions against it...."[45] After claiming that
people deny the true nature of contemporary North
American women's lives just as many "denied the reality of
the Nazi Holocaust," Ms. has insisted that women "live in
the midst of a reign of sexist terror comparable in magni-
tude, intensity, and intent to the persecution, torture, and
annihilation of women as witches from the 14th to the
17th centuries in Europe."[46] It has told us that gang rape "is
a key feature of male bonding rituals within patriarchal
societies" and characterized the traditional nuclear family
not as a place where violence and abuse sometimes occurs
but as a structure which keeps "its members in terror" and
produces "violent, distorted definitions of love" that not
only oppress women but require children "to humiliate
themselves, over and over again, before power."[47]

Regarding women (all assumed to be truthful) in child

custody battles, another *Ms.* article declares:

> A custodially embattled mother is not unlike a
> runaway African slave in the nineteenth century;
> a Jew in Nazi Europe; a peasant, a professor, a
> housewife, or a child in flight from the world's
> gulags, killing fields, and torture chambers. Except
> there is no "north"; no "Israel"; and no "United
> States" to shelter a woman in flight from male
> domestic violence.[48]

Young women—who may be understandably hesitant to
identify with feminism given some of what *Ms.* is currently
publishing—are said to fear "commitment to something
larger than the self that asks us to examine the consequences of our actions." Readers are informed that such
women avoid the women's movement because they "don't
want to be called to account."[49] In another piece, the magazine criticizes the Holocaust Memorial Museum in
Washington, D.C., on the following basis, among others:

> No use was made of feminist work on sexual abuse
> or bodily invasion and violation—neither the
> substance of this knowledge nor the strategies
> used to create the safety in which women can bear
> remembering…. This museum did not become a
> safe place for women's testimony about the sadism
> of sexualized assault.[50]

While trashing the length and breadth of modern civi-
lization, and criticizing practically everything for being
tainted by tyrannical male norms, some of the solutions
and personalities *Ms.* offers as alternatives fall somewhat
short, however. Early in 1995, for example, *Ms.* profiled
Zsuzsanna Budapest, a writer who claims to be genetically

descended from a long line of witches, in its arts section. Her books are recommended enthusiastically by the magazine. One, titled *The Goddess in the Office*, is described as "a marriage of common sense and magic" that includes:

> ...runes (ancient magical symbols) to use in managing an unruly computer, herbs to purify the workplace, and spells for getting a raise or a promotion. If you are being harassed, Budapest recommends using your full range of powers— from organizing and seeking justice through legal avenues to performing a hex that would reform Clarence Thomas.[51]

Critical thinking, it seems, is not something to be applied to feminism (or, at least, not to those feminists Ms. likes). If you, as Budapest apparently does, spout the right lines about patriarchy and female oppression, no one seems to worry too much about how preposterous your other ideas may be.

But is the state of mainstream feminism really this bad? Is the situation really so bleak? Surely, when this sort of thinking runs up against our male-dominated society, its message gets blunted, its more outrageous claims become tempered by harsh reality. Surely real people in the real world know that these ideas are over the top. Surely no one takes this kind of stuff seriously.

The short answer is: yes and no. Not everyone accepts these ideas as gospel. Many of us who consider ourselves feminists don't, for example. There is also opposition to such thinking from people who might be called anti-feminists. And for this, we can thank our lucky stars. Because, if absolutely everyone said they thought the same way, we'd know we'd left democracy behind and were now living under totalitarianism.

It's for this reason that people who criticize the women's movement should be taken in stride. What makes feminists so special, anyway? Who says we alone are above criticism? Those who dish it out on a regular basis shouldn't be surprised to find themselves on the receiving end once in a while. Every negative word, every objection, is not a symptom of a "backlash" orchestrated to oppress women. To believe this is to waste valuable energy fighting non-existent enemies and to alienate people who might otherwise be important allies.

We must never underestimate how influential feminist ideas have been, and this knowledge should sharpen our desire to hold them up to scrutiny. Feminist thought has been incorporated into criminal law, educational regulations and police guidelines. It affects the way the media present various issues and how people in positions of power gauge voter opinion. In a remarkably short period of time, feminist ideas have been translated into public policy. They influence which problems society considers most important and which ones it ignores. They help decide which projects receive assistance (often in the form of public tax dollars) and which don't. They contribute to our collective consciousness in myriad, often unrecognized, ways.

Anyone who thinks feminism has had nothing more than a nominal effect on people's attitudes should consider the matter of pornography. In the 1970s, "dirty" magazines were viewed as harmless fun by mainstream society. To be sure, there were people who objected to them on religious grounds, but in popular culture, individuals who got agitated over sexually explicit material were likely to be considered prudes who needed to lighten up a little. Few men worried that they'd be causing offence if they admitted, in mixed company, to subscribing to *Playboy*. Indeed, many people considered it a sign of sophistication to have a copy on the coffee table, since it suggested that they'd thrown

off the strait-laced attitudes of the 1950s, when TV and
movies portrayed respectable married couples sleeping in
separate twin beds.

Then came anti-pornography feminists such as
Catharine MacKinnon. And, within not much more than a
decade, attitudes have swung around 180 degrees. From
television sitcoms to Ann Landers's columns,[52] when people talk about porn these days they're likely talking about
something noxious. Rather than a celebration of sexual liberation, diversity and experimentation, rather than a sym-
bolic rejection of earlier ignorance and shame—or even a
neutral phenomenon—porn is now considered degrading.
In a public opinion poll conducted in April 1993, 55 percent of Canadians (64 percent of women and 45 percent of
men) answered "Yes" when asked: "Do you think that adult
magazines are discriminating to women?" When people
were asked whether such magazines should be available in
corner stores, the majority of respondents (56 percent)
were opposed to the idea.[53]

This rapid shift in public attitudes regarding porn is
remarkable, especially when one considers that it took
place at precisely the same time that many people were
preaching tolerance toward homosexuality. The irony is
that, while large numbers of feminists were defending
diversity in the form of lesbian sex, they were simultane-
ously trying to re-stigmatize expressions of (straight) male
sexuality. As a result, there are now many workplaces
where it would be a foolish man indeed who admitted he
was running out on his lunch hour to return the pornographic video he'd rented. He would become a social pariah
among many male, as well as female, co-workers.

But this is exactly where the problem lies. If the feminist ideas having such a profound impact on the real world
were straightforward ones that unmistakably promoted fairness and equality, there'd be little cause for concern. If the

feminism that is increasingly affecting people's everyday lives were consistently driven by the belief that "the majority of men are honest and decent," I would never have written this book. But it is my contention that this is not the case. Rather, the kinds of objectionable feminist attitudes I've outlined above are working their way into some rather high places. Once there, they are often being accepted at face value and given official sanction by some of our most powerful decision-makers.

In a way, the dynamics of this situation aren't difficult to understand. As extremist ideas become increasingly indistinguishable from mainstream feminist aims, the more likely it is that elected representatives who question arguments being advanced by the women's movement will be accused of not caring about female equality. (Extremists do tend to be a short-tempered lot.) And in a society where women live longer than men and slightly outnumber them to begin with—thus forming a majority of the electorate— politicians can't afford to be accused too often of shafting women. I'm not saying elected officials are quaking in their boots at the thought of annoying feminists, but I am arguing that women are one of a number of powerful constituencies that any intelligent government will attempt to mollify.

This, then, helps explain the Canadian Panel on Violence Against Women, something I consider a national embarrassment. The panel was struck in the wake of what has become known as the Montreal Massacre, in which fourteen women engineering students at the École polytechnique de Montréal were murdered in 1989 by a gunman who first separated female classmates from male ones and declared that he hated feminists. In July 1993, the panel's final report was made public. It cost $10 million, took two years to complete and represented the efforts of nearly one hundred individuals, including nine full-time panellists, eighteen advisory committee members and a staff of fifty-eight. The nine central personalities, one of whom was male, all had experience and expertise in the area of violence. For example, they'd run crisis centres or been associated with the family court system.[54]

The press release distributed by Status of Women Canada, a federal government body, called the five-hundred-page report "the world's first comprehensive national study of violence against women." Indeed, the Tory government of the day—which feminist groups attacked before and after the fact for its "neo-conservative" agenda and what they termed its "devastating" impact on women's lives due to funding cuts—couldn't praise the report enough. It was called a "powerful" document that "brings us to a new level of awareness and understanding about violence against women and its links with women's inequality."[55]

But the self-described "feminist lens"[56] through which the report's authors chose to view the subject at hand was hopelessly skewed. Anyone who believes that the kind of extremist thinking I've been discussing is confined to a small group of individuals on the margins of society should consider the following passage, from this document's introductory pages:

> Canada's image abroad is that of a country with a high standard of living—a country dedicated to promoting peace in the world; a country where women have access to post-secondary education, and freedom of expression; a country where women are free to pursue the occupation they choose and to move about without constraint.
>
> But the panel learned that Canadian women are all too familiar with inequality and violence which tether them to *lives few in the world would choose to lead.* [my italics]

This doesn't say that *some* Canadian women are victimized by violence and therefore endure admittedly dreadful lives. Rather, it declares that being a woman per se in 1990s Canada means being consigned to a life "few in the world would choose to lead." If this is really the case, why does the panel devote an entire chapter to the special problems faced by immigrant and refugee women after they reach our soil? If being a contemporary Canadian woman is so rotten an experience that few people around the globe would choose it, why not simply declare that immigrant and refugee women are mistaken if they consider this country an improvement over what they left behind?

That's only the beginning. Elsewhere we read that verbal abuse is part of "the strategy of men to control women," and that the fact that children witness wife abuse isn't an unfortunate by-product of domestic violence but "a powerful tool in reinforcing already overwhelming patriarchal norms of male dominance, female submission and the use of violence."[57] Moreover, the report declares: "In a society whose very structure condones male violence, all men, whether or not they are violent, derive substantial benefit from its institutionalization."[58]

The allegation that all men "benefit" from the current arrangement of our society is common in feminist literature. The *Encyclopedia of Feminism*, for instance, defines "patriarchy" as a "universal political structure which privileges men at the expense of women."[59] Hand in hand with the suggestion that males sat down and deliberately designed matters (as opposed to our society having assumed its present form as a result of often contradictory historical, political and economic forces) is the strong implication that those who benefit from a certain state of affairs are also morally responsible for it.

Nowhere, however, have I seen anyone acknowledge that there is sometimes an enormous difference between these two ideas. I benefit from the fact that I was born in an industrialized country in the late twentieth century. My life has been one of the most privileged in the history of humanity. I have never gone hungry. I have always had a roof over my head and clothes on my back. Despite what the violence report's authors might think, millions of people who have had the misfortune to be born into less favourable circumstances would change places with me in an instant.

But am I personally responsible for this accident of fate?

If not, what is the point of implying that my husband—who, by another accident of fate, was born with a pair of testicles rather than a pair of ovaries—should somehow be held responsible for the flawed state of the society he inherited as surely as did I? This is one of the ways in which feminist thought has led to honest, decent men being blamed not only for the violence committed by their outlaw brothers but for the sins of their fathers as well. It suggests that no matter how sensitive and caring and compassionate a man has been, no matter how many pro-choice marches he's attended, dirty diapers he's changed, dishes he's washed or toilet bowls he's scrubbed, it doesn't matter. He's male, therefore he's derived "substantial benefit" from our unequal system, therefore he's guilty.

Indeed, he may as well behave like a violent brute, because he's never going to get any credit from the sort of people who wrote the above quote. He may have tried his level best his entire life to treat others with kindness and respect, but in their eyes he isn't a unique individual with his own personal history. All that matters is that he belongs to a group—a group they've decided is beastly and vicious.

This is stereotype. This is sexism. This is what feminism started out protesting.

Nor does the report stop there. When it informs us that "the concept of patriarchy" is central to its analysis,[60] it becomes evident that the panel cares more about feminist dogma than the bruises and broken bones of real Canadian women. We're told that the five hundred pages that follow address not violence against women per se but "violence women suffer because of their gender."[61] The panel makes a point of letting us know that it is firmly rejecting the more inclusive term "family violence" (which it calls inaccurate and misleading) in favour of "woman abuse."[62] Woman abuse, says the panel, is committed by men. Indeed, over and over again, we read about "male power," "male violence," "violent men" and "men's authority to be violent toward women."[63]

Marilyn French, Catharine MacKinnon and Ms. magazine all insist it's men who do horrible things and women who get hurt.[64] They, too, urge us to focus not on the violence itself but on the sex of the perpetrator, because they want us to see these incidents as part of an overarching scheme to oppress women.

I'm not denying that this analysis is persuasive to a degree. In some parts of the world, young unmarried women suspected of engaging in sexual activity (and, therefore, of dishonouring their families) are killed by male relatives who are unmistakably using violence as a means of enforcing compliance with rigid gender roles. Men who batter their wives often say the women "stepped out of line" in ways that are connected to behaviour expected of them as women. It would be foolish to deny that this is one piece of the domestic violence puzzle—perhaps even the largest, most important piece.

But it isn't the only one. No single theory can possibly explain everything. And it's women who pay the price when people insist on looking at complex social problems with feminist tunnel vision. Because this approach renders the violence women suffer at the hands of other women invisible.

It denies the trauma experienced by a thirty-two-year-old Toronto woman with a mental disability who received broken ribs and a dislocated shoulder during the year she lived with her abusive female roommate. It says the roommate, who was sentenced to eighteen months in jail in 1994, and who reportedly choked her victim, kneed her in the groin, struck her in the face with a drinking glass, burned her with cigarettes, banged her head against a wall, assaulted her with a belt, drugged her, forced her to cook and clean and threatened that she'd be "beaten beyond recognition" if she ever went to the authorities, doesn't exist.[65]

It implies that only some kinds of violence against women are real. If you're a frail grandmother or a fifteen-year-old who has the bad luck to be brutally assaulted by a woman rather than a man, there's no room in the panel's report for you. Your pain doesn't count. If you happen to be murdered by another female, as was American Grammy-award-winning singer Selena early in 1995, your tragedy doesn't matter.[66]

Canadian taxpayers paid $10 million for a study that was supposed to be about female anguish. Instead, it turned out to be, first and foremost, about something else: male misconduct. This is where extremism leads. When people are put in the uncomfortable position of choosing between feminist dogma and real female suffering, the dogma—not women—prevails. The whole truth about women's lives gets ignored.

When the panel then turns its attention to the issue of power in our society, once again it elects to mouth feminist platitudes rather than admit matters can't always be reduced to predictable formulas. It says:

> In a relationship, society has given the man the
> power over a woman from the point of earliest

> acquaintance. Men exercise this power not only in intimate relationships and not only in sexual matters but in any social context where contact between women and men occurs.[67]

Men are always in positions of power. They're never nervous, unsure of themselves, frightened or worried about measuring up in the presence of *any* woman *ever*. Really. Have these people never seen a pimply-faced young man reduced to tongue-tied blushing in the presence of a self-assured young woman?

Are males in a position of power when their teachers and professors are females who mete out passing or failing grades? Are they in a position of power when the boss they can't seem to do anything right for is a woman? Are they in a position of power when they see a well-dressed, beautiful woman on the street and believe that they themselves are too unattractive, earn too little money, or are too short even to stand a chance with her? Are they in a position of power when, like the man whose brother wrote to Ann Landers, their wives stalk them and threaten them with death?

Many of my women's studies professors (who, as rigorous scholars, never allowed their feminism to distort the truth) wouldn't have accepted such simplistic twaddle from a first-year student. But this report has received the stamp of approval from Canada's federal government. And tangible, real-life consequences ensue from this fact.

For example, when I inquired, as a journalist in early 1995, as to why two different Ontario government ministries had spent a total of $15,000 in taxpayers' money funding a highly questionable feminist conference (at a time when other worthy projects were being hit by cutbacks), I was informed that the decision to do so had been based on the findings of this very report.[68] What further use will be made of this document in the coming years, how many more dubious decisions it will be used to defend, is anyone's guess. Subsequent to its release, however, copies were distributed to public libraries across the nation. An accompanying video, intended for rental by schools, churches and public service organizations, was produced. Understandably, people (many of whom will be young and impressionable) who read parts of the report or watch the video will hesitate to question the underlying assumptions in materials that have, after all, been given high official sanction. A Community Kit was also assembled, the contents of which are supposed to help concerned, well-intentioned people educate those around them about such matters.[69]

And so, sloppy thinking spreads like a virus. It infects the air that people who've never heard of Marilyn French or Catharine MacKinnon breathe. This extremist view of the world, of relations between the sexes, of who's to blame and who's not, of who commits violence and who doesn't, lodges inside people's hearts and minds. It becomes part of us.

If feminists defend irrationality they are in no position to complain if men resist all evidence and go on believing until the end of time that women are inherently weak, unreasonable and given to fits of the vapours.... It is only through insisting that the evidence should be looked at carefully that women are able to attack the prejudices of men. Feminists cannot possibly support irrationality in any form.

–*Janet Radcliffe Richards*[1]

CHAPTER TWO

He Says, She Says

Try to visualize this scene: a young woman with freckles and auburn hair is strapped down to a bed. Thick, belt-like restraints encase her ankles. Others are looped around her wrists and secured near her waist. The woman, whose name is Gretchen, is not struggling.

Five other people are in the small room with her, gathered around, watching. She has been injected with a barbiturate—sodium amytal—long discredited as a "truth serum."

A man sits by Gretchen's bed asking questions. "Let's finish this," he says. She knows what he wants to hear. She believes her life will improve if she co-operates. Finally, in an agonized voice, she says the things for which he's been waiting. At last, she provides the details he's been trying to pry out of her for months.

The man continues in a flat voice. He registers no shock, no surprise, at what she's revealed. It's clear he knew all along this was coming, that it was just a matter of time.

But then Gretchen begins to pull at her restraints, to thrash and writhe. Her face becomes contorted, her voice hoarse. She is now hysterical. Her struggles are so violent that the other people in the room have to grasp her limbs and hold her down.

This entire episode is filmed. Later, Gretchen is shown the video. Again she becomes hysterical and again she is restrained. This, too, is filmed.

Welcome to mental health care in the '90s. The above scenario is called "therapy." It took place in 1992, in a psychiatric hospital in Texas. Gretchen's story comprises the first thirty minutes of an hour-long documentary film about multiple personality disorder (MPD). This is an illness in which two or more distinct personalities are believed to inhabit a person's body.

The film was released in 1993 by Home Box Office and was broadcast as part of TVOntario's Mental Health Week in early 1995. The several health care professionals who appear in it share three assumptions:

- One thing causes MPD—childhood sexual abuse.
- This abuse was so terrible that patients such as Gretchen have "repressed" their memories of it.
- The way to treat/cure MPD is to help the patient "recover" these memories so that they can be confronted in the patient's conscious mind.

Two years after being diagnosed as an MPD sufferer, and during the course of a four-month stay in a specialized psychiatric ward that "focuses on recovering repressed memories," Gretchen has finally retrieved images of being sexually abused in a bathroom as a child. We're told, at the end of the segment, that she "now feels she knows who her abuser is."

What the film doesn't disclose is that, although MPD was officially recognized by the American Psychiatric Association in 1980, debate continues over whether or not the illness truly exists. The World Health Organization, for instance, remains unconvinced, and some experts argue that there hasn't been a single documented case in which a person who had not previously undergone therapy—or who hadn't heard about this disorder via the media—developed MPD on their own. They say some mentally ill patients are highly suggestible and are being cued (often unconsciously) by their therapist to behave as though they possess different personalities.[2] Some of these personalities claim to be unicorns, angels, lobsters, gorillas and demons.[3]

Prior to 1970, only two hundred cases of MPD had been diagnosed worldwide. Then, in 1973, the best-selling book *Sybil* was published. *Sybil* was about a woman who'd experienced childhood sexual abuse and who, after 2,300 therapy sessions, displayed sixteen separate personalities. A film, starring Sally Field, followed in 1977. Since then, an estimated thirty thousand cases of MPD have been identified. Many of these diagnoses originate with a small coterie of U.S. specialists.[4]

Even if MPD does exist (it's possible therapists were so unfamiliar with the illness in the past that they didn't recognize it when their patients displayed symptoms), what causes it is another whole debate. And even if it were agreed that MPD is the result of childhood trauma—as opposed to a chemical imbalance, for example—there's still a third area of dispute over what *kinds* of trauma might trigger it. Currently, there appears to be no good reason to believe that, of all the distressing things that happen to people as youngsters, sexual abuse alone produces this condition. Another famous case of MPD—involving a woman known as Eve White, whose story is told in the 1957 book *The Three Faces of Eve* and a 1957 film of the same name—

had no abuse whatsoever in her background. She had been traumatized by seeing a drowned man at the age of two, by touching her dead grandmother's face when she was five and by witnessing an injury to her mother's arm.[5]

Nevertheless, the idea that MPD is invariably linked to sexual abuse has been adopted by an influential segment of the mental health community. More importantly, for our purposes, it has also been embraced by mainstream feminism. The film discussed above, which is titled *MPD: The Search for Deadly Memories*, is co-narrated by Gloria Steinem, who gives no indication that she is troubled by what has been done to Gretchen. Near the beginning, referring to MPD patients, Steinem asks:

> Why have they become tormented and broken into different personalities? What is the childhood pain that lies buried in the unknown depths of their minds? How can they search for the deadly memories that hold the secrets to their past and the promise of their healing?

Gretchen is obviously seriously disturbed. She regularly experiences panic attacks, triggered by common sights and sounds, such as the noise produced by a vacuum cleaner. Her body is, in places, a mass of scar tissue—the result of "hundreds" of self-inflicted lacerations. There's no denying, therefore, that she needs professional help. But does the kind of help she's receiving qualify as responsible mental health care? Surely there's cause for concern if, rather than adjusting the therapy to fit the unique circumstances of the patient, a therapist compels one patient after another to conform to a pre-established script. And if the only way a therapist can get a woman to admit she was sexually abused as a child is to strap her down and shoot her up with a hypnotic drug—which the film tells us "acts like a truth serum" but instead produces a state similar to alcohol intoxication[6]—surely we should be asking what in heaven's name is going on in North America's psychiatric wards.

Near the beginning of the film we learn that the reason Gretchen is trudging across town by foot and cannot afford a car is because "all the money she has goes to therapy." Later, she frets over the fact that the abuse she's been working so hard to remember bears little relation to her conscious memories. Prior to the sodium amytal scene—the first occasion on which specific details of abuse emerged—she says of the suggestion that she was sexually molested:

> That doesn't fit with what I *know* that I experienced and that I saw and that I heard. Everything fits but it doesn't fit. I had a wonderful life. I have lots of happy memories. I had lots of wonderful things in my childhood. [original emphasis]

Gretchen is mentally ill. But she's not stupid (we're told she's an honours student in college). And she's desperately trying to understand what's the matter with her. "I don't want people to think I'm crazy," she says at one point. "I don't want to appear abnormal in any way. I want to fit in."

She's therefore particularly vulnerable when someone who calls himself an expert tells her he knows what will cure her. She wants to believe. She wants to get better. And when everyone she encounters during her four-month stay in the specialized psychiatric unit not only insists that there's a magic key but tells her exactly what it is, should we be surprised that "memories" of childhood sexual abuse then begin to surface?

How can this be considered acceptable mental health care? Why is it okay to subject Gretchen to treatment of this sort? Why is it okay for therapists who may well be doing her more harm than good to take all her money?

Why is it permissible to destroy the image Gretchen and thousands of other women (an estimated 90 percent of those diagnosed with MPD are female[7]) have of their childhoods on the basis of a highly controversial psychiatric theory? And what is North America's most prominent feminist doing not only applauding it all, but making a video to let the world know she applauds it?

This wasn't a situation in which Steinem agreed to be part of a project and then couldn't back out despite later reservations. Rather, we're informed at the end of the film that it was all *her idea*. One assumes that she would be the first to protest if it were publicly known, for example, that appendectomies were being performed on mostly female patients by doctors with a lot of conviction but little evidence that such a procedure would cure acute depression. What's different about this?

No reasonable person would deny that childhood sexual abuse is a terrible and ugly reality. How prevalent it is (the statistics are all over the map) is almost beside the point; any number of cases is too many. Nor can it be disputed that, until recently, such abuse remained unrecognized by society as a whole. This meant that victims could expect little help from the authorities or others in whom they might confide. It meant that they suffered alone and felt ashamed, suspecting that they had somehow brought the abuse on themselves. Victims also worried, often justifiably, that they'd be rejected by family and friends, who would likely be unprepared to cope with the situation if it became known.

Sadly, these tragic facts have now become more grist for the feminist mill. Today, child sexual abuse is seen as just one more example of how men deliberately cripple female lives at every turn. Marilyn French, remember, lists sexual molestation of female children among her ten things the "vast majority of men in the world do one or more of."

She says, further, that:

> All patriarchists exalt the home and family as
> sacred, demanding it remain inviolate from prying
> eyes. *Men want privacy for their violations of*
> *women*.... All women learn in childhood that
> women as a sex are men's prey. [my italics][8]

Journalist Sylvia Fraser, Canada's most famous incest
survivor, reports that her memories, which came flooding
back to her at the age of forty-seven, were not induced by a
therapist. I have no reason to disbelieve this statement or
her insistence that she was abused by her deceased father.
But this feminist goes well beyond such claims when she
writes, in a March 1994 magazine article, that:

> I was, in reality, *bred by my parents* as my father's
> concubine.... What we take for granted as the sta-
> bility of family life may well depend on the sexual
> slavery of our children. What's more, this is a cyni-
> cal arrangement our institutions have colluded to
> conceal. [my italics][9]

The Canadian Panel on Violence Against Women also
tells us that beliefs "about privacy and the separation of
'home' from the 'other' world increases women's vulnerability." It adds, a few lines later:

> We are taught, encouraged, moulded by and lulled
> into accepting a range of *false notions* about the
> family. As a source of some of our most profound
> experiences, it continues to be such an integral part
> of our emotional lives that it appears beyond criti-
> cism. Yet hiding from *the truth* of family life leaves
> women and children vulnerable. [my italics]

Catharine MacKinnon, too, maintains that "the private is a sphere of battery, marital rape and women's exploited labor."

In this way, privacy and family are reduced to nothing more than aspects of the master plan, which is male domination. Democratic freedoms and the need to keep the state's nose out of our personal affairs are rendered meaningless. The *real* reason our society cherishes privacy is because men have invented it as an excuse to conceal their criminality. If people still insist that the traditional family is about love and mutual aid—ideals which, admittedly, are sometimes betrayed—they're "hiding from the truth." The family isn't a place where battery and marital rape sometimes happen but where little else apparently does. Sick men don't simply molest their daughters, they operate in league with their wives to "breed" them for that express purpose.

The fact that child sexual abuse remained a dark secret until recently is also considered proof of a conscious plot to ensure a steady supply of victims. But this view overlooks the fact that it's only during the past few decades that our society has become more aware of, and sensitive to, all sorts of social issues. We don't call people "bums" any more, we call them "the homeless." Interracial marriages are more common (and accepted) these days, "crippled" children's hospitals have been renamed, and openly homosexual politicians run for office (and get elected). All these changes are so recent that they have taken place within my lifetime. Even the *physical* abuse of children is discussed with an openness today that was unheard of before an influential paper on "Battered Child Syndrome" was first published in 1962.[10]

North American society has gone through a tremendous amount of consciousness-raising in the last while, and we're all better off as a result. Back in 1970, Canada's landmark *Report of the Royal Commission on the Status of Women*, for example, failed even to mention violence.[11] While domestic abuse was surely occurring back then, many feminists were clearly unaware of its existence. Rather than the issue being kept quiet as the result of a male conspiracy, it seems more likely that society as a whole needed to be educated.

Now that the highest levels of government have acknowledged that child sexual abuse exists, feminism is going one step further and trying to convince us that it occurs more often than we think—i.e., that far more men are pedophiles than we'd ever imagined. While that may, in fact, be the case, the way in which these people are attempting to prove their point further suggests that the women's movement has taken leave of its senses. One of the side effects of this fixation on male malevolence is that the interests of real women are once again being ignored—not to mention principles such as reason and justice.

Let's return to the film. After learning about Gretchen, we are then introduced to John, a forty-year-old police officer. Steinem calmly informs us that John shares his job "with several personalities who have different abilities. He switches when different police skills are needed and *is always aware of what his other personalities are doing* [my italics]." One personality is apparently good at driving in high-speed chases. Other "alters" have different styles of marksmanship. We are shown a clip of John's commanding officer, who says he makes a fine policeman, and are told that John has received "many awards and commendations" during his thirteen-year career.

Steinem tells us that John remembers a stable childhood home and being well provided for as a youngster. But he has always heard "voices" inside his head and has now been diagnosed as having twenty personalities, "many of [whom] are frightened children who appear only in therapy."

According to these children, John was actually viciously abused while he was growing up. In addition to being shoved down a staircase and tortured with electrical currents, he was also, says Steinem, "sexually abused by both male and female perpetrators." In response, his psyche apparently "created a personality whose job it was to have sex." Steinem tells us he also has a history of depression, unexplained mood swings and difficulty controlling his temper. John himself admits that no physical evidence—such as scars or medical records—exists to corroborate these allegations, and he concedes that he wouldn't be able to prove any of this in a court of law.

Unlike John, neither Gretchen nor Barb—the film's third MPD sufferer—is aware of what's happening when her other personalities manifest themselves. Indeed, Gretchen says:

> I requested, when we started this, that please,
> when someone is out, will they please write the
> date, the day and the time [in her journal] and
> where they were and who they might have seen.
> If they would please give me an idea of where the
> body's been.

Barb's various personalities take drug overdoses, punch walls (breaking her hand in four places), inflict burns on her face, write hundreds of dollars' worth of bad cheques and, on one occasion, set her car on fire with her inside (she woke up in intensive care, on a respirator).

John's awareness obviously presents an inconsistency. When the film was released in 1993, the American Psychiatric Association's definition of MPD had two parts. Part A required a person to possess two or more distinct personalities. Part B decreed that these personalities must "recurrently take *full control of the individual's behavior* [my italics]."[12] If what Steinem tells us is true, if John was "always aware of what his other personalities" were doing, he didn't meet this second requirement—and therefore wasn't a real MPD patient.

It seems to me that there are a few possible explanations for this rather startling discrepancy. The first is that Steinem was mistaken about John's true self always being in control—a rather significant error, considering the nature of the work he does. The second is that this clearly disturbed police officer suffers from some other mental illness or combination of mental illnesses and was misdiagnosed, leaving Steinem in the unenviable position of commending his maltreatment by the mental health profession. The third is that Steinem, as well as others involved in the production of this film, weren't in possession of the most basic facts concerning MPD, even though three high-profile MPD experts are listed in the film's credits, and these people would have been as familiar with the APA's requirements as I am with the back of my hand. The fourth is that some of those involved in the making of the film *knew* John didn't qualify, but a decision was taken to stretch the truth a little—in a documentary intended to "educate" the public.[13]

Whatever the case may be, Steinem's reputation as a reliable, credible source of information is tarnished by this film, as is feminism's reputation by extension.

But that isn't the last of the video's questionable assertions. Thirty-four-year-old Barb also has a history of severe depression. We're told she has few memories of her life prior to her early twenties. Her therapist explains that Barb developed MPD in order to cope with the disparity between what was really going on in her childhood home and its outward appearance. Her father (who is not identified by name but appears in a photograph) was a prominent dentist and university professor. According to Barb's

various alters—which include a teenaged boy—her father
tortured her with his dentist drills (in her mouth, but also
on other parts of her body) and "burned up a grey cat."
Intones Steinem's male co-narrator: "Barb's father was not
her only abuser. He frequented the local bars where he
made friends that shared his interests." Barb informs us that
"a lot of men" were eager to have sex with a young girl and
were willing to pay her father in order to do so. We're told
she had several abortions, the first when she was thirteen,
and that she developed ulcers as a child.

What we don't hear is whether or not there's one iota of
documented proof of any of this. Since Barb's father is
dead, he's not in a position to dispute these horrific allegations. Yet the filmmakers don't seem to think independent
verification is important. They apparently accept these
accusations at face value, assuming that we will too.

And maybe these events really did happen. They're
surely not impossible. But then again, what if they're
merely the result of a profoundly ill young woman being led
to believe that a sexually abusive childhood must have
caused her illness? What if Barb's tormented psyche simply
made this stuff up? What if her father's good reputation is
being dragged through the mud unjustly? Those responsible
for this film don't appear to have asked themselves these
questions. Instead, Steinem closes with the following:

> Multiple personality disorder shows the extraordi-
> nary capacity of the mind to invent ways of bearing
> the unbearable. And these people also show us that
> when allowed to give up its secrets, the human
> mind can heal itself.

Except, we don't know that these people have been healed.
Gretchen may be. We're told that, following her stay in the
psychiatric hospital, she returned to school and finished

her degree. But we don't learn what has happened to her since. If all her problems have been resolved, we aren't informed of it.

John is anything but healed. At the end of the film we can only surmise that he continues to "switch" personalities on a regular basis, and that he continues to visit his therapist, where he sits cross-legged, hunched over a teddy bear, speaking in children's voices about horrific victimization. When we last see Barb, despite the fact that she's apparently been aware of her former abuse for some time, she hasn't recovered either. On the contrary, she's checking herself into a psychiatric hospital out of concern that she might harm herself (or perhaps her three young daughters). Says the narrator, "We were with Barb and her family when a dangerous time had come again."

This theory about how to cure MPD is an interesting one, but the examples provided by Steinem's own film don't support it.

The documentary raises yet another issue, however, and that's one of ethics. Catharine MacKinnon thinks women who consent to pose for porn should be considered legally incompetent. I think a much stronger case could be made that these three mentally ill people were not the sort of individuals who should have been asked to participate in a film that, among other things, involved the taping of intimate one-on-one sessions with their therapists. I'm astounded that the three therapists apparently had no concerns about what effect the production of this film would have on their patients' progress. Gretchen tells us she wants to fit in. Being followed around by a film crew—to class, her art studio and the library—is unlikely to have assisted much in that regard. And is it not possible that knowing a film crew was present when she was injected with sodium amytal put even more pressure on this disturbed young woman to "retrieve" the kinds of details her therapist wanted to hear?

We're given to believe that Gretchen had no conscious memory of what she said under the influence of this drug. The first time she finds out that she has, in fact, "remembered" abuse is when she's shown the video of it later. Is it ethical to film the reactions of someone being informed of such a terrible thing for the first time? Is this not exploitation? Furthermore, is it not possible that one of the reasons Barb's condition appears to have deteriorated near the end of the documentary is because the experience of having a film crew in her life may have been too much of a strain?

What sort of judgment has Steinem exercised here? Although usually mindful of the abuse and misuse of power in our society, she remains untroubled by the fact that John is being permitted to walk around with a police-issue revolver—as well as by the knowledge that, while still sorting out his own relationship to such issues, he is investigating child abuse cases and is a member of a task force on the subject. Moreover, although she suggests that John's child alters emerge only in therapy, this isn't true of all of them. At one point during the documentary we see him, in his own living room, with no therapist in sight, "switch" to a ten-year-old who has trouble reading the words in a news clipping. Is it appropriate to allow a ten-year-old anywhere near a loaded gun?

Steinem appears blissfully unaware that, according to one researcher, patients "frequently become suicidal and attempt to mutilate themselves" *after* they're diagnosed as MPD rather than before.[14] Nor is she impressed by the dozens of studies, dating back to the 1930s, that have determined that sodium amytal is anything but a truth serum. Declares one recent examination of the available evidence:

> The degree of agreement in the literature…is striking: numerous studies were reviewed for the present

article but *not a single investigator* endorsed this procedure [amytal injection] as a means of recovering
accurate memories of past events. Barbiturate-facil-
itated interviews intended to uncover memories of
childhood sexual abuse *may be worse than useless,*
because they may encourage patients' beliefs in com-
pletely mythical events. [my italics][15]

Gloria Steinem not only took part in the production of
this film but further agreed to be the keynote speaker and
guest of honour at the 1994 annual conference of the
International Society for the Study of Multiple Personality
and Dissociation—the organization that bears a good deal
of responsibility for the fact that women are now being
strapped down, doped up and badgered until they tell therapists what they want to hear.[16] Gretchen's mother claims
she has written to Steinem, both at Ms. and at her home
address, but reports that Steinem (like HBO) has declined
even to respond.[17]

Sometimes, when you're a true believer convinced of
the righteousness of your cause, you don't worry too much
about ethics. You think the ends really do justify the
means; that your good intentions are sufficient in themselves; that the harm you do isn't real harm. Mainstream
feminism seems to have a full-blown case of this malady
these days, and nowhere is it more in evidence than in the
way in which it has dealt with the issues of sexual abuse,
MPD, repressed memories—and, to add a further twist,
allegations of something called satanic ritual abuse. In
their laudable desire to have the terrible tragedy of child
sexual abuse acknowledged, addressed and prevented, feminists are gambling the credibility of the entire movement.
Their propensity to view "women and children" as victims
has created a situation in which any and all claims of abuse,
no matter how far-fetched, must be believed—as a matter

of feminist principle.

Ms. magazine's January/February 1993 issue provides a prime illustration of this. Its cover bears a drawing of a naked infant caught up in the coils of a monstrous serpent. "Believe It! Cult Ritual Abuse Exists" reads the headline. Inside, six pages are devoted to a first-person account written under a pseudonym. The author tells us that, while in therapy, she started talking about the satanic cult she'd belonged to when she was four to five years old. She accuses this cult of altering her "thought patterns" through "brain-washing and severe psychological abuse" and assures her readers that "cult leaders are knowledgeable about how to perform ritualistic abuse so it will not be detected."[18] She writes:

> …cult members are smart; there was a doctor in our cult who taught members how to "discipline" children so as to leave no scars. Some examples are torture with pins and needles, forcing a child to take mind-altering drugs, and submerging a child in water, particularly as part of a satanic baptismal ritual. Other tactics include withholding of food and water, sleep deprivation, and forced eating of feces, urine, blood, or raw flesh.[19]

The author tells us her mother and her own best friend were strapped to an altar and ritually gang-raped. She says she also witnessed the ritual murders of two children, one of whom was her baby sister:

> My mother became pregnant a few months after I was inducted into the cult. About seven months later, the cult decided she was carrying a girl child. Her labor was induced and the infant delivered prematurely by the cult doctor at our house.[20]

We're told the child was decapitated a few days after being delivered and eaten by cult members and that, since its birth wasn't recorded, its death went unnoticed as well. How this could be the case since, aside from their Saturday night rituals in the woods, she describes her family as being an "otherwise ordinary middle-class" one, living in a small city, isn't clear. Did friends and neighbours not think it odd that a woman seven months pregnant would suddenly lose her child but never be hospitalized? Did the writer's paternal grandparents, who she says were not part of the cult but lived "in the same town" and saw her family "frequently," not find it strange, either?[21]

The article quotes from a Los Angeles County Commission for Women task force report on ritual abuse which claims, among other things, that "most victims dissociate their memories" of cult abuse. This is another way of saying they repress them. The *Ms.* article maintains that people who've been abused by satanic cults may not be consciously aware of this fact, and that those who've had cult contact at a young age are more likely to develop MPD than other victims.[22]

Not one piece of corroborating evidence accompanies this fantastical tale, however. Since the author, her family and the community where these events allegedly occurred aren't identified, there's no way to verify any of it. As with the film about MPD, we're just supposed to take *Ms.*'s word for it. But it's actually worse than that, because the article hints, none too subtly, that if you remain unconvinced, you're aiding and abetting this horrific abuse. Near the end, it reads, "[b]ecause society tends to doubt stories of ritual abuse, this attitude carries over into the court system." A few lines later, a quote from a publication produced by the Illinois Coalition Against Sexual Assault alleges that "[c]hildren are revictimized because people cannot face the truth." The *Ms.* article continues:

The truth is that *ritual abuse exists*.... It exists
because violence is perpetrated against women
and children, and then passed on to the next
generation. Ritual abuse is at the extreme end of
a continuum of abuse.... Society's denial makes
recovery much more difficult for survivors.
Those who have suffered from ritual abuse need
the same respect and support that would be
given to survivors of any tragedy. [original
italics][23]

According to the available evidence, however, there is
currently no rational basis for believing that satanic ritual
abuse is real. A 1992 report prepared by the U.S. Federal
Bureau of Investigation admitted that while the notion of
"a few cunning, secretive individuals in positions of power
somewhere in this country regularly killing a few people as
part of some satanic ritual or ceremony and getting away
with it is certainly within the realm of possibility,"[24] hard
proof remains elusive. As the report's author, Supervisory
Special Agent Kenneth Lanning, would later tell a journalist: "There is not one single scrap of evidence for the existence of these cults. Not one. Nowhere. Zero."[25]
Lanning says it is extremely difficult to commit crimes
on a large scale without becoming careless and leaving at
least some physical evidence behind. Human nature being
what it is, he says, the more people who are involved in
ongoing and blatantly illegal activity, the more likely it is
that internal conflicts will arise within the group, which
will prompt some members to make self-serving disclosures
to the authorities. His report concludes, in part:

The explanation that the satanists are too
organized and law enforcement is too incompetent
only goes so far in explaining the lack of evidence.

For at least eight years American law enforcement
has been aggressively investigating the allegations
of victims of ritual abuse. There is little or no
evidence for that portion of their allegations that
deals with large-scale baby breeding, human
sacrifice and organized satanic conspiracies. Now
it is up to mental health professions, not law
enforcement, to explain why victims are alleging
things that don't seem to have happened.[26]

When, in 1994, the National Center on Child Abuse
and Neglect in Washington, D.C., made the findings of its
own investigation into ritual abuse public, its conclusions
were wholly consistent with the FBI's. The following quote,
which relates to part one of a five-part study, is representative:

In summary, a very small group of clinicians, each
claiming to have treated scores of cases, accounted
for most of the reports of ritualistic child abuse.
Reports by adult survivors were particularly
extreme, involving acts such as murder, which
should have left some traces of hard evidence.
However, hard evidence for satanic ritual abuse,
especially abuse involving large cults, was scant to
nonexistent. Evidence for lone perpetrators or very
small groups (e.g., two people) who abuse children
in ways that include satanic themes was uncovered,
although such abuse was infrequent.[27]

Declared Dr. Gail Goodman, who supervised the research
team that compiled data on more than twelve thousand
cases of alleged ritual abuse, "If there is anyone out there
with solid evidence of satanic cult abuse of children, we
would like to know about it."[28]

A similar report, prepared for the Department of Health in Great Britain, was also released in 1994. Although it cautions that there is a "considerable difference between North American and British cases" since there have been no allegations involving pre-school children in Britain (as sometimes happens on this side of the Atlantic), it too found no evidence of satanic abuse. Rather, it describes people who claim that such things happened to them in their youth as "damaged individuals, with a known history of various forms of abuse, neglect or family problems."

The report further says:

> Three substantiated cases of ritual, not satanic, abuse were found. These are cases in which self-proclaimed mystical/magical powers were used to entrap children and impress them (and also adults) with a reason for the sexual abuse, keeping the victims compliant and ensuring their silence. *In these cases the ritual was secondary to the sexual abuse which clearly formed the primary objective of the perpetrators. The rituals performed in these cases did not resemble those that figured in the allegations of the other 81 cases.* [original italics][29]

Additionally, early in 1995, Randy Emon, a retired California police sergeant, made the following public declaration on an Internet discussion group:

> As a retired cop who totally believed in the SRA [Satanic Ritual Abuse] phenomenon, I actively searched for hard evidence. All I *ever* received were the anecdotal accounts of the "survivors." I perpetuated this myth by participating in the following videos: *In the Name of Satan; Devil Worship—the Rise of Satanism; America's Best Kept*

Secret; [and] *Halloween, Trick or Treat*. I can state
with absolute certainty, that if you review what
I said in those videos and then ask me to prove
what I said in a court of law, I could not provide
any corroborating evidence to support what I had
said.... The fact is—I succumbed to the same
hysteria as many of my colleagues have also done.
The evidence I have totally proves the existence
of teen involvement, and the loner criminals
using Satanism as an excuse to commit a crime.
Everything I said in those videos and at police
seminars (I've taught about 5,000 cops) regarding
SRA was provided to me from "survivors" who
went through therapy, visualization, who read
a book or were involved in 12 step therapy
programs. Yes, that's what I based my expertise
upon—unverified rumors.[30]

True believers, many of them feminists, remain unimpressed by such reports and testimonials, however. Agent
Lanning says that his findings have been dismissed by persons who insist he's really a satanist "who has infiltrated the
FBI to facilitate a cover-up."[31] Medical anthropologist
Sherrill Mulhern notes that those who believe in ritual
abuse have responded less than sensibly to the absence of
concrete proof:

The lack of corroborative material evidence for
the satanists' monstrous crimes simply proved
that they [satanists] were far more sophisticated
than the police. Doubters were portrayed, at best,
as examples of society's refusal to recognize the
horror of child sexual abuse and, at worst, as cult
collaborators.[32]

One feminist, writing in a Canadian newspaper, recently compared people who express scepticism about the existence of ritual abuse to those who dispute the Holocaust. "Ritual abuse deniers, like Holocaust deniers, are trapped in an untenable position," wrote Judy Steed. "The Holocaust really did happen."[33] People who doubt the trustworthiness of "recovered memories" have also been accused by feminists of displaying "authoritarian opposition to women having equality in our society" and of "covering up the crimes of incestuous parents."[34]

In its Fall 1992 issue, the Canadian feminist magazine *Herizons* devoted a special section to ritual abuse which included two first-person accounts. A note from the editors makes it clear they feel they are "breaking the silence" on a taboo by publishing this material, just as earlier feminists had "peeled back the protective layers of patriarchal violence." (I'm not certain *Herizons* can be considered a "mainstream" feminist publication, since Canada has no equivalent to *Ms.*, but it demonstrates that a belief in ritual abuse is not uncommon among Canadian feminists.)

R.J., a twenty-five-year-old woman who admits to long-term psychiatric problems, related hospitalization and self-mutilation, "recovered" her memories of cult ritual abuse in therapy. She says these involved images of: "'little boy babies' hanging from their genitalia (presumably dead), as well as visions of a blond woman in a white gown, stretched out on a stone table—a man in black held a dagger above her heart."

Amethya, the second person to tell her story, says her memories were retrieved four months after she began going to a feminist therapist. Soon afterwards, she was diagnosed as having MPD. She claims her abuse began when she was *less than a month old*, that members of the satanic cult she belonged to were often punished by "being closed in a coffin with [a] mutilated dead body," and that she witnessed her ten-year-old best friend being impaled on a stake and burned alive. She also recalls:

> ...torture, electrical shocks, drowning attempts,
> being buried in deep pits with human bones,
> sadistic sexual abuse.... Other experiences we
> suffered were cannibalism, child and adult
> prostitution, pornography, drugs, and witnessing
> countless rapes, tortures and deaths of other
> victims.[35]

In response to these articles, a Canadian dissident feminist named Marjaleena Repo submitted a critique to *Herizons* in which she asked: "Since when does being a 'feminist' mean being either gullible, brain-dead, or both?" She ended her impassioned, detailed challenge to much of what the magazine had printed with the following, which I have her permission to reproduce here:

> A number of years ago I worked in a mental hospi-
> tal where I met many people, men and women,
> with serious and elaborate delusions about their
> lives. They were being persecuted and tormented
> by sinister people in this world—the Mafia and the
> KGB among them—as well as aliens from outer
> space. Some thought of themselves as Christlike
> figures who continued to experience crucifixion.
> They pointed at their scars and injuries to "prove"
> that they had been tortured by laser rays and
> unwanted "operations." I listened to their stories
> with empathy, because they were obviously suffer-
> ing and clearly believed in what they were saying.
> But...at no time did I go along with, or encourage,
> their delusions, which I came to see as metaphors
> for their life experiences.

Something similar is needed with the current
crop of "ritual abuse survivors." Instead of going
along with disturbed and either highly manipulative or easily manipulated, suggestible individuals,
true feminists—and feminist publications worth
their salt—must refuse to be hoodwinked into
believing every impossible and irrational story
so long as it's being told by a woman and implies
female victimization. We women have enough
real problems to deal with, without having to
invent new ones. And these problems of substance
will be ignored and unsolved, if our energies and
empathies are pulled into the direction of non-
existent crises in our midst.[36]

Herizons declined to run Repo's piece. The rejection letter she received began: "It is clear that you and the editors
of *Herizons* have a different opinion on the experience of
the women in the articles on Ritual Abuse. We stand by
our initial articles and will not be publishing yours." It
went on to say that the magazine would continue to print
articles on abuse that explore the "different realities"
women experience.

In addition to the *Herizons* coverage, a Vancouver feminist newspaper published an article sympathetic to ritual
abuse survivors in June 1995.[37] And ritual abuse was also
recognized by the Canadian Panel on Violence Against
Women, which turned the issue into an "all or nothing"
proposition. According to the panel, there "is a clear parallel between the long-standing disbelief of sexual abuse survivors and the present disbelief of ritual abuse survivors."[38]

Apparently, one isn't entitled to make intelligent distinctions, to separate that about which, speaking in general
terms, there is no dispute (child sexual abuse) from that
about which there is a great deal of dispute (satanic ritual

abuse). Feminists, it seems, are supposed to suppress our critical faculties whenever a controversy that involves women arises. Nor are we supposed to feel any uneasiness when the sidebars accompanying the Ms. ritual abuse cover story tell us that some therapists don't consider MPD "a disorder at all, but a very effective coping technique" and then recommend a book that "encourages multiples to 'see themselves as the creative, sturdy, smart survivors that they are.'" We aren't supposed to be troubled when Ms. recommends *The Courage to Heal*, the highly controversial "survivors" bible, written by Ellen Bass and Laura Davis, noting that it contains "an excellent short chapter on cult abuse."[39]

A subsequent issue of Ms. reports that *The Courage to Heal* has been called one of the twenty "most influential women's books of the last 20 years." Recently, lawsuits were filed against the authors by two women, who alleged that the book caused them to "remember" childhood abuse that never happened. When the lawsuits were quashed, Ms. called it a victory that countered "the backlash against the concept of recovered memory."

I should state here that I don't support such lawsuits against book authors. I don't think rapists should be able to blame pornography for their actions, and I don't think authors should be held legally responsible for what people do with the information they provide. That said, I can't claim to be entirely unsympathetic to these two women. The larger concern in this instance, though, is Ms.'s utter refusal to recognize the complexity of these issues. Although its coverage of the lawsuits suggests that anyone who criticizes *The Courage to Heal* should automatically be dismissed as unsympathetic to women, the opposite may be closer to the truth. Indeed, Ms.'s disregard for whether or not this book may be having a deleterious effect on thousands of female lives appears astonishingly cavalier to this

feminist. The magazine ends its short bulletin by saying
that, with the lawsuits out of the way, "survivors can get on
with the healing."[40]

But parts of *The Courage to Heal* seem to have far more
to do with manufacturing illness than healing it. Exactly
what sort of healing is being encouraged when readers are
assured: "If you are unable to remember any specific
instances like the ones mentioned above but still have a
feeling that something abusive happened to you, it probably did."[41] And, on p. 22: "If you think you were abused
and your life shows the symptoms, then you were." Readers
are also told:

> If you don't have any memory of it, it can be hard
> to believe the abuse really happened. You may feel
> insecure about trusting your intuition and want
> 'proof' of your abuse. This is a very natural desire;
> but it is not always one that can be met (p. 82).

What kind of health flows from chapter headings such
as "ANGER—THE BACKBONE OF HEALING"?[42]
Pointing to passages such as the following, one of the
book's critics has observed that its authors "prescribe a cul-
tivation of rage" to their readers:[43]

> If you're willing to get angry and the anger just
> doesn't seem to come, there are many ways to get
> in touch with it. A little like priming the pump,
> you can do things that will get your anger started.
> Then, once you get the hang of it, it'll begin to
> flow on its own. (p. 124)

> You may dream of murder or castration. It can be
> pleasurable to fantasize such scenes in vivid detail.
> Wanting revenge is a natural impulse, a sane

> response. Let yourself imagine it to your heart's
> content.... Suing your abuser and turning him in to
> the authorities are just two of the avenues open....
> Another woman, abused by her grandfather, went
> to his deathbed and, in front of all the other rela-
> tives, angrily confronted him right there in the
> hospital. (pp. 128-29)

The Courage to Heal, it must be noted, is only one of many such self-help books. This particular publishing niche has grown rapidly in recent years, and it's not uncommon to find several volumes on this topic in any good-sized bookstore. They bear titles such as *Secret Survivors* (which has a glowing endorsement from Gloria Steinem on the cover),[44] *The Right to Innocence* and *Incest and Sexuality*. As feminist Carol Tavris has observed, they also have a ten-dency to feed into and off one another:

> ...the authors of these books all rely on one
> another's work as supporting evidence for their
> own; they all endorse and recommend one
> another's books to their readers. If one of them
> comes up with a concocted statistic...the numbers
> are traded like baseball cards, reprinted in every
> book and eventually enshrined as fact. Thus the
> cycle of misinformation, faulty statistics and unval-
> idated assertions maintains itself.[45]

The definition of what constitutes sexual abuse in these books can also be alarmingly broad. For example, Beverly Engel, the author of *The Right to Innocence*, tells us that her alcoholic mother occasionally gave her "wet" kisses on the mouth, walked in on her while she used the bathroom and looked at her in ways that made her feel uncomfortable when she was undressing. "It was not until very recently that I came to terms with my mother's behavior," Engel writes, "and saw it for what it really was—sexual abuse."[46]

The assumption that any woman who claims to have been sexually violated *was violated* is the one that guides rape crisis centres, of course. And in that context, it makes sense. When a woman phones up a hotline or shows up for a consultation, she's looking for empathy and support. Therefore, disbelief gets suspended. It isn't the role of sexual assault counsellors to cross-examine women about what really occurred. That's the job of the police and the courts. But mainstream feminism in the '90s wants to chain us all to that one particular window sill. It wants us to pretend that there aren't any other legitimate ways of thinking about these matters. If we don't want to be called anti-feminists, or worse, we're all supposed to act like perpetual rape crisis counsellors, to believe any and all allegations that come out of the mouths of female persons.

Some of us consider this unreasonable. In Tavris's words: "If a woman suspects that she has been abducted by UFOs, that the FBI is bugging her socks or that a satanic cult forced her to bear a child that was half human and half dog, must she (and we) likewise assume that 'it probably really happened'?"[47]

At its best, feminism has been about asking questions, about challenging conventional wisdom and supposed societal "truths," about exposing the logical fallacies behind sexist beliefs. But as the above feminist responses to issues such as MPD, recovered memories and ritual abuse make clear, this tradition has been abandoned. Now, intelligent inquiry finds itself trampled into the dirt by a stampede of careless emotion. When faced with complex issues, feminism now tries to shut down debate, to stop people from raising objections. It now demands that "true" feminists abandon rational thought and accept—on faith alone—highly suspect allegations.

Another area of concern is this: what happens when childhood sexual abuse, MPD and recovered memories intersect with rape crisis centres? One of the *Herizons* articles on ritual abuse says that these centres are "becoming more experienced in working with ritual abuse survivors." Amethya, who claims her abuse began when she was less than a month old, is identified at the end of her piece as a "counselor working in the area of violence against women." The editors of *Herizons* preface the ritual abuse section with this warning: "If reading these articles provokes extreme reactions or triggers memories, you may want to find someone to talk to about your reactions, or *call a crisis line* [my italics]."[48]

In February 1992, Columbia University established its own rape crisis centre in response to criticism from students that it wasn't doing enough to address the problem of violence against women. During the first semester it was in operation, seventy-nine people used the centre's services. Only about 10 percent of those, however, were seeking assistance regarding a recent occurrence in their lives. The rest wanted to talk about earlier incidents, and many of these involved childhood sexual abuse.[49]

In 1993 an independent consultant was asked to assess the Sexual Assault Centre in the small city of Hamilton, Ontario. The centre had been criticized in the local media, and its funders (two levels of government plus the United Way) wanted a review of the program they were supporting to the tune of half a million dollars a year.[50] The report, written by people obviously familiar with and sympathetic to feminist concerns, identified the childhood abuse cases as a serious problem. It pointed out that more than 80 percent of the centre's caseload involves clients "who were sexually abused as children."

According to the consultants, this causes two main difficulties. The first is that the reason the centre exists at all, the reason it is so generously funded and the reason it enjoys broad public support is because it has a mandate to assist women who've suffered a recent sexual assault. But childhood sexual abuse clients are draining its resources. Even worse, at the time the report was written, no priority was being given to recently assaulted women. This meant that women who'd just been raped were looking at a nine- to eighteen-month-long waiting list in order to get into a support group at the centre. Such women also complained that centre personnel were "too busy" to accompany them to court or didn't stay with them for "as long as they were needed."[51]

The second difficulty identified by the report is that, despite the dramatic shift in the kinds of cases it deals with, the centre had failed to modify either its staff training or its programs. Centre personnel were, therefore, prepared to deal with only 20 percent of the people who walked through their door. While the centre appears to have assumed that the same kinds of responses are appropriate for both types of clients, the independent consultants disagreed. They concluded that:

> ...although there are similarities between the needs
> of recently assaulted women and women who are
> survivors of child sexual abuse, the differences far
> outweigh the similarities.
> Counselors who work with child sexual abuse
> require training in specific skills for this task.[52]

In other words, both groups of women were being short-changed as a result.

What the report didn't talk about, however, are the implications of publicly supported rape crisis centres being pulled into the childhood sexual abuse/MPD/ recovered memory vortex. I would like to stress, once again, that I know sexual abuse *does* occur and I support programs that help the victims of such crimes put their lives back together. I also know that there are many reputable, responsible mental health professionals who would never dream of pressuring their clients into conforming to a set script, who would never in a million years strap someone down and shoot them full of "truth serum" in order to get them to admit to being sexually abused. But the problem is that there are people in the profession who clearly do operate this way—and they have influential champions such as Gloria Steinem. The problem is that women who read books such as *The Courage to Heal* may become convinced they were abused (despite having only the vaguest idea how) and then call up a rape crisis centre. The problem is that people who believe they were abused by satanic cults since they were infants are having their delusions taken seriously *and reinforced* by publicly funded rape crisis centres. This is not an appropriate use of tax dollars—or charitable ones, for that matter.

I'm not sure what the answer is, but this issue should be receiving far more attention than it does. Every crisis centre on the continent should have a definite policy on such matters. It would be a great loss if these centres were to forfeit their public support and their funding because they aligned themselves too closely with questionable childhood sexual abuse claims. It would be a terrible irony if, by trying to help a broader range of people, these centres ended up without the resources to assist their original set of clients—victims of recent sexual assault.

The debate over childhood sexual abuse is not an academic one. It affects real people in the real world. And one group of individuals that is often virtually absent from these discussions is the alleged perpetrators, the accused abusers. Feminists aren't supposed to have any sympathy for these people. In our perpetual-rape-crisis-counsellor mode we're always supposed to side with the "victim," to accept her story no matter how preposterous it might be. But life is more complicated than that. The accused are also human beings, who may themselves be victims.

In late 1993, I attended the annual convention of the Ontario Criminal Lawyers' Association, held in Toronto. That year's conference focused on false sexual abuse allegations and the intricacies of human memory. It was picketed by feminists with signs that bore messages such as: "Please beware of the childish and abusive and disrespectful use of language re: children and women's lives." According to the pickets (whom I went out to talk to), some parts of the conference were offensive. They singled out, for example, a presentation listed on the program—"Child Sexual Abuse Syndrome—Not!"—being given by a Florida psychologist, Dr. Harry Krop.

What they seemed unaware of is Krop's genuine sympathy and concern for bona fide abuse victims. It was Krop who, in 1977, established the first child sexual abuse treatment program in the state of Florida. Since then, he has counselled thousands of such victims and doesn't need to be reminded that real instances of abuse are all too common. But Krop is one of a growing number of professionals who are now expressing concern about the danger of false allegations and unjust convictions at a time in our history when sexual abuse accusations are mushrooming. After I'd told the pickets I considered the conference important because some accused persons are innocent and deserve to be represented by lawyers aware of the issues, they responded with that old feminist standby: only a small minority of those accused of sexual violence are truly innocent.

None of these people would have suggested that the experiences of South Asian immigrant women aren't important because such women comprise only a tiny percentage of the North American population. Instead, they would have argued that these women are entitled to sensitivity and understanding from society at large. Moreover, all of these feminists would consider rape intolerable— even if it happened to only five women a year.

It seems to me we have to be consistent. Either we're compassionate human beings who value justice for its own sake, or we think that the suffering of some is less important than the suffering of others. Anyone who's comfortable with this last option is invited to step right up and join the front of the line of those that society has decided not to give a darn about this week.

Sadly, even Ann Landers, an eminently sensible woman, has fallen into this trap. In September 1993, she published a letter from a man falsely accused of date rape. He reported:

> Just before the case was to go to trial, all charges
> were dropped. Prosecutors found conclusive
> evidence that the woman was lying. So after
> 14 months of a living hell and nearly $20,000 in
> legal fees, my ordeal is over.

He ended his letter by saying he's convinced that many other men are currently serving prison sentences for sexual assaults they didn't commit. "My heart goes out to all of them," he wrote. Ann's response?

> So does mine, but I'll bet an equal number of men
> who are guilty of rape are free as the breeze. Too
> often, the woman is reluctant to file charges and
> risk the publicity, so she keeps quiet. Or she files,
> the court is not convinced of the man's guilt and
> he's off the hook.[53]

Ann doesn't say anything that's untrue, of course. But her response is the equivalent of telling someone who's just broken their arm that they should stop whining because the person across the street broke their leg. Surely both injuries deserve similar amounts of medical care, as well as compassion.

Ann devotes just three words to men who have been falsely convicted *by the state*; who may have lost their reputations, their savings, their homes and their families because the state came and arrested them, tried them, convicted them and is now keeping them behind bars. Moreover, it does *real* victims of sexual violence or abuse no good whatsoever to jail innocent people. It accomplishes nothing. It merely adds more anguish and sorrow to a world that contains too much of these things already.

Many people are never actually charged with offences such as child sexual abuse, but that doesn't mean their lives aren't shattered. As a journalist, I've received letters from parents, in their seventies, who say their adult daughters sought therapy for depression or following a marriage breakdown and subsequently ended up accusing their families of satanic ritual abuse. Such "victims" frequently cut off all contact with their relatives, effectively abandoning their elderly parents and depriving them of access to their grandchildren. This is a heavy burden for parents to bear in their later years.

In fairness to Ann Landers, she later responded sympathetically to people who claimed to be falsely accused of sexual abuse. In December 1993 she printed a letter from LITTLE ROCK, ARK., who wrote:

> As a father who has been unjustly accused, I can testify to the shock, pain and grief that results from the accusation by an adult daughter. Estrangement from my children and grandchildren followed. A

therapist had convinced my daughter that all her
problems were the result of "repressed" anger at me
for having abused her sexually 25 years ago.

Ann tells him she's received "hundreds of letters" similar to
his and, after printing another, advises readers that not all
sexually dysfunctional adults were abused as children and
that false memories are more common than people believe.
She continues:

> Unfortunately, anybody can say anything about
> anyone, and the accused is then in the position of
> defending himself. All too often, if the maligned
> individual is a high-profile personality, the feeding
> frenzy begins, the headlines are a foot high, and
> the TV coverage is relentless. By the time the true
> facts are made public, the victim is thoroughly
> discredited and his reputation in shreds.

Ann had already printed another such letter, a month
earlier, from TULSA. It included the following:

> My sister has literally torn our family apart with her
> unfounded accusations of sexual abuse. She decided
> to latch on to this as the reason for her teenage
> promiscuity and her failed marriages. She made her
> devastating accusations against our father publicly,
> but privately has admitted that she doesn't really
> have any actual memory of these events. Her
> excuse is, "They must have happened because my
> life is such a mess."[54]

Laura Pasley spent half a decade convinced she was the
victim of severe sexual abuse that her therapist insisted was
really ritual abuse. Her story, published in *Skeptic* magazine,

said that the women in her therapy group weren't even permitted to discuss the effect such allegations might have on their families:

> The visions in my head were of severe physical and sexual abuse. The images were so incredibly bizarre, yet they seemed so real. My picture of my family became distorted. Was it the drugs the doctors had me on, was it television shows or traumatic events I had witnessed over the years, or was it actual memories? I did not know but Steve [her therapist] said they *were fact* and to deny them meant that I did not want to get well. He said I was in denial, I was running, I was "protecting" my family, I was staying sick to "cover up" for my family. [original italics]

Pasley tells us that patients were often advised to write hostile letters to their parents which accused them of horrible acts and which divorced them, and that these letters were written with and read out loud to the other members of her therapy group. She says she was told the group was her "new family" and that she wouldn't be able to recover if she didn't move away from her "dangerous" relatives:

> Steve had me believing my mother had been trying to kill me for years. Not in an obvious attempt, but in the things she would do for me. I was bulimic. If Mama bought us groceries and any of them were easily ingested "binge foods," Steve said it was to kill me. At one point, I took some badly needed groceries back to her, threw the bag and asked her if she was trying to kill me because there were some cookies and chips in the bag.

Pasley also neatly encapsulates the dilemma that people accused of long-ago sexual abuse face:

> My family's response to accusations I made would not have mattered. If they said nothing, it was because they were guilty. If they cried innocence, they were trying to hide something. If they did not remember something the way I remembered it, they were in denial. There was always an answer.

Near the end of her piece, Pasley describes what happened to her in therapy as "the con job of all con jobs." She reports:

> All my energy, all my money, everything I had went to them. When I woke up, my daughter was 12 years old and I [had] missed it. I missed some of her most precious years while searching endlessly for the next "memory."

Many "survivors," however, have yet to wake up. And when they do, some of them discover another albatross around their neck—the crushing guilt they feel over the strain they've placed on innocent family members' health. Pasley tells us about one woman in her therapy group who falsely accused her parents of satanic ritual abuse but reconciled with them a short time before her mother died of a heart attack. The woman remains wracked by guilt "each and every day."[55]

The issues of child sexual abuse, MPD and recovered memories are complex ones fraught with danger. But there is little or no acknowledgment of this within mainstream feminism. Gloria Steinem's MPD film doesn't concede this. *Ms.* magazine doesn't. To its credit, the longest of the three articles in *Herizons* spends four lines cautioning that not everyone who claims to be a satanist is necessarily a ritual abuser, and says that if people "lose sight of that fact we just might find ourselves in the midst of a modern-day witch-hunt."[56] Sadly, the author is more concerned about stereo-typing people who belong to a fringe religious group than in the harm being done to those falsely accused of canni-balism and of molesting their one-month-olds.

A women's movement that insists all accusations of sex-ual violence must be believed no matter what—and that calls people who express reservations about such matters "backlashers"—is a feminism that cares more about its own dogma than it does about real women's lives.

Gretchen, Barb, R.J., Amethya and Laura all turned to people in the mental health field for help. If these women have suffered any abuse, it isn't difficult to argue that much of it may have been at the hands of "experts" whom they trusted. There's more than one way to victimize women. When mainstream feminism actively applauds such victim-ization, its credibility vanishes.

If you prick us, do we not bleed? if you tickle us, do we not laugh? if you poison us, do we not die?

–William Shakespeare
The Merchant of Venice

CHAPTER THREE

Double Standards, '90s Style

In April 1994, three men burst into a Toronto café. It was around 11:00 p.m. and the trendy establishment, which served gourmet coffees and decadent desserts, contained more than two dozen patrons. These people were ordered to hand over their cash and other valuables. When the robbers left, a twenty-three-year-old woman named Georgina Leimonis lay dying from a gunshot wound to the chest.

By American standards, Toronto is a clean, safe place to live. This kind of apparently random violence might happen in New York City, but it's not the sort of thing to which Canadians are accustomed. In the aftermath, the media declared that Toronto had "lost its innocence" that night. Members of the public stopped by the shut-down café to pay their respects with bouquets of flowers, which soon overflowed onto the sidewalk.[1]

As it happened, the three robbers were black. There was resulting concern, in certain quarters, that the incident might undermine race relations in the city. Newspaper editorials stressed that it was unjust to view these robbers as being representative of the black community. A high-profile black spokesperson delivered a speech in which he pointed out that most blacks lead quiet, normal, law-abiding lives. "The whole community shouldn't be criminalized by the actions of a few," he said. "I am appalled at anyone who would do that."[2]

Unlike the United States, Canada doesn't compile race-based crime statistics in any formal or consistent manner. Following the café shooting, a few commentators called for this, but the suggestion went nowhere. Other people argued that even if such figures showed that blacks commit more crime than other groups, this still wouldn't demonstrate a "cause-and-effect relationship between race and crime"[3]—in other words, the statistics themselves would not be overly meaningful. While they would have the potential to besmirch the reputation of an entire group of people, they would tell us little about *why* that group was either committing or appeared to be committing more crime, and little about what society as a whole might do to help correct the problem.

Which is all well and good. But on each December 6 since 1989, Canada —with the vocal support of practically every segment of its population—has been commemorating the deaths of the fourteen female engineering students gunned down in the Montreal Massacre by a man named Marc Lepine. Speeches are made in Parliament, rallies are held across the country, the media is flooded with angst. And in this case, people have little compunction about saying that Lepine *is* representative of *all men*. When we talk about this event we don't say Lepine was a profoundly troubled individual whose behaviour tells us little of importance about the group to which he happened to belong. We don't say that most men lead quiet, normal, law-abiding lives. We don't say that the fact that more men than women commit crimes doesn't demonstrate a cause-and-effect relationship between gender and crime.

Admittedly, the situation is more complicated in this case. Lepine made it easy for us. He told us he was committing these offences because he hated feminists. Apparently, he believed he hadn't been accepted by the engineering school because female students were taking places that should have gone to men. He baited the line—and we swallowed it, along with the hook and the sinker. As dissident feminist Amy Friedman has observed: "The act itself was named by the killer, and we accepted his explanation. Marc Lepine said he was out to get feminists, and we took him at his word. We allowed Lepine to write the scenario for us."[4]

Allow me to draw a distinction here. I believe it's important that we have discussions about why (according to U.S. data) blacks commit more crime than whites and why men commit more crime than women. But there is a difference between having a rational, intelligent, ongoing debate about these issues and simply accepting at face value whatever explanation is offered by a particular criminal or group of criminals.

Let's suppose, for instance, that the men who took part in the café robbery had gone to the trouble of articulating their thoughts and feelings. Suppose they had muttered, while threatening people, taking their wallets and shooting one of them: "You're just a bunch of middle-class scum. You suckers actually get up in the morning and go to work. We hate people like you, with your smug, stable lives, because you represent something we haven't been able to achieve."

Would we, in such a case, have allowed these ravings to become the focal point, the lens through which we viewed the entire incident? Would we still be referring to them five years later? Or, after duly reporting such comments, would

we have relegated them to the sidelines, collectively deciding that the life that was lost was the important thing, not
the twisted logic of the criminals?

To use another example, Susan Smith, the South
Carolina woman who confessed to drowning her two young
sons in 1994 (after falsely telling police she'd been car-
jacked), may say she did so because her boyfriend told her
he wasn't able to face the responsibilities associated with a
ready-made family.[5] But should we allow this excuse to
dominate what we write and think about this tragedy? Or
do we conclude that Smith is a sick woman whose pathetic
explanation doesn't deserve much attention, that what
really matters is that she deliberately snuffed out the lives
of two beautiful little boys?

Yet Marc Lepine's stated rationale has been enshrined
as the correct, final interpretation of his horrific acts—as
the thing that deserves to be remembered. Why? Because
mainstream feminism's explanation for Lepine's behaviour
happens to coincide with the man's own ravings. While
most feminists would denounce in an instant anyone who
said the black robbers in the café were merely acting out
the violence that blacks as a group are more prone to committing, many consider it an article of faith that Lepine was
merely acting out (in an extreme fashion) the violence that
men as a group are more prone to committing.

This is a double standard of the worst kind. It is logi-
cally inconsistent and morally offensive. It now appears
that it isn't double standards per se that feminists object to,
it isn't logical inconsistency per se that we oppose. Rather,
double standards that work against men, that stereotype
them deplorably, are not merely acceptable to feminists,
they are being promoted by us. And the rest of society has
gone along for the ride.

Let me put this another way: suppose Lepine had separated not the women from the men but the whites from the

non-whites. Suppose he'd been a neo-Nazi who said he hated non-whites because they were taking up spots in the engineering school he thought he deserved, and then he shot fourteen of them to death. Would this incident have become a symbol of white racism? Would we have been told that all whites were responsible for what occurred? Would politicians have insisted his actions were the logical extension of the more subtle kinds of racism whites perpetuate against their fellow citizens on a daily basis? Would the date have been declared a national day to reflect on white racism?

It's possible, but I don't think so. I suspect it's far more likely that people would have kept things in perspective. While not denying that this was a terrible tragedy, and not denying that race was certainly an element, we would have said: "Look, the man was a psycho. Most whites are heartsick at his actions. This society still has a long way to go before eradicating racism, but it serves no purpose to hold up the crazed behaviour of a lone neo-Nazi as being representative of the way whites treat non-whites." No doubt certain leftist commentators and less moderate spokespersons from non-white communities would have insisted that the incident reflected the true state of race relations, but I think most people would have considered this an extreme position that had more to do with a certain political outlook than with everyday reality—particularly the Canadian reality.

Notice, however, that when feminism advances an equally extreme position, this patriarchal, male-dominated, misogynous, backlash society falls for it. In late 1994 a *man* wrote an opinion piece in the country's national newspaper defending the decision to spend more than a quarter of a million dollars not on violence prevention but on fourteen pink granite benches in Vancouver, each bearing the name of a slain female engineering student as well as "a small hollow that will gather rainwater, the tears of and for the women who were murdered that day, and who are murdered every day." The political and social climate being what it is, this person also defended the inscription accompanying these benches, which reads, in part: "In memory, and in grief for all the women who have been murdered *by men* [my italics]." We're told that to remove the word "male" from "male violence" is to render it "a causeless phenomenon, like the weather."[6] But this leads us right back to the café robbery. Should we, then, make a point of mentioning that the people responsible for taking the life of an innocent patron were three *black* robbers, so as not to obscure the identity of the group that should be blamed?

The report prepared by the Canadian Panel on Violence Against Women explicitly rejects the notion that men who commit violent crimes are troubled individuals who should be viewed as such. Indeed, it criticizes Canadian institutions for regarding men's violent acts as "individual pathological responses by 'sick' men" and declares that a man who uses violence is really "affirming his power, which he wants to preserve at all costs and which makes him neither monstrous nor sick."

From this perspective, then, men never lose their cool and lash out angrily at whoever is nearby. Rather, they are always calmly and deliberately carrying out a political agenda of oppression whenever they mistreat female persons. The report says that violent men "make conscious choices including their choice of victim, the places and circumstances of their violence and the degree of force they use."[7]

Do the authors of this report live in the real world? Surely we can all agree that there's sometimes a political subtext to male violence, that some men do believe they are entitled to punish and control women, that their violence is justified, and that society gives them the right to behave this way. It would be foolish to deny this. But there are also vast numbers of men who grew up being told they weren't supposed to hit a girl and were raised to view males who assault females as despicable bullies. Men often feel trapped, inadequate, overwhelmed, confused, resentful and unappreciated. Those who haven't developed constructive strategies for dealing with such emotions may behave horribly, but the reasons for their behaviour are part of the complex tapestry of everyday life. The idea that men are *always* acting on a single, identifiable political impulse whenever they behave violently toward someone who happens to be female is thinking that honours neither truth nor humanity.

The panel says it is interested in dispelling myths. Accordingly, it insists it is a myth that women are in any way responsible for the violence committed against them:

> One of the most pervasive is the myth that places responsibility for violence on the victim rather than on the perpetrator: women provoke, tease and taunt men, invite their sexual advances and then push them away. Women annoy, disobey and confront, thus leading or contributing to the violence they encounter. They were wearing the wrong clothing, drank too much alcohol, walked alone at night, etc.
>
> We flatly reject any analyses that place *any degree of responsibility* for violence on the women themselves *no matter what their actions*, appearance, demeanour or behaviour. [my italics][8]

Let me state categorically that I'm as outraged as the next feminist by the idea that some man would think that by merely being out on the street late at night, for instance, I'm asking to be raped. But is it reasonable to say that nothing I *ever* do can be viewed as contributing to crimes that may be committed against me?

As dissident feminist Camille Paglia has argued, if you drive to New York City, leave your keys in plain sight on the hood, and someone then steals your car, that person should be tracked down and punished. If you sleep with your doors wide open and someone comes in and burglarizes your home, that person, too, should be brought to justice. But this doesn't change the fact that you have behaved stupidly.[9] Is it reasonable to maintain that you haven't *contributed* to what has transpired, to assert that someone else is 100 percent responsible for what occurred?

Let's say my husband and I get into a raging fight. I slap him in the face and threaten him with a frying pan. Am I not *somewhat* to blame if he grabs my wrist and, in the struggle, it becomes sprained? Women aren't in the right all the time—far from it. And while feminism was responsible for bringing us down off our Victorian pedestal, it now appears intent on placing us back up there.

A couple of pages later, the Violence Report continues:

> Men who are violent bear *sole responsibility* for their violent actions.... Abusive behaviour cannot be explained away by loss of control or unfavourable circumstances. Problems with relationships, stress, alcohol, anxiety, depression and unemployment may contribute to violence against women, but they are neither acceptable excuses nor root causes. [my italics][10]

If that's the standard we're going to hold men to, why do women who commit violence against other women get to "explain away" *their* inappropriate behaviour? Why do lesbians who batter other lesbians get to blame it on the stress that a society hostile to lesbians places them under? What's so unique about this sort of pressure that nothing remotely approximates it? The report reads:

> Although research into the incidence and prevalence of [lesbian battering] is virtually non-existent in Canada, women who spoke to the Panel contend that it is the result of institutionalized heterosexism which isolates lesbians and adds pressure to their relationships.[11]

This is one of the rare occasions in which the panel is forced to acknowledge that women can be victimized by people born with ovaries rather than testicles. And how does it respond? First, by neglecting to mention that U.S. research on this problem does exist and that it suggests lesbians batter their partners at about the same rate as men batter their wives.[12] (The panel cites U.S. sources—including *The Courage to Heal*—elsewhere, so why not here?) Second, it accepts an excuse from women it has already said won't be tolerated from men. It lets it stand. Shamefully, the report neither challenges nor denounces it.

But the double standards don't stop there. In its section devoted to native women, the panel suggests that native women who commit criminal offences shouldn't be held accountable for their behaviour the way other people are, since they're really just victims of the system. Indeed, the report reads: "For Aboriginal women in conflict with the law, a prison sentence is the final act of violence imposed on them by a society that has oppressed them since birth."[13] The panel urges the development of an alternative justice system that would respond to criminal acts by native women within the context of their own cultures. But when it comes to native men, the report reverses itself. It says culture shouldn't influence the way native men are treated by the legal system, and that taking culture into account amounts to racism:

> Aboriginal culture should not be considered in
> determining whether or not to lay criminal
> charges. Nor should it be used by law enforcers
> to decide whether or not to act on a complaint
> of spousal abuse. This is systemic racism because
> different standards of treatment are applied to
> Aboriginal people than to non-Aboriginal
> people.[14]

As Trent University professor John Fekete has observed in his book *Moral Panic*, the report goes further still in a subsequent chapter when it "extends this double standard with one stroke to all women and men."[15] In that particular section we read that men who do terrible things are criminals and should be treated harshly. Women who do terrible things, on the other hand, are simply misunderstood. In this way, the panel declares that the only real criminals are male:

> Women who have committed crimes need healing
> models identical to other women and correctional
> environments that allow them to regain power over
> their lives. They have more in common with other
> women than with male perpetrators of crime.[16]

While men are expected to dread being sent to prison because it's an unpleasant place where people are deprived of "power over their lives," according to the panel, prisons should be designed to empower inmates of the feminine gender.

These state-sanctioned feminists aren't the only ones who think double standards that favour females are okay. In the introduction to *The War Against Women*, Marilyn

French protests against prejudice, which she defines as the "prejudgement of people based on their inherent, unchangeable sex or color." She then spends the next couple of hundred pages pre-judging men based on their sex. She explicitly decries double standards but then, in the context of a book that criticizes men for denigrating everything female, boasts that "the clitoris is the superior organ" when compared with the penis because it is "compact, protected, and unique—it has no other function but producing sexual pleasure."[17]

French holds men responsible for the way they turn out, but not women. She expects men to struggle actively against their upbringing, but she doesn't blame women who fail to struggle against theirs. As we've already seen, French doesn't think women should be criticized for the brutal acts they commit—such as female genital mutilation—since society is forcing them to do these things. Elsewhere, in the context of talking about women who abuse alcohol or drugs while pregnant, she says:

> Like men, women in despair, unhappy women,
> behave in self-destructive ways. A society that was
> really concerned about this behavior would address
> the causes for the hopelessness. Most of the babies
> harmed by self-destructive maternal actions are
> part of the underclass that society condemns to
> death every time it chooses to spend money on
> weapons rather than social programs.

If women behave irresponsibly and inflict harm on others, we should try to figure out why and fix things. But if men do the same, according to her thesis, there's only one explanation: it's because they've been socialized to *want* to be violent, nasty people.[18] Ultimately, then, her position boils down to: excuses for women, moral censure for men.

Feminism consistently tells men to shape up, to stop being jerks, that they're the problem. As Wendy Dennis writes of the contemporary North American male in her book *Hot and Bothered: Sex and Love in the Nineties*:

> Even though he's been bending over backwards
> to adjust to [women's] ever-changing needs, over
> the years he's taken a fair bit of flak for behaving
> like the male creature he was raised to be. He
> has also heard—and endured in manly silence—
> interminable lectures about how he must mend
> his ways. In fact, the story of his life in the after-
> math of feminism has largely been a story of
> censure, blame, belittlement and distaste for the
> male person that he is.
>
> For one of the implicit, if unadmitted, tenets of
> feminism has been a fundamental disrespect for
> men.[19]

Men hear about women's rights and their own responsibili-ties. Among the Canadian violence panel's recommenda-tions regarding the educational sector is one that says schools "must create the strongest possible equality model" by, among other things, "emphasizing the rights of girls and women and the responsibilities of boys and men to respect these rights."[20]

Yet feminism doesn't treat women half as harshly as it does men. Its message to women, even now, is: "There, there, it's not your fault." Think about it. A middle-aged, balding senior partner shows up at the office Christmas party with an attractive, very young woman on his arm. Her skirt's up to here and her cleavage is down to there. Behind his back, the man is snickered at—and criticized— for spending time with a "bimbo." It's obvious to everyone what he really sees in her, and feminism views him with contempt for being more attracted to the woman's breasts than to her brains. But what about the young woman? Do we chastise her with anywhere near the same vigour for being attracted not to the man (surely they don't all have sparkling personalities) but to his sports car and his European vacations? Hardly. It's true, the older wives at such parties don't go out of their way to make her feel comfortable, but feminism itself attempts to.

In *The Beauty Myth*, Naomi Wolf argues that women know, instinctively, that if we dress in certain ways we have a better chance of getting what we want from people who are male. This is often the case. But she then proceeds to argue that, as a result, women don't have a choice about how we behave. She says a woman who puts on spike heels and lipstick before asking "an influential professor to be her thesis advisor" shouldn't be considered "a slut" because she's merely doing what a woman has to do in a hostile world.[21]

Leaving aside the issue of whether wearing lipstick and heels qualifies as sluttish behaviour, to say that this imaginary female has simply been swept along by the tide and therefore isn't responsible for her actions is a grave insult to all those women who've managed to work their way up academic and corporate ladders without sleeping with their bosses. Wolf, like MacKinnon, says we don't really exercise free will, that we don't really have choices. But this position, once again, denies the complexity of the world around us. There are very few situations that come down to only two options. Even if all the cards we've been dealt are low ones, we still *choose* from among them and decide in which order to play them.

If a knife-wielding man threatens me as I'm getting into my car in a parking lot, I can yell loudly and try to attract attention, give him a shove and attempt to run away, or do what he says and get inside. Even if I choose the latter, I can still try to lean on the horn or to exit by the passenger door. I can struggle violently, remain calm until he lets his guard down, talk to, scream at or ignore him. If he tries to force me to perform fellatio, I have the option of complying or of biting his penis off. Women aren't rag dolls being pulled this way and that by forces immune to anything we might say or do. We spend our lives around other human beings, not caught up in the grip of King Kong-sized adversaries. How we respond matters. We have the ability not only to affect our own destinies but to make history.

Contemporary feminism, though, is prepared to accept this idea only sometimes. It does say that women should organize and agitate and demonstrate. But then we have Wolf telling us that women won't really have a choice about whether to dress up before going to an interview with a prospective thesis adviser until we not only rewrite the last several hundred years (an impossibility) but advance a few more hundred into the future. She says, of this hypothetical graduate student:

> She will have a choice when a plethora of faculties
> in her field, headed by women and endowed by
> generations of female magnates and robber
> baronesses, open their gates to her; when multina-
> tional corporations led by women clamor for the
> skills of young female graduates; when there are
> *other* universities, with bronze busts of the heroines
> of half a millennium's classical learning; when
> there are *other* research-funding boards maintained
> by the deep coffers provided by the revenues of
> female inventors, where half the chairs are held by
> women scientists. [original italics][22]

This pretty much condemns the women who are alive right here and now to perpetual victimhood—and the excuses feminism never tires of making for their frailties, faults and misdeeds.

Feminism doesn't hold women up to the same harsh standards that apply to men. It doesn't tell women who suffer from anorexia to get a life, to stop obsessing about superficial matters such as their appearance and to start putting their energies to better use. Feminism doesn't demand that women who are being battered stand up for themselves the very first time and every time a man tries to push them around. It doesn't demand that they leave abusive situations (even if that means going on welfare) because they have a responsibility to ensure that their children don't grow up in such circumstances. Feminism doesn't tell young women that giving birth to a child when you're fifteen is a one-way ticket to poverty. It doesn't say there's no excuse for not using birth control in the '90s. It doesn't tell teenaged girls it'll take longer to close the gender wage gap if they keep dropping out of school and settling for low-paying jobs. Instead, we say that anorexics, battered wives, young single mothers and high school dropouts all deserve understanding and compassion. We demand programs to assist them and blame the school system for being a "hostile environment."

I have no problem with compassion and understanding. When I think of friends who have been anorexic, for example, I know it's callous even to suggest that this problem can be dismissed outright. But what's good for the goose is good for the gander. Why don't men deserve the same consideration? Why, at a time in history when everyone insists women are men's equals, do women still get a shoulder to cry on and men get a cuff upside the head? Why do we bend over backward trying to understand why women behave in less-than-perfect ways but don't spare a tear for men who end up as basket cases? Why are men held fully responsible for their defects but not women? Why is it okay to be nasty to men as a group but not to women as a group?

In 1991 Ms. magazine published a piece by novelist Alice Walker (*The Color Purple*) about Winnie Mandela, the now-estranged wife of South African president Nelson Mandela. Ms. Mandela is a controversial figure. In May 1991, she was found guilty of four counts each of abduction and of being an accessory to assault—activities that ended tragically in the death of a fourteen-year-old boy. Since the publication of Walker's piece, Ms. Mandela has been suspended from an African National Congress position amid allegations of fraud and continues to be a source of mortification for her husband.[23] While it's possible, as Walker suggests, that Ms. Mandela is entirely the victim of an elaborate plot to discredit her, it appears just as likely that she is an unstable person who has let the celebrity of being the wife of the revered Nelson Mandela go to her head. In a classic case of the appalling double standards that prevail in the women's movement, the Ms. article leaves one with the distinct impression that even if Ms. Mandela had helped her bodyguards kidnap, confine and assault the four young men in question, even if she herself had slit the throat of the youth who died, she shouldn't be held accountable. Crimes are only crimes, then, when they're perpetrated by people you dislike or whose politics you disagree with? I doubt the family of the slain fourteen year old finds such thinking very comforting.

While Ms. runs a "No Comment" column that calls attention to the sexist attitudes displayed in mainstream advertising, it has no compunction about printing, in large lettering, in its "international news" section, a Saudi Arabian saying that reads: "Trusting a man is like trusting a sieve to hold water." Or another from Sweden which declares, "A woman's heart sees more than ten men's eyes."[24]

These double standards are important, because they

spill over into mainstream culture. The squeaky wheel gets the grease, and feminists have become expert at insisting loudly that the female experience of the world is far worse than the male experience. That message seeps into our consciousness, it influences how we all view social issues.

How many times have we heard, for example, that three to four times more teenaged girls than boys attempt suicide? How often have we put down a newspaper or magazine after reading this figure more convinced than ever that the world is an inhospitable place for females?[25]

In truth, that number tells only part of the story. What it doesn't reveal is that many more young males than females actually kill themselves. According to 1992 U.S. data, *six times* more males aged fifteen to twenty-four took their lives than females in the same age group. In Canada, 1990–1993 figures reveal that *five times* more males than females in this age group committed suicide.[26]

Only in a topsy-turvy world could actual deaths receive less attention than *attempted* suicides. Dead bodies are the end of the line. They are a testimony to utter hopelessness. There are no more chances with a dead body, no more opportunities to try to work things out.

Unless we want to argue that young women are more incompetent than males of the same age, we have to conclude that most young women who attempt suicide don't mean to kill themselves. They're trying to signal their desperation; they're calling for help. On the other hand, partly because males are socialized to believe that admitting they have problems is the same as admitting that they are failures as males, these young men don't appear to believe help will be forthcoming, or that they are entitled to it.

We haven't heard about the suicide crisis that's robbing North America of its young men because feminism has played into and helped to reinforce pre-existing, sexist double standards. Our society has never considered men's suffering to be as important as women's. It's always been assumed that "real men" take stress, abuse, danger, fatigue and so forth in stride. Men have been trained to view such things as challenges to be met, trials by which to gauge one's self worth, rather than conditions to complain about. They grow up knowing that, in the event of a natural disaster, it's women and children who are entitled to seats in the lifeboats first.

Men's activist Warren Farrell refers to football, which high school boys learn they will be considered manly for playing, as "smashface."[27] I thought this was a tad extreme until the Toronto Argonauts of the Canadian Football League ran a series of advertisements in 1995 featuring slogans such as:

- "Disabled list? Hey, if it ain't broke, they're not trying."
- "There's nothing like seeing a gory blind-side tackle to the kidneys to really make you feel alive!"
- "It's like slowing down to look at a gruesome road kill. For 3 hours."

There's no female parallel in our culture. There is no context in which the pain and damaged bodies of living, breathing young women is blatantly celebrated.

The combination of this entrenched double standard with feminist navel-gazing has proved to be a potent one. In some respects, it continues to be a deadly one, too. Consider that in 1993, 208 females of all ages were murdered in Canada. In that same year, 488 males aged fifteen to twenty-four took their own lives. While the media devoted loads of coverage to violence against women it barely mentioned young male suicides.[28]

Only so much air time and only so many pages of print

get devoted to social issues. If a society is inclined to take female suffering more seriously to begin with, and if it is told again and again that women are the ones who are really having a terrible time of it, other concerns recede into the background. Communities have limited dollars and limited numbers of volunteers with which to address social problems. When these resources are being concentrated overwhelmingly in one direction, others are inevitably neglected.

And suicide rates aren't the only indicator that males are worse off than females. As Betty Friedan recently pointed out, American women currently live eight years longer than men do. (In Canada, the gap is six years.) Nor can this difference be attributed to innate biological superiority since, at the turn of this century, women survived their husbands by only one year.[29] Imagine the outcry from feminists if these numbers were reversed: if five times as many women were taking their own lives in their youth and if those who managed to reach retirement age were going to their graves seven years sooner!

Furthermore, the attention being paid to women's health issues and the accusations of bias in the medical profession (according to Marilyn French, "many doctors...take pleasure in mutilating women's bodies"[30]) have combined to obscure the fact that men die more often than women do from all fifteen of the leading causes of death in the United States. From heart disease to motor vehicle accidents, it is men—not women—who are over-represented.[31] This doesn't mean research into women's health problems shouldn't continue, or that the male medical establishment can be absolved entirely of charges of insensitivity and downright closed-mindedness regarding their female patients. But it does tend to cast doubt on the notion that a massive male medical conspiracy bent on victimizing women has been in operation over the past several decades.

If such a conspiracy exists, it's surely been one of the least effectual in memory.

Now let's look at violence. Despite everything we've been hearing and reading, the truth of the matter is that, in 1992, American men were four times more likely than women to be murdered. In Canada, men accounted for 67 percent of the nation's homicide victims in 1993, and were robbed twice as often.[32]

Feminists routinely gloss over the grim realities of male life by overlooking large chunks of the violence statistics. Instead, we tend to concentrate on sexual assaults and point out that, while men are more often attacked and murdered by strangers, women are more frequently victimized by someone they know, and perhaps love and trust. While I agree there's something to the argument that it's *worse* to be attacked by a person you know, especially in a home you've considered "safe," I also think it's possible to exaggerate this aspect. The other side of the coin is that the world writ large is less dangerous for women than it is for men, and it may be that experiencing violence at the hands of someone you know is easier to anticipate (and perhaps take precautions against) than the kind of out-of-the-blue violence men are more likely to encounter. In John Fekete's words:

> Many women would be relieved to hear that they need not worry about getting knifed or even hurt; and that [statistically] their abrasions in life, such as they are, will come from people they associate with. An acquaintance relationship that goes over the top, and a society in which this happens, are still closer to the orbit of what is understandable and predictable, and perhaps preventable, than perpetual risk from strangers.[33]

Indeed, despite the fact that women are frequently assaulted in their homes, a Statistics Canada report on crime victimization in 1993 found that "[f]emales who were separated or divorced had violent victimization rates almost seven times that of married females." In other words, living with a man isn't necessarily the arrangement in which women are most at risk.[34]

Now, let's turn to education. American, Canadian and British data all tell us that boys are currently doing measurably worse in school than girls. Yes, there are studies that claim adolescent girls' self-esteem plummets. There are others that say teachers devote less classroom time to girls than they do to boys. There are still others that say the sexual harassment girls experience in school makes them *want* to cut classes more. But the cold hard facts are that high school girls are currently outperforming boys in virtually every activity. The most successful boys still tend to take slightly more senior math and science courses and to score slightly higher in these subjects on standardized tests. Boys also participate in more school-related sports. But in every other area—whether you look at reading, student government, overall academic achievement or absenteeism and drop-out rates—girls are faring better than their male counterparts. Girls also report more often than boys that their parents expect them to continue their education.[35]

Feminists, one suspects, deserve to take a bow for much of the success girls are now enjoying, but few people are paying attention to the other side of the coin. Precious little noise is being made on behalf of these boys, innocent children who surely deserve our concern. If the numbers were reversed, a chorus of feminists would be condemning a system that doesn't give girls a fighting chance, that undercuts them from their earliest years. The media could be counted on to ensure that results showing girls trailing boys made it into the headlines. But when the Toronto Board of

Education released results of its most recent high school student survey, the media emphasized that black students and those of Portuguese descent were doing less well than others. The fact that boys from *all* ethnic backgrounds were performing at lower levels than their sisters was scarcely noticed. Nor did any feminist I'm aware of admit publicly that such results demonstrate that young females aren't quite as beleaguered as we've been assuming.[36]

In an earlier time, boys who weren't academically inclined could still find high-paying, relatively unskilled jobs. But automation, economic restructuring, the global economy, demographic shifts and information technologies are all having profound effects on North American employment prospects. Today, many unskilled jobs have disappeared or are in the process of being phased out. Thus, at a time in our history when young adults need a high school diploma more than ever, the fact that boys as a group aren't keeping up with girls as a group, and will likely lead disadvantaged lives as a result, isn't receiving the attention it warrants. This is because, in a very real sense, if a story doesn't conform to our preconceptions, if it doesn't show women being short-changed or victimized in some manner, it's not considered news.

Incidentally, some of those high-paying jobs that poorly educated young men have been spending large numbers of their waking hours performing are also unpleasant, dangerous ones. In the United States, men accounted for 94 percent of occupational fatalities during the 1980s. According to 1993 Canadian data, 96 percent of those killed on the job were male, while men suffered three times as many non-fatal injuries at work as women did.[37] In *The Myth of Male Power*, Warren Farrell points out that young men are twenty-four times more likely to be killed while performing farm labour than young women are, and he notes: "The more a worker's beat requires exposure to sleet and the heat, the more likely is the worker to be a man: ditch digging, previously the work of chain gangs of prisoners, was protested as exploitative of prisoners."[38]

Feminists rarely acknowledge factors such as these when they complain that women are still concentrated in pink-collar ghettos. Nor do they acknowledge that the expectation on the part of many women that they will marry a man who earns more money than they do gives them the flexibility to pursue career options that are less lucrative but perhaps more appealing. Given a choice between repairing hydro lines outdoors or supervising children in a day-care centre for less than half the pay, many women *choose* to do the latter. Says Farrell:

> We frequently hear that women are segregated into low-paying dead-end jobs in poor work environments such as factories. But when *The Jobs Related Almanac* ranked 250 jobs from best to worst based on a *combination* of salary, stress, work environment, outlook, security, and physical demands, they found that twenty-four of the twenty-five worst jobs were almost-all-male jobs. Some examples: truck driver, sheet-metal worker, roofer, boilermaker, lumberjack, carpenter, construction worker or foreman, construction machinery operator, football player, welder, millwright, ironworker. All of these "worst jobs" have one thing in common: 95 to 100 percent men. [original italics][39]

Although it can be argued that men, as a group, have been paying dearly for their higher wages in a number of ways, they are still being blamed for this apparent inequity. Feminists view the current income imbalance as resulting from male malevolence rather than a societal double standard that says it doesn't matter so much if men undertake dirty, dangerous jobs or perform work that permits them little time with their families. Feminists describe women's progress in the employment world as far too slow and conclude that it must be entirely men's fault, without acknowledging that some of the responsibility rests with women themselves.

When Canada was making its most recent appointment to the Supreme Court in 1992, three women declined the position before it was awarded to a man. We can talk about glass ceilings and structural discrimination. We can say there are too few women in positions of power. And yet, these three women apparently turned down a chance to rise to the absolute pinnacle of their profession because the job demands would disrupt their family lives too much.[40]

In the last few pages, then, we have quickly scanned suicide rates, life spans, leading causes of death, violent crime, education, occupational fatalities and unpleasant jobs. This data can't be denied or manipulated out of existence. While we can try to change the subject or divert attention away from such issues, the fact remains that, in a significant number of quantifiable ways, males—not females—are losing out in this society.

But feminism continues to self-obsess. It has become so preoccupied with women's (often legitimate) grievances that it has lost sight of the bigger picture. I think it's time we started asking why feminism closes its eyes to the above facts, why it refuses to admit that males often get a raw deal too. Why in heaven's name can't we just acknowledge that the world contains both ponds and streams?

A philosophy that dismisses these issues out of hand doesn't deserve our allegiance. In late 1993, Letty Cottin Pogrebin, a founding editor of Ms., began a column in that publication with the words: "Have you ever noticed that whenever women take center stage, someone rushes into the social control booth and yanks the spotlight back to men?" Pogrebin goes on to insist that questions about why the Ms. Foundation's Take Our Daughters to Work day didn't include boys as well as girls are merely "Me-Too" and "What-About-Us" reactions on the part of selfish males who can't bear to see girls enjoy "their one moment in the sun." She then presents the self-esteem studies and refers to eating disorders, depression and the lack of female occupational role models as proof girls are in more desperate need of encouragement than boys.[41] The data we've just looked at, however, is completely absent from her analysis. It doesn't exist. From the feminist perspective, males are never, ever worse off than females.

Feminism used to be about making sure *all* the relevant data was taken into account, about ensuring that female experiences and perspectives were added to the information already under consideration so that a balanced perspective was possible. Today, feminism seems to be more about picking and choosing the facts and figures that make your argument while deliberately ignoring everything else.

Which brings us to the clothing issue. In *The Beauty Myth* Naomi Wolf complains that career women are sometimes hassled, judged and denied opportunities because of the way they dress, how much they weigh and whether or not they wear make-up. Marilyn French also notes that rules regarding female attire are a means by which gender conformity is enforced.[42] In 1992, hundreds of feminists across Canada demonstrated for the right to go topless in public after a young woman was arrested and convicted of committing an indecent act a year earlier by walking barebreasted along some of the main streets of a small university city in southern Ontario. They based their position on the fact that men don't face criminal charges for similar behaviour.[43] When these kinds of sexist conventions hurt women, therefore, feminists make their views known.

However, let's go back to the two young men discussed

earlier, one of whom was arrested and the other assaulted for wearing "women's" clothing. To my knowledge, feminists failed in both cases to declare their solidarity with these young men. Nor do they seem to mind that women continue to enjoy far more flexibility with respect to formal wear than men do (a jacket and a tie is a jacket and a tie, after all), or that male elected representatives to Canada's national parliament aren't permitted to participate in debates while wearing turtlenecks, even though women are.[44] Feminists also remained silent when, in 1994, a male Canada Post employee was threatened with dismissal for refusing to cut his hair and trim his beard.[45]

If true gender equality is our goal, surely sexist conventions deserve to be protested *all* the time, not just when they work against women. Feminists, of all people, should know that being forbidden from doing something solely because of your sex is anything but liberating. Therefore, we shouldn't stand for arguments that say men actually have it better than women do because they don't have to worry about make-up and because no one notices if they wear the same suit to the office twice in one week. This is similar to arguing that women were lucky when only a handful of jobs were open to them, since it wasn't so difficult to make up their minds about what they wanted to do.

Perhaps the most telling example of how comfortable feminists are with sexist double standards that operate in our favour is the military one. In the United States, young men are still required, by law, to register for the draft when they reach the age of eighteen. Those who refuse to do so may be jailed for up to five years and fined up to $250,000. They can be restricted from holding government jobs and, in some states, are prohibited from attending certain schools or receiving student loans.[46]

In 1967, world heavyweight boxing champion Muhammad Ali refused, on moral grounds, to fight in the Vietnam

War. He spent the next four years of his life in a prison cell.
Not only was he deprived of his liberty, but a period of time
that should have figured prominently in his athletic career
was taken from him. Other young men became draft-
dodgers who, to this day, have yet to receive official par-
dons. Both former U.S. vice-president Dan Quayle and
President Bill Clinton have been forced to explain why
they didn't fight in Vietnam and have had to stare down
ugly insinuations that they must be cowards. As an
acclaimed documentary film series on the American Civil
War reported, social pressure on men to do their military
duty extends back into history. According to the series, first
aired on PBS in 1990, Southern men who preferred not to
join the war effort were goaded into doing so by women
who made it clear they wouldn't marry men who were
afraid to fight.

Women haven't had to face any of this. They haven't
been shipped off, young and scared, to risk their lives and
sanity in a war they didn't understand or care about.
Women haven't had to worry about whether they'd be able
to pull the trigger when ordered to kill other human
beings, or about disgracing themselves if they failed to
behave as instructed under such circumstances. Women
haven't been compelled, by their government, to kill and
kill again in gruesome hand-to-hand combat. They haven't
been jailed or forced to flee their homes and families for
refusing to do so.

Moreover, while there clearly are men who enjoy war,
who savour the adrenaline rush and the danger, if all men
were the aggressive brutes our society supposedly turns
them into *we wouldn't have to threaten them with jail or
ostracism* in order to get them to register for the draft and
join battles already in progress.

Those feminists who think it's right and proper for
today's young women to be compensated for injuries their

great-grandmothers suffered would do well to remember that the righting of past wrongs cuts two ways. Half a million American males died in the Civil War. Another 100,000 were killed in World War I, 400,000 in World War II and 60,000 in Vietnam. Altogether, the total exceeds one million. These figures don't include soldiers whose lives were never the same again, who returned from the fighting paralyzed, blinded, suffering from shell shock, minus limbs or emotionally traumatized past all hope of recovery.

If today's young women should be compensated for wrongs other women in history have suffered, there can be little reason not to compensate young men, also, for sexist policies that worked against their male ancestors. And in that case, we should be drafting only women for military service and sending only women off to the world's combat zones until such time as one million American and one hundred thousand Canadian females have lost their young lives and been shipped back home in body bags.

Why isn't a movement that advocates fundamental equality between women and men protesting these sexist draft policies? There is nothing remotely just about women enjoying all the privileges but not all the responsibilities of full citizenship. In Farrell's words: "Registering all our 18-year-old sons for the draft in the event the country needs more soldiers is as sexist as registering all our 18-year-old daughters for child-bearing in the event the country needs more children."[47] Is the women's movement concerned about such sexism? I'm afraid not.

Double standards tend to perpetuate double standards. Feminists who are convinced that women are the only aggrieved sex, under seige from all directions, and who consider men violent brutes, suffer from a view of the world so skewed that no matter what outrageous claim is made, if it "proves" female victimization they're prepared to believe it.

Although feminists carefully dissect "male" data, treating it with both suspicion and scepticism, evidence that originates from feminist sources is automatically presumed to be true. This sort of double standard, then, helps explain the embarrassing phenomenon known as "feminist fictions."

In *Revolution From Within*, Gloria Steinem tells her readers that "about 150,000 females die of anorexia each year" in the United States. Steinem cites Naomi Wolf's *The Beauty Myth* as her source for this information, and, indeed, Wolf's book does provide this figure. She says it comes from the American Anorexia and Bulimia Association. But rather than quoting their literature directly, Wolf herself has found the statistic in another book. Wolf does go to the trouble of telling us, though, that this number means that "more die of anorexia in the United States each year than died in ten years of civil war in Beirut." Beirut, she says, was front-page news. In her view, the fact that a disease that's claiming the lives of so many young women isn't consistently on the front pages of our newspapers is just one more indication of how indifferent our society is to female well-being.[48]

Wolf devotes an entire chapter to the issue, referring to "emaciated bodies starved not by nature but by men." She compares anorexia to a famine in the Netherlands during World War II and to the Holocaust. At one point, she says: "Women must claim anorexia as political damage done to us by a social order that considers our destruction insignificant because of what we are—less. We should identify it as Jews identify the death camps...." Wolf argues that a woman's body can't tell the difference between being an anorexic living "in an affluent suburb" and being a concentration camp inmate. That may be. But in addition to exploiting the deaths of Holocaust victims in a scandalous manner, this is about as meaningful as saying that your body can't tell the difference between performing manual labour in a coal mine for pay and working there as an indentured slave. It signifies nothing.[49]

The real story, though, is that nowhere near 150,000 women die from anorexia and bulimia in the United States every year. Many women may suffer from these diseases, but the most obvious reason why the front page of your morning paper doesn't tell you that women are dropping like flies is because they are not.

Christina Hoff Sommers is a philosophy professor and the author of Who Stole Feminism? Having learned in driver's ed that a total of 50,000 Americans are killed in automobile accidents every year, she found the 150,000 anorexia figure rather high. She contacted the Anorexia and Bulimia Association in order to double-check it and was told the organization had been grossly misquoted. As it turns out, a 1985 newsletter released by the group had reported that there were between 150,000 and 200,000 sufferers in all of the United States. In fact, American government figures show that only 54 women died of anorexia and bulimia combined in 1991.[50]

Nevertheless, the myth has taken on a life of its own. In April 1992, for instance, Ann Landers told her readers that "[e]very year, 150,000 American women die from complications associated with anorexia and bulimia." Ann got this information from yet another book. Since then, the bogus statistic has also begun turning up in college texts.[51]

Unfortunately, this isn't the only example of inflated claims that exaggerate female victimization. In January 1993, Time magazine reported that a March of Dimes study had identified wife battering during pregnancy as a major cause of birth defects. The idea that some men batter even their pregnant spouses is a particularly grotesque one and is commonly included in lists of violence statistics, but this particular allegation took things further than ever before. Over the next few months, these same "study" results made their way into various newspaper articles. However, when the March of Dimes was contacted by Sommers, it said no such document existed. According to her, the chain of events went like this:

> [The *Time* magazine journalist] had relied on information given her by the San Francisco Family Violence Prevention Fund, which in turn had obtained it from Sarah Buel, a founder of the domestic violence advocacy project at Harvard Law School who now heads a domestic abuse project in Massachusetts. Ms. Buel had obtained it from Caroline Whitehead, a maternal nurse and child care specialist in Raleigh, North Carolina.

Whitehead told Sommers the whole thing was the result of a misunderstanding. While introducing Buel as a speaker at a 1989 conference, Whitehead referred to a March of Dimes protocol aimed at screening pregnant women for domestic abuse. Buel apparently misheard Whitehead and afterwards began disseminating the birth defects myth both verbally and in writing, without bothering to track down a copy of the alleged document. Nearly a year after printing the false information, *Time* magazine published a retraction. Observes Sommers:

> Unfortunately, the anorexia and the March of Dimes "study" are typical of the quality of information we are getting on many women's issues from feminist researchers, women's advocates, and journalists... When they engage in exaggeration, oversimplification, and obfuscation, the feminist researchers may be no different from other such advocacy groups as the National Rifle Association or the tobacco industry. But when the NRA does

a "study that shows...," or the tobacco industry
finds "data that suggest...," journalists are on their
guard. They check their sources and seek dissenting
opinions.[52]

Violence statistics of questionable merit probably make
up the largest part of feminist myths. They pop up in all
sorts of places and are often distributed by highly regarded
public institutions, including governments, the police and
public libraries. Writing in *Newsweek* in 1993, Sarah
Crichton tells us some college students are being given flyers containing suspect information as part of their freshmen
orientation:

> As Penn State's Sexual Assault Awareness pamphlet
> reads, in can't-miss-it type: "FBI statistics indicate
> that one in three women in our society will be
> raped during her lifetime."
> Except there are no such FBI figures.

Crichton goes on to explain that the FBI's data is so out of
date that no one takes it seriously. But somewhat conservative, trustworthy numbers from the National Victim Center
suggest that one in seven American women are victims of
forcible rape.[53]

During a five-month period in 1994, Ann Landers published letters claiming that two to four million women are
assaulted or raped by their boyfriends or spouses each year,
that 80 percent of the women who leave abusive mates are
subjected to further violence from them, that "a man beats
a woman every 12 to 15 seconds," that twelve million
American women have been raped at least once and that
"nearly half of all women will be battered at some time in
their lives."[54]

A Statistics Canada study released in late 1993 reported

that 29 percent of married women had been assaulted by their spouses (this included anyone who'd ever been "grabbed" during an argument).[55] The Canadian violence panel's data, which was made public the same year, indicated that 98 percent of the females surveyed had experienced violence. (Since obscene telephone calls qualified as "violence," it's surprising the total wasn't 100 percent.)[56] Both these sources were subsequently cited repeatedly in "Dispelling the Myths," a twelve-page booklet about sexual assault published by the Ontario government in 1994.[57]

Much of the research from which these numbers have been culled contains serious flaws, however. Often, the people who've been polled aren't representative of the population at large. If the only women who have filled out your survey are those seeking refuge in battered women shelters, for example, you may have discovered important things about *their* situation, but you've learned little or nothing about the lives of the vast majority of women. Also, if the people you've sampled don't correspond to the general population in terms of education, income or race, your data will be skewed. A similar problem arises when information that has been collected about the likelihood of women who suffer from one type of disability being assaulted is extrapolated to *all* disabled women. Surely women who are paraplegic or developmentally handicapped are far more vulnerable than those who require hearing aids.[58]

On other occasions, only women are polled about violence and abuse. If we don't ask men the same questions, we aren't able to say for certain whether these experiences are common to all human beings. And indeed, when researchers do go to the trouble (and expense) of asking both sexes about matters such as sexual harassment and domestic abuse, they are often surprised to find the sexes have more in common than many people— particularly feminists—suppose. But data suggesting similarities doesn't always make it into the public arena.

In late 1991, for example, the Ontario minister respon-
sible for women's issues, Marion Boyd, announced Wife
Assault Prevention month and disclosed details of an
$858,000 ad campaign that featured the slogan: "WIFE
ASSAULT; IT *IS* A CRIME. THERE'S NO EXCUSE."
She also took the opportunity to inform the provincial leg-
islature of an alarming statistic. According to the minister:

> Research shows that one in five men living with a
> woman admits to using violence against her. This
> violence takes many forms, including slapping,
> throwing objects at her, beating her up, threatening
> her with a knife or gun and even using weapons
> against her.

This information came from a study conducted by a
University of Calgary sociologist named Eugene Lupri. The
portion that dealt with violence committed by males
appeared in a Canadian journal and did, indeed, appear to
confirm the minister's remark. Part two of the study,
involving female violence, apparently couldn't find a
Canadian publisher. It eventually saw the light of day in a
German publication. In the words of David Lees, the journalist who tracked it down:

> ...[it] contains nothing that should surprise
> anyone, male or female, who has survived—or
> clings to—a troubled relationship or who takes
> the saddened view that we should be better people
> than we are. It documents the probability that both
> sexes evolved on the same planet and bring to their
> affairs the same disagreeable tendencies. Violence
> in the home, in other words, observes no gender
> boundary.[59]

For clarity's sake, I've summarized the results as follows:

Admitted to:	Wives	Husbands
threatening to hit or throw something at their partner	15.9%	9.1%
pushing, grabbing or shoving their partner	13.1	11.9
slapping their partner	7.6	5.0
hitting or trying to hit their partner	9.0	5.4
kicking, biting or hitting their partner with a fist	6.3	6.4
beating up their partner	6.2	2.5
threatening their partner with a gun or a knife	3.6	2.1
using a gun or a knife against their partner	.8	.5

Some people admitted to doing things that fell into more than one category, but when the dust finally settled it was determined that 17.8 percent of the men and 23.3 percent of the women among the 1,530 people surveyed admitted to behaving in a "violent" manner toward their spouses.[60]

The irony, of course, is that a government concerned about the violence taking place in Canadian homes spent the better part of a million dollars on an ad campaign that targeted *only* wife assault. Indeed, according to the very research it chose to cite, the ads should have been targeting female violence if, for some reason, it was necessary to single out one gender.

Feminists have developed another set of excuses for not taking seriously results that challenge their assumptions. They argue that this kind of data is biased since it doesn't tell us anything about the *context* in which women committed such violence. Maybe these women were acting in self-defence, and if so, who could blame them? Fair enough. But in that case, it's equally true that we don't know what context the men were acting in, either.[61] When Winnipeg researcher Reena Sommer recently asked people whether or not they resorted to domestic violence in self-defence, nine out of ten women said no.[62]

And then another objection is raised. Contradicting the standard line that patriarchal society condones and encourages male violence against women, they now acknowledge that it's less socially acceptable for men to hit women than vice versa. Therefore, they say, the results can't be trusted because men's sense of shame is causing them to under-report or minimize their violence.[63] It's worth remembering, though, that no such protest is voiced as long as the findings make only men look bad.

The excuses continue. Even if women commit more domestic violence than men, we are told, women suffer more injuries as a result. First of all, it's difficult to come by reliable information about this matter. Prior to the 1970s, many rapes didn't make it into the official statistics because women were afraid of the shame and blame they'd be exposing themselves to by reporting them. (Large numbers of rapes continue to go unreported, but there's no denying that the social climate has changed considerably over the past twenty-five years; today people are far less likely to "blame the victim.") Men may be at a similar point in their history with respect to domestic assault.

They may still be too afraid of being ridiculed by police officers, medical personnel and judges. As a result, when they show up in emergency wards, they have a powerful incentive to say their injuries were incurred in some manner other than spousal abuse.

A number of studies do suggest, however, that women are seriously injured much more frequently during domestic disputes than are men. Much of this can be attributed to the fact that men tend, on average, to be physically stronger than women. When a man does behave violently, therefore, he's more likely to inflict serious damage. As Lees observes, "greater strength brings with it a greater obligation for restraint."[64] But all of this is ultimately a side issue. Such facts don't make it okay for women to assault their spouses.

The Canadian Violence Panel report includes "psychological violence" among the crimes men commit against women. This is defined as "taunts, jeers, insults, [and] abusive language," as well as a "deliberate withholding of various forms of emotional support." The author of "several landmark books on violence against women" recently told *Ms.*, "in my view, a lot of women are battered who are never hit, because you can, you know, be subject to control without any physical violence."[65] But if such things are true when women are on the receiving end, they're true when men are, as well. The "silent treatment" can be resorted to just as easily by a woman as by a man. There is no good reason for thinking that females are any less adept at emotional and psychological abuse than males are, or that they participate in it any less frequently.

One of feminism's last lines of defence is that when men do experience abuse, it's easier for them to leave such a situation because they aren't as economically dependent as women are. Ergo, men still don't deserve the attention and concern women receive.[66] Once again, this is beside the point. It also indicates how feminists have now come to assume that the female experience is "the norm" in certain areas—something we've long berated men for. It may be true that *most* men earn more money than their wives, but many men do not. In 1992, wives were the major breadwinners in one out of every four Canadian families.[67] And although economic factors may be the biggest obstacle for a woman trying to escape an abusive relationship, they aren't the only obstacle. For a man, a more pressing concern might be that contact with his children would be drastically reduced should he leave, since he can't count on being awarded custody.

Moreover, while women tend to be more economically dependent on their spouses, men tend to be more emotionally dependent. Farrell refers to this as the "all your emotional eggs in one basket" phenomenon. Most men have fewer emotionally significant relationships than do women. While it isn't uncommon for women to spend hours talking about their problems and sharing intimate details of their lives with friends, men are less likely to do so. Because they usually have less-developed support networks, walking away from the main source of emotional sustenance in their lives (even if it's negative sustenance) isn't an easy thing for men to do.[68]

Feminism may be satisfied with double standards and excuses, but in the real world, women are no angels, and at least some domestic violence appears to be a two-way street. In November 1993, Ann Landers published a letter from CONCERNED IN MICHIGAN about an incident he'd witnessed in his rear-view mirror between a couple in the car behind him. "I was struck by the fact that they both were unusually good-looking," he wrote, "when suddenly, I saw the woman hit the man in the face." The letter continued:

The guy didn't show much reaction, which
suggested to me that she had probably hit him
before. I could see them shouting and exchanging
harsh words. When the woman bent to the floor
to pick up something, the man tried to choke her.
There was more shouting and tears as she broke
away.

The man made a move and she flinched,
throwing her hands up protectively. As they pulled
into the next lane and passed me, I saw her hit
him again.

In June 1994, Ann printed another letter from a ST.
LOUIS WOMAN who described her husband as being
prone to ordering her around, shoving her and treating her
roughly in bed. One day, she decided she'd had enough:

When Ike shoved me again, I let him have it. It
turned into a real fight and I beat the tar out of
him. I have never seen him so mad. Over the next
few months, he started a few more fights and I beat
him every time.

The bottom line is, our marriage is much better
now.

As Ann said, if "it works for you." But in a climate where
feminists insist, and society believes, that only men behave
violently in the home, Ike would be criminally convicted
for doing things for which his wife would never even be
prosecuted.[69]

Perhaps the most telling example of gender double standards I've come across is the December 1994 letter published in "Dear Abby," the advice column of Ann's twin
sister, Abigail Van Buren. LOOKS LIKE A BLIMP said she
needed advice before she ended up taking her mate's life.

She told Abby she had a short temper, a weight problem and a stressful job which paid three times as much as her husband's. She then explained the difficulty:

> When I get home, I feel like a volcano ready to
> explode, and my poor husband is usually on the
> receiving end of my wrath. This is dangerous
> because I'm bigger and stronger than my husband
> and can easily overpower him.
>
> I'm ashamed to admit that to spare him from
> my terrible rages, I've had to move him into the
> garage, which is really unfair to him.

I'll say. There's no question this is a bizarre letter and that people such as this are probably few and far between. But can you imagine the reaction if the genders were reversed? Can you imagine what Abby would say to a man who, rather than using his larger income to get a room somewhere, told her he'd decided it was best that his wife lived in the garage?

Abby responded at length, urging the woman to join Overeaters Anonymous. She explained the organization's philosophy, its international presence, and told readers how to get in touch with a chapter in their area. She assured LOOKS LIKE that when her appearance improved she'd like herself better and would "be kinder" to her husband as a result. That was all. There were no strong words to condemn the decision to exile someone you presumably love to the garage, as though they were the family pet.[70]

While our society insists women must be treated with dignity, respect and sensitivity, it seems that males are still expected to square their jaw and "take it like a man."

There is a postscript to this chapter. A year and a half after the 1989 Montreal Massacre, in which Marc Lepine murdered fourteen young women, wounded thirteen other people and then turned the gun on himself, the person in charge of security at the school revealed that the tragedy had claimed an additional three lives.

The first was a young male student who'd been present that terrible day. He left a suicide note that, in the security chief's words, explained that "he could not accept that, as a man, he had been there and hadn't done anything about it." Unable to cope with their son's death, both his parents took their own lives several months later.

The security chief also revealed something else. He said that the twenty-five-year-old killer had sat outside the registrar's office for about forty minutes on the afternoon of the murders; that he had stretched out his legs in a manner that had obstructed people's passage in the hallway. Apparently, no one spoke to him. Psychologists have since speculated that "by drawing attention to himself, Lepine was probably hoping someone would stop him."[71]

If we do not take care, we run the risk of planning a scheme in which the only freedom women get is the freedom to do what their liberators want them to do.

—*Janet Radcliffe Richards*[1]

CHAPTER FOUR

Office Politics

Did you know that the real reason I'm writing this book has nothing to do with fairness, honesty, compassion or humanity? Did you know that I'm not writing it because a movement I used to believe in has gone terribly wrong and I'd like to try, in a small way, to help repair the damage? Susan Faludi, the author of *Backlash: The Undeclared War Against American Women*, knows this.

Faludi and I have never met. We've never corresponded. And although I've read writing by and about her, as far as I'm aware she's never laid eyes on one word I've set to paper. But in the March/April 1995 issue of Ms. magazine, Faludi says that dissident feminists such as myself are neither honest nor sincere. We don't give two hoots about feminism. What we really are, she insists, is part of a "media-assisted invasion of the women's movement." We represent an "artificially engineered reproduction effort" by right-wing forces to replace "real" feminists with fake ones, *à la* the B-movie *Invasion of the Body Snatchers.* We're all just trying to "turn the media spotlight" our way, to opportunistically cash in on conservative-inspired unease over feminism. We're just pretending to be feminists so the television cameras will give us our fifteen minutes of fame.[2]

Faludi doesn't talk about me, a Canadian newspaper columnist, but on the list of women she denounces as pretend feminists are writers who share many of my concerns: Rene Denfeld, the author of *The New Victorians: A Young Woman's Response to the Old Feminist Order,* and Camille Paglia, the author of *Sexual Personae; Sex, Art and American Culture;* and *Vamps and Tramps.* Katie Roiphe is attacked for her book *The Morning After: Sex, Fear and Feminism,* as is Christina Hoff Sommers for hers, the full title of which is *Who Stole Feminism? How Women Have Betrayed Women.*

I think it's vitally important that *Ms.*, and feminists such as Faludi, read and discuss these works, since it appears that an important shift is beginning to take place in the hearts and minds of some feminists. I also think it's understandable that people who feel passionately about such issues sometimes get a little hot under the collar and say things they later wish they hadn't. But one of the advantages of being a writer is that you have an opportunity to think carefully about things before signing your name to them. And when you're doing magazine work, unless you've blown your deadline in a major way, you have a further period of time to reconsider, to call up your editor and have the petty or moronic things you've said changed before the article rolls off the presses and gets sent off into the wide world to take its place in libraries and databanks.

I can only assume, then, that Faludi's recent *Ms.* article is an accurate reflection of her considered position, and that *Ms.* thinks this "exposé" (which was hyped by a banner on the magazine's cover) qualifies as thoughtful debate. Such notions are depressing in the extreme, since Faludi's article is little more than an insult-slinging, name-calling session.

According to Faludi, the authors on her list are *faux* feminists, pseudo feminists, pod-feminists and anti-feminist feminists. They employ "low-rent logic," "gleefully" pounce on feminist mistakes and promote "erroneous, easy opinions parading as serious and daring ideas." Rather than looking "forward to creating a better future," she knows they're actually opposed to improvements in the lives of women who differ from themselves, since their views are really "just right-wing thought undercover." You get a feel for the tone of her piece from the following passage:

> While the Roiphes and the Sommerses claim to
> be going against the cultural grain, they are really
> auditioning for the most commonly available,
> easiest parts to get in the pop culture drama: the
> roles of the good girls whose opinions are dutifully
> in line with prevailing prejudice.

If one disregards the illustrations, the headlines and the quotations in large lettering that accompany the article, the text itself amounts to six and a half pages. Faludi uses the word "conservative" ten times and terms such as "right-wing," "rightward leaning" and "far right" a further eight times in this short space. She also refers to Dan Quayle, George Bush, Norman Mailer, George Gilder, Phyllis Schlafly, Newt Gingrich, Clarence Thomas, Ronald Reagan, Jerry Falwell and Pat Buchanan—sometimes more than once. Having read the books Faludi is critiquing, I doubt any of these authors would agree with much of anything the above listed right-wingers have to say. But rather than discussing these women's ideas with something approaching even-handedness, Faludi settles for smearing them by continually implying a direct link between their ideas and the far right.

When I was in university, I had a professor who used to say that whenever anyone tries to tell you there are only two choices—either you agree with them or you're the enemy—you know you're being fed propaganda. Faludi's piece declares that people who have serious concerns about the direction in which the women's movement is headed are the enemy. Essentially, she says there are only two choices: either you accept feminism as it is or you're a right-winger.

This is either/or thinking. This is us/them thinking. This is thinking that doesn't believe in a middle ground, in compromise, in unlimited possibilities.

But life is more complicated than this. It *is* possible to be critical of the left without necessarily running into the arms of the right. In politics, there are always more than two options. Just as one can be highly critical of the way a school board is being run without being opposed to education, those who criticize the current state of the women's movement can still be ardent feminists.

Faludi's approach is precisely the sort that Ms. likes to berate other people for adopting. Rather than dealing with the substance of these women's concerns (Faludi looks at a few points only briefly and superficially), she attempts to impugn their motives, to uncover their "real" reasons for writing and saying the things they do. A 1992 Ms. editorial complained about this sort of thing when the woman who accused William Kennedy Smith of acquaintance rape encountered it:

> Always the interrogators thunder: "What is your real reason for coming forward? Ambition, money, attention, scorned love, revenge? What is your real motivation?"

When it comes to rape, feminism says we're always supposed to presume that women are telling the truth. But according to Faludi, when women criticize feminism, we're supposed to presume they're really liars harbouring ulterior motives. Near the end, the same *Ms.* editorial talks about women's "pain and rage" in a general sense and says that when such feelings are finally fully articulated, the message "will at first be disbelieved. They will try to deny it, denounce it, defuse it, rename it."[3] Do these tactics sound familiar?

Faludi's criticisms don't stop there. She chides these authors for their attempts to discuss gender issues in calm, measured tones. These women are condemned by her for not being sufficiently angry at the world—something she apparently feels is a requirement of the "true" feminist. She writes:

> [T]he "I am a feminist, but..." crew are not
> feminists at all. They frown on any feminist display
> of political passion or anger; they are cool mouth-
> pieces, appropriate for the cool media to which
> they aspire. It is this lack of heat and passion, this
> lack of anger, that gives them away.

Doris Lessing is a world-renowned novelist who was a communist in her youth until she became aware of the great wrongs communism was committing in the name of making the world a better place. In her non-fiction book titled *Prisons We Choose to Live Inside*, Lessing discusses the problem of ordinary, decent people becoming carried away by political passion, and the harm they are capable of inflicting while under such an influence. She says:

> One mass movement, each set of mass opinions,
> succeeds another.... Each breeds a certain frame

of mind: violent, emotional, partisan, always
suppressing facts that don't suit it, lying, and
making it impossible to talk in the cool, quiet,
sensible low-keyed tone of voice which, it seems
to me, is the only one that can produce truth.

Lessing warns that one "learns nothing, about anything,
ever, when in a state of boiling ferment, or partisan enthu-
siasm."[4]

Isaiah Berlin is a British political scientist whose books
include *Karl Marx*, *Four Essays on Liberty*, *Russian Thinkers*
and *Against the Current*. When the University of Toronto
presented Berlin with an honorary doctorate in late 1994,
his acceptance speech noted that the horrors of the twentieth century, the "oppression, torture, murder which can be
laid at the doors of Lenin, Stalin, Hitler, Mao, [and] Pol
Pot," weren't caused by "ordinary negative human sentiments"—but by ideas. Such atrocities were carried out by
people whose "eyes were fixed upon some ultimate golden
future" and who were, therefore, prepared to "kill and
maim with a tranquil conscience."

Berlin doesn't view heat, passion or anger as positives in
the political arena, either. Rather, he says:

[W]e must weigh and measure, bargain, compromise,
and prevent the crushing of one form of life by its
rivals. I know only too well that this is not a flag
under which idealistic young men and women may
wish to march—it seems too tame, too reasonable,
too bourgeois, it does not engage the generous
emotions.

In reference to the revolutionary argument that one has to
break a few eggs in order to make an omelet, Berlin cautions that it is precisely when we are willing to forgo being

"reasonable" that we are in danger of starting down the path toward coercion and tyranny, to "destruction, blood— eggs are broken, but the omelet is not in sight, there is only an infinite number of eggs, human lives, ready for the breaking: and in the end the passionate idealists forget the omelet, and just go on breaking eggs."[5]

Faludi is entitled to her opinion that those who fail to display political anger and passion are suspect. But there are wise, learned souls who strongly disagree with her. Indeed, some of them might say she is mistaking dangerous fanaticism for political commitment.

Faludi also accuses dissident feminists of proclaiming, in essence:

> I don't believe women face discrimination any-
> more; I don't see any reason for women to organize
> politically; I don't think the pay gap, sexual harass-
> ment, rape, domestic violence, or just about any
> other issue feminism has raised are real problems.

If this is the case, why did Camille Paglia help draw up sexual harassment guidelines at the college where she teaches?[6] Why does Katie Roiphe write so sympathetically about anorexia and agree (with reservations) with much of what Naomi Wolf says about young women who suffer from this disease?[7] Why does Rene Denfeld complain so bitterly that the attention feminism is paying to goddess worship doesn't do a thing for the millions of women who "have to cope with unequal pay, lack of affordable child care, nonex- istent job opportunities, and raising families without health insurance"?[8] Why does Christina Hoff Sommers protest the inequities in rape crisis services?[9]

These women all call themselves feminists. They care deeply about many of the same issues Faludi does. Faludi may think she's been appointed supreme arbiter, that she gets to decide who's a feminist and who's not, but that isn't the case. The last time I checked, not only did we feminists not require identity cards, but Faludi was in no position to be unilaterally revoking them.

The problem is not that these women aren't feminists, it's that they're not Faludi's kind of feminist. They don't believe the women's movement is above criticism. They think high-profile feminists such as Marilyn French, Catharine MacKinnon, Gloria Steinem, Naomi Wolf and, yes, Susan Faludi should be vigorously challenged when they make mistakes and highly questionable pronouncements. They think a spade should be called a spade, and that we should all be prepared to admit, from time to time, that the empress isn't wearing any clothes.

Perhaps the most distressing part of Faludi's piece is her insistence that red is really green, that the sun is really the moon. She maintains that, the criticisms of dissident feminists to the contrary, the contemporary women's movement is an open, tolerant one, which in no way tries to stifle dissent.

If that's true, why didn't *Ms.* invite each of the feminists whose work Faludi attacks to contribute a short piece of her own, outlining her position, rather than commissioning Faludi to "expose" them? Why does the magazine pull mostly one-liners from their work, presenting these quotes in large print with no sources, context or page number, and no indication of whether the words appearing in bold are that way in the original or not? Why, rather than showing us attractive photos of these women—as it does with others who appear elsewhere in the magazine—does the magazine give us line-drawing caricatures? Sommers's caricature is wearing a T-shirt with percentages written all over it, Roiphe's has blinders that obstruct her vision, and Denfeld's is punching a bag that has a woman's face on it (she's an amateur boxer). Only one other person is represented by a caricature in that issue of the magazine: Newt Gingrich, the right-wing Republican.

Such treatment may be Ms.'s idea of open and honest dialogue, of welcoming views that conflict with its own, but most people would consider it something else. Nevertheless, within the context of this sort of presentation, Faludi insists that while some feminists do "think only their opinions are the right ones,"

> ...for every feminist trying to dictate policy in one direction, there's another challenging her. Heated exchanges, not censorship, characterize feminists' approaches to difficult subjects like pornography, surrogate motherhood, or [the abortion pill] RU 486.

You could have fooled me. Perhaps Faludi should take another look at the "RAGE + WOMEN = POWER" issue of Ms. By my count, the subject of pornography comes up seven different times, and on *every* occasion it's considered a bad, sexist, horrible thing. On page 11, a letter to the editor describes our society as one "where we raise men on pornography and violence against women." Another, on the following page, complains that men "are comfortable purchasing women's sexuality cheaply and easily at newsstands and video stores."

Pages 50 and 51 display an enormous photograph of a feminist anti-porn march. There's a large banner that reads "WOMEN AGAINST PORNOGRAPHY. STOP VIOLENCE AGAINST WOMEN." Assorted picket signs declare: "PORN HURTS WOMEN," "PORN IS VIOLENCE AGAINST WOMEN" and "PORN IS VIOLENCE DISGUISED." In book reviews appearing on page 58, we're told that it's "sad" that a particular author has "buckled" and decided to part ways with anti-porn feminists. We also read that young women who, among other things, don't agree with the feminist anti-porn critique provide "a depressing case study in the success of backlash propaganda."

On pages 86 and 87 we find a feminist theory piece about prostitution, which criticizes those "women who recognize rape and battery as violence" but continue to defend pornography. Finally, the last two pages of the magazine are devoted to a guest column written by a black male who draws links between sexual harassment and pornography. He says pornography "demeans and degrades women and men," that it "corrupts our sexuality" and fosters "aggression and abuse." The piece ends with him saying it's time for porn to "be thrown into the trash."[10]

If this is what Faludi means by a "heated exchange" of opposing ideas, if this is what she means by one feminist pulling in one direction and another feminist pulling in another, she has a notion of these concepts that's rather different from mine. Robin Morgan, the long-time editor of Ms., is the person who coined the phrase "Pornography is the theory, rape is the practice."[11] By no stretch of the imagination could it be said that Ms. has given equal time, over the years, to feminist anti-censorship ideas, never mind pro-porn ones.[12]

In a published speech titled "The Sexual Liberals and the Attack on Feminism" (which, incidentally, is referred to positively in the Ms. "rage" issue), Catharine MacKinnon makes it clear that she doesn't consider women who defend or enjoy pornography to be feminists. She calls them "liberals," and she considers the term to be an insult. She spends in excess of two pages disagreeing with the position of a group called FACT, the Feminists Against Censorship Task Force. She has every right to do so, of course, but then she gets nasty. "The Black movement has Uncle Toms and Oreo cookies," she says. "The labor

movement has scabs. The women's movement has FACT."
On another occasion, MacKinnon has compared feminists
who oppose censorship to "house niggers who sided with
the masters." She has also declared that if "pornography is
part of your sexuality, then you have no right to your sexuality."[13]

Faludi and MacKinnon aren't the only ones, though,
who think they get to decide who's a feminist and who's
not, in this ever-so-tolerant movement in which people
treat each other with respect despite differences of opinion.
Robin Morgan's editorial in the May/June 1993 issue of Ms.
declared flatly that pop singer Madonna is not a feminist
and that any "attempt to characterize her as such...reveals
an unfortunate lack of understanding about feminism." It
continued, several lines later:

> Madonna may be talented; she's clearly in rebellion
> against her Catholic upbringing; she's taken
> admirable stands in urging voter registration and
> in the fight against HIV/AIDS. But a feminist?
> Quite a stretch—for a performer marketing herself
> in the acceptable objectifying style, and acting
> "outrageous" in ways calculated not to undermine
> but to enhance the patriarchal establishment,
> pornographic and otherwise.[14]

There's only one way to interpret Madonna's performances,
and if you didn't know that, then you, too, obviously aren't
a real feminist. Would someone please let me in on the big
secret: where are the checklists and scorecards kept? Where
can I fill them out and discover once and for all whether or
not I pass the Feminist Purity test? Or do I have to sleep on
a stack of mattresses and discern the pea tucked beneath
the very last one? As Denfeld has commented with respect
to this editorial:

> The question is not whether Madonna's depictions of sexuality make her a feminist, the question is whether they prohibit her from being deemed one.
>
> Morgan…would answer yes. Women of my generation might answer, "Who cares, and since when is it your business?"[15]

Gloria Steinem, too, thinks she's entitled to pass judgment on who's a feminist and who's not. In an interview with the *Advocate* magazine in May 1992, Steinem said of Camille Paglia: "Her calling herself a feminist is sort of like a Nazi saying they're not anti-Semitic. She's not a feminist. She's Phyllis Schlafly with sex added."[16]

This is an opportune time for me to say a few words about Paglia. I've read her work and I've heard her speak. I think she's an obnoxious, acid-tongued egotist. I think some of the things that come out of her mouth are as appalling as the comments of people such as MacKinnon and Marilyn French that I've been going on about. I think her catty, personal attacks on other feminists are uncalled for. But when I went to hear her speak in late 1992, I spent the entire evening in stitches. Her irreverence was such a relief from the earnest, pained feminism I was used to. She was the first person I'd ever heard who was willing to criticize out loud the famous-feminists-on-high, who was willing to admit they had flaws, too.

To her credit, Paglia, unlike these others, doesn't take herself too seriously. She admits she has a "boisterous, wise-cracking, machine-gun American verbal style" and a manic personality. She acknowledges that she is "an overeater and *overstater*, a gourmandizer of the grand manner [my italics]." Moreover, she jokingly says, with respect to her new lover, "I lost a big part of *my act* when I couldn't complain about my sex life any more" [my italics]."[17] I don't have to agree with half of what Paglia says to concur with Sommers that she's "one of the most brilliant, original thinkers" in America. Therefore, I say the woman's entitled to make up her own mind about whether or not she's a feminist. And, regardless of what Steinem may think, Paglia loudly declares that she *is*.[18]

In the same Ms. editorial in which Morgan said Madonna wasn't a feminist, she also answered another question she said she was being asked frequently: What do you think of Camille Paglia? Her response: "I don't. Why should we waste energy on a publicity-obsessed, intellectually bereft, rather pathetic person trying to revive the lie that women want to be raped."

That's not what Paglia says at all. She makes it quite clear that rape "is an outrage that cannot be tolerated in a civilized society" and acknowledges that acquaintance rape "has been a horrible problem for women for all of recorded history."[19] But she believes women should use common sense. Just as they wouldn't drive to New York City and leave their keys on the hood of their car, they shouldn't get drunk at fraternity parties and then go upstairs to a boy's room if they're not interested in sex. She makes comments such as, "I feel that sex is basically combat" and "You have to accept the fact that part of the sizzle of sex comes from the danger of sex. You can be overpowered."[20] But this is a far cry from saying women want to be raped.

The women's movement's response to Paglia is a good barometer of just how closed the feminist world can be. Steinem's answer, when she was asked at a feminist gathering about Paglia, has become almost legendary. "We don't give a shit about what she thinks," she's reported to have said from the podium.[21]

Yet these people still insist on maintaining the fiction that "feminists don't all think alike." Maybe so, but you can be a woman, running for elected office, pro-choice and in favour of tougher rape laws, and still be publicly denounced by Steinem for being a "female impersonator" because you're a Republican.[22] You can be a novelist who writes an opinion piece for *The Washington Post* about how feminism has alienated large numbers of ordinary women and have Faludi respond in a magazine interview, "Who is she to be commenting on feminism?" while Steinem calls you "a water bug on the surface of life."[23] You can be Sommers, who, after taping an interview about her book with CBS TV's Connie Chung, learned that Steinem had contacted Chung personally in an attempt to get the show canned.[24] Feminism is supposed to belong to all women, but she who criticizes it had better have a thick skin, because not only might she be publicly reprimanded by Big Sister feminists, half the people she thought were her friends might well stop talking to her, too.

In Betty Friedan's words, twenty-three-year-old Katie Roiphe "was virtually crucified for her [book's] attack on the excessive focus on date rape among college feminists."[25] Women's studies professor Gail Dines, for instance, quoted in *Newsweek*, called Roiphe a "traitor," said she was the "Clarence Thomas of women" and that she was reinforcing the "white-male patriarchy."[26] Roiphe was subjected to this sort of thing, even though her book decries feminist intolerance. In the introduction, she writes:

> At Harvard, and later at graduate school in English
> literature at Princeton, I was surprised at how
> many things there were not to say, at the arguments
> and assertions that could not be made, lines that
> could not be crossed, taboos that could not be
> broken. The feminists around me had created their
> own rigid orthodoxy. You couldn't question the
> exist-ence of a rape crisis, you couldn't suggest that
> the fascination with sexual harassment had to do
> with more than sexual harassment, you couldn't

say that Alice Walker was just a bad writer, and the
list of couldn'ts went on and on.

Roiphe continues: "Everything was cut and dried. It was
feminists against the backlash, us against them, and
increasingly I was 'them.'"[27]

Amy Friedman was born and raised in Ohio but now
lives near Kingston, Ontario. As a college freshman in
1972, she was one of the first seven women to be assigned
to what had previously been an all-male dormitory at
Columbia University. She campaigned for the Equal Rights
Amendment, participated in the women's health movement, learned car repair and lost a job when she refused to
sleep with her boss. In the late 1980s, she began writing a
column for Kingston's *Whig-Standard* newspaper. Alarmed
by what appeared to be a growing victim mentality within
the women's movement, she started asking questions about
the direction things were taking—and found herself vilified
by local feminists.

Her book *Nothing Sacred: A Conversation with Feminism*
describes how merely expressing doubts, merely talking
about such matters in a public forum, prompted other
women to attempt to silence her. She reports that, after the
appearance of a column in which she implored men and
women to try to listen to one another, her supervisor at the
community college where she was teaching received a telephone call from a feminist history professor who urged the
college's women's studies department to demand a public
apology. On another occasion, when she wrote about being
raped years earlier on a subway platform in New York
City—and suggested that life does go on—she was
informed by other feminists that she'd dealt with her
assault in "too white and too middle class" a way. While
feminism used to insist that each woman's experience was
important and legitimate, Friedman's view of the incident,

her manner of coming to terms with the associated trauma, was now being callously dismissed on obscure political grounds.

She describes one such conversation she had around this time:

> ...[with] a woman on the verge of graduation from Queen's School of Law with a job secured in a Toronto law firm at a starting salary well above the average middle-income family's, a white woman in her thirties, an intelligent, well-educated, sophisticated, lovely woman, [who] talked to me about her life, her experiences, the changes she had gone through in Law School. She called herself oppressed.

When Friedman gently challenged the woman's use of such an adjective, she became hostile. Says Friedman:

> I suddenly perceived something that I began to think of as the Feminist Forehand Smash. It consisted of this: I am female and I am telling you my feelings, so you must be still and listen to me.
>
> And that seemed simply another version of the male power gambit: I am male and I can overpower you and so you must be still and listen. And if you don't.... Feeling was substituted for force, but it worked the same way. This woman's feelings, obviously to her, demanded my silence...

Friedman says she is now considered "a threat, an enemy, a member of the backlash brigade, an anti-feminist." She knows, from first-hand experience, that genuine diversity of opinion isn't encouraged on either side of the Canada-U.S. border. Rather, in her words, some feminists "had given themselves the right, indeed the privilege and responsibility of pointing out just who was good and who was bad, who was the enemy and who was friend."[28]

In November 1990, journalist Danielle Crittenden delivered a speech to a Women in the Media conference in Toronto in which she discussed the relationship between women's issues and responsible journalism. She noted:

> We are all aware that there has come to be a "political line" on women. True, this line fluctuates enormously. At one moment it is heresy to suggest that women do not yearn to pick up briefcases and emulate the career patterns of men; at another, it is heresy to suggest they do. But at any given moment there is a line: Depart from it, if you're a man, and it makes you a sexist; if you are a woman, a traitor.

Crittenden said the pressure she has felt to adopt a particular slant while writing about women's issues has not come from sexist male editors but from other female journalists. She observes that it would be a tragedy if women "should fall into the trap of sternly enforcing new stereotypes upon themselves" in the name of liberation.[29]

Margaret Atwood (the Canadian author whose work includes The Handmaid's Tale and The Robber Bride) has also written of this phenomenon. She says:

> For me, the dangers of dictatorship by *ism* are largely metaphorical: I don't have a job, so no one has the power to fire me. But for some members of what I now geriatrically refer to as the younger generation, things are otherwise. When younger women writers come to me, at parties or under cover of night, to whisper stories about how they've been worked over—critically, professionally, or

personally—by women in positions of power,
because they haven't toed some stylistic or ideological line or other, I deduct the mandatory fifteen
points for writerly paranoia. Then I get mad....

If the women's movement is not an open door
but a closed book, reserved for some right-thinking
elite, then I've been misled. Are we being told yet
once again that there are certain "right" ways of
being a woman writer, and that all other ways are
wrong?

Sorry, but that's where I came in. Women of
my generation were told not to fly or run, only to
hobble, with our high heels and our pantygirdles
on. We were told endlessly: *thou shalt not*. We don't
need to hear it again, and especially not from
women. [original italics][30]

Atwood writes that she, too, has felt pressured by feminists
who'd like her to say she personally encountered sexism
when dealing with male publishers, particularly as a beginning writer. But she insists this wasn't the case, and that
she's not about to rewrite history just because other feminists claim the publishing industry is stacked against them.

Often, much of what you're not supposed to say as a
feminist writer is closely connected to issues of race. I
believe it's vitally important that people be aware of and
sensitive to the concerns of racial minorities, that we
always be open to perspectives that contrast with our own.
But there's a difference between treating other people with
respect and being expected to agree with everything they
do or say. Unlike *Ms.* magazine, which declares on its 1995
subscription inserts that "anyone who has experienced
something is more expert in it than the experts," I don't
believe that direct experience *automatically* trumps everything else. In other words, I think it's important for whites

to participate in discussions about race, and that we should-
n't be silenced by people who imply that our skin colour
makes us incapable of grasping the issues at hand.

One of my earliest newspaper columns about the
women's movement dealt with the racial politics associated
with Toronto's 1991 International Women's Day (IWD)
march. When the piece appeared in *The Globe and Mail,* a
friend who's a veteran of the feminist trenches called to say,
"I agree with you, but I think it's a good thing your number
isn't listed in the phone book." In the piece, I had
expressed my uneasiness over the fact that the main slogan
for that year was: "WOMEN SAY: STOP THE RACIST
WAR FROM OKA TO THE GULF. MAKE THE LINKS."
(The Oka Crisis took place near Montreal in late 1990
when a small town attempted to extend its golf course onto
land which local natives claimed as their own. The town
sent in the police to ensure that work could begin only to
encounter armed resistance on the part of the natives. The
standoff lasted 78 days.)

I wrote that it was overly simplistic to reduce either
Oka or the Gulf War to pure racial terms. I also took issue
with two of the march's three policy statements. One called
for self-determination for aboriginal people, Palestinians
and black South Africans. The second opposed racism. I
said that while these were worthy causes, they shouldn't be
dominating a *women's* event. To borrow an example from
Denfeld, this is the equivalent of allowing gay issues to
dominate a march organized by the National Association
for the Advancement of Colored People. Some blacks may
be gay, but most aren't, and a black organization that does-
n't concentrate on issues common to most blacks risks
becoming irrelevant to the very group of people it's supposed to be serving.[31]

Shortly afterward, the paper published a rebuttal written by the chair of the Coalition of Visible Minority

Women and a representative of the National Action Committee on the Status of Women. While I was gratified that we were at last having a public discussion about the issues, the tone of the rebuttal was another matter. Read one passage:

> Racism is a priority for the women's movement in Canada today. It is appalling that Ms. Laframboise calls a day devoted to racism "an opportunity for solidarity lost and squandered." It is frightening that she holds a degree in women's studies. Under the banner of feminism, Ms. Laframboise sets out to maintain that celebrations in Toronto are "not relevant to most women."

The message was unmistakable: other feminists considered it "appalling" and "frightening" that I dared to question the women's movement status quo.[32]

For the past several years, I haven't belonged to any women's groups, precisely because I don't need the hassle of dealing with people who are as likely as not to be annoyed with me for what I write each week. I have grassroots political experience and a modest public profile—both of which would be assets to many organizations—but I've chosen to stay away because it's clear to me that the women's movement of the 1990s tries to keep people on a very short leash, and I'm not willing to play good puppy dog.

Because my social and professional life doesn't depend on what other feminists think of me, I'm relatively immune to the feminist office politics that end up consuming so much valuable time and energy. While I can't think of a single friend (male or female) who isn't a feminist, when we have our differences, we agree to disagree rather than behaving like children in a schoolyard who point their fingers and say: "I'm a feminist and you're not." Many women,

though, aren't so lucky. If they want to help out at a battered women's shelter or a rape crisis line, if they want to
take part in a demonstration, they run a high risk of being
caught up in interminable political skirmishes. And that's
everyone's loss.

It's no exaggeration to say that in Toronto, and perhaps
in all of Canada, women-of-colour issues are currently
wrestling with violence issues for first place on the feminist
agenda. I left the last pro-choice I attended in disgust when
someone took the megaphone and started going on about a
supposedly racist Royal Ontario Museum exhibit. What she
was talking about had absolutely no connection to reproductive rights. It had no connection to the political party
outside whose offices we were demonstrating. It was,
instead, an example of how contemporary feminists insist
that "all issues are women's issues." According to this view,
it therefore follows that there is a "correct" opinion with
respect to each one of them.[33]

Any woman who wants to call herself a feminist soon
senses that she must not only bring her views into line on a
whole range of immediately recognizable "women's" concerns, she is also expected to hold fairly uniform ideas
about gays and lesbians, racial issues, the disabled, goddess
worship, the environment, the Gulf War and the exhibit
running over at the museum. The theory is that if all the
people represented by each of these different constituencies join together in a united political front of right-thinking individuals, then paradise on earth is assured. But the
reality is that the longer the list of set opinions you're
expected to hold grows, the less likely it is that any one
person is going to agree with it. While the average Jane
Doe might have been comfortable aligning herself with a
movement that stood for the first three points, she might
have doubts (some of them serious) about the next four—
and so she stays away. Consequently, the united front fails

to materialize, and exhausted activists end up blaming the patriarchy, capitalism or public apathy for what is really the result of their own muddle-headedness.

In February 1995, a letter to the editor appeared in a Canadian newspaper outlining one woman's disillusionment with the women's movement in general and the National Action Committee on the Status of Women (NAC) in particular. It read, in part:

> I am a feminist, in the sense that I believe women should have equal opportunity and should be free from all threat of discrimination and violence. But I didn't measure up to NAC's politically correct standards because:
>
> • I held a management position in my job. A NAC leader once told me I was "part of the problem" for women in the workplace and that my own problems as a woman manager were "of no consequence."
> • I was white, middle-class, able-bodied and heterosexual. I stopped attending International Women's Day events because I got tired of being made to feel guilty for the supposed sins of my peers.
> • I used new reproductive technologies to treat my infertility. NAC has viewed these new technologies as exploitation of women by the male-dominated medical-pharmaceutical complex. They have also tried to exclude the major stakeholders in the debate (infertile women and their partners).
> • I stayed at home with my child. The NAC family-policy committee was sure that my baby would be better off in day care, that I was turning back the clock on women's gains.[34]

In my view, this woman is correct when she talks about Toronto International Women's Day events having been as much about guilt as anything else in recent years, and she's not the only one who has been voting with her feet. During the 1990s, the annual IWD march has attracted 2,500 or fewer participants annually, down considerably from the 5,000 to 8,000 who used to show up in the '80s. (By comparison, Toronto's annual Lesbian and Gay Pride Day parade draws crowds ranging from 25,000 to 500,000.[35]) This decline in participation has corresponded to an increasing emphasis on race. Below is a list of official IWD slogans, which give an indication of the prevailing winds:

- 1986—"WOMEN SAY NO TO RACISM
  FROM TORONTO TO SOUTH AFRICA"
- 1987—"FIGHTING RACISM AND SEXISM
  TOGETHER" (notice which comes first)
- 1988—"WOMEN UNITED TO RIGHT
  RACISM, SEXISM AND ECONOMIC
  INEQUALITY"
- 1991—"STOP THE RACIST WAR FROM
  OKA TO THE GULF"
- 1992—"500 YEARS OF RESISTANCE—
  RECOVERY FROM DISCOVERY" (a reference
  to the native perspective on the Columbus
  quincentennial)

In 1993, the official slogan, "NO TIME TO STOP, OUR STRUGGLE MUST CONTINUE," was accompanied by four demands. Three of the four mentioned racial issues. Only 2,000 people participated in the 1994 IWD march. The media reported that one of the organizers called it an historic year because, "for the first time in Toronto, the annual celebration was organized by women of color."[36]

Not quite. As far back as 1986, the Canadian feminist newspaper *Broadside* was reporting that black feminists had had significant input into Toronto's IWD events that year. According to the paper, a group of black women had expressed dissatisfaction with "the decision-making process" employed by the IWD organizers:

> The result of the Black Women's Collective statement was that direction was taken from the leadership of Black women in every aspect of organizing the day: from the rally, to the order of contingents in the march, to the march route, to the topics at the fair workshops, to the entertainment of the day, to the kind of music that was heard at the dance.[37]

Although the Canadian women's movement is frequently accused of having ignored non-white issues, a representative of the Committee Against the Deportation of Jamaican Women addressed the first Toronto IWD rally in 1978. (Her speech resulted in a unanimous demand that deportation orders for domestic workers be rescinded.[38]) The 1979 IWD march sent a telegram of solidarity to Iranian women protesting attacks on female civil liberties following Ayatollah Khomeini's rise to power.[39] In 1985, the keynote speaker was African-American activist Angela Davis.[40] In 1990, a young woman named Sophia Cook was invited to be a guest speaker—apparently because she is black and had been shot by a white policeman while a passenger in a stolen car. That same year, the fact that an advertised IWD party turned out to be an aggressively black-music event prompted complaints.[41] And in 1992, native women's insistence that alcohol was a tool of white oppression deprived the march of its biggest fundraiser when the post-demonstration dance was designated alcohol-free.[42]

When one combines this list with the IWD slogans appearing above, it becomes evident that race has received rather a lot of attention—especially considering that Statistics Canada tells us that non-whites represent only 10 percent of the overall population. (Admittedly, this figure is estimated to be more than twice that in Toronto and Vancouver.)

It is my contention that IWD attendance remained high in the short term because many of us didn't mind emphasizing race for a while. But we've grown tired of being told not only that we oppress our sisters but that we haven't shown any willingness to share power or to acknowledge racial concerns when the history of this particular event tells a vastly different story.

In June 1993, thirty-five-year-old Sunera Thobani, a graduate student who'd been living in Canada for just four years, wrote a newspaper opinion column for *The Toronto Star* in which she claimed the Canadian women's movement had benefited only a minority of women. Feminism, so the argument goes, has been dominated by white, middle-class women who have selfishly promoted their own agenda while ignoring the concerns of everyone else.[43]

This is absolute nonsense. During the past two decades, the central feminist issue in Canada has been access to abortion. The battle has been fought on the streets and in the courts. Feminists picketed and demonstrated. We organized fundraising events and circulated petitions. If the women's movement had merely been addressing middle-class concerns this would never have happened. As we pro-choicers have been fond of telling politicians (and anyone else who'd listen), middle-class women have always been able to arrange safe abortions. They've had the money and the connections to secure one quietly and locally, or to travel elsewhere. Abortion access became a rallying point because the lives of less privileged women were at risk.

White, middle-class feminists poured their time, energy and money into this struggle precisely because they recognized a social inequity and were determined to do something about it.

A similar argument can be made with respect to affordable child care, another feminist mainstay. Women who are in a position to hire nannies need this far less than do other groups. Ditto for battered women's shelters, since women with money have more options when it comes to leaving violent situations than those without means.

Nevertheless, Thobani's article suggested that the picture was far grimmer, that different groups of Canadian women had always been at each other's throats rather than genuinely supportive of one other. Even more disturbing, however, was her insistence on narrowing matters down to an either-or scenario: "Either the women's movement will forge ahead *under the leadership* of the women most marginalized in society [my italics]," she wrote, or it would be seen to be slamming the door on them. Translation: minority women would consider themselves badly treated if control of the women's movement wasn't handed over to them. She went on to say that disadvantaged women "understand our society *better* than those who live in the four walls of their relative privilege [my italics]." Translation: circumstances don't provide each of us with different perspectives, they provide minority women with a superior world-view.

Thobani, then, wasn't talking about merely expanding the feminist agenda to include points of view she felt had been historically absent. She wasn't envisioning an equal, mutually respectful working relationship among all women. Rather, she was saying that the leadership of feminist organizations should be decided on the basis of criteria that included skin colour. Three days after this piece appeared in the country's largest daily, Thobani became the first woman-of-colour president of NAC, Canada's biggest and most influential feminist organization—by acclamation.

Racial politics had already left their mark on NAC, however, before Thobani assumed leadership. A year earlier, the organization had issued an ultimatum to the Canadian Panel on Violence Against Women. Although the project was two-thirds complete by then, NAC suddenly declared that three more women-of-colour panelists should be added immediately. Two of the people already on the nine-member panel were visible minorities. Since non-whites comprise roughly 10 percent of Canada's population, two people out of nine therefore amounted to 22 percent—hardly a glaring case of under-representation. But this wasn't good enough for NAC, whose proposal would have inexplicably bumped non-white representation up to 42 percent. NAC said it was prepared to withdraw its support and to do everything in its power to discredit the panel's findings if its demands weren't met.[44] The composition of the violence panel remained the same, and NAC publicly dissociated itself from it shortly afterward.[45]

In mid 1994, Canadian women were given another indication of where NAC's priorities lay when a woman named Maureen Kempston Darkes became the new president of General Motors of Canada, Ltd., the country's largest company. Many of us considered this an important achievement, a powerful symbol of how women are altering the face of the corporate world. We thought it especially encouraging that the event had taken place in such a male-dominated industry. When a radio station telephoned NAC for its response to this historic occasion, however, the organization's spokesperson responded with the following, regarding Darkes: "She's white, isn't she? Skin colour brings privileges."[46]

Perhaps the most disturbing example of racial infighting in the Canadian women's movement, though, concerns feminist June Callwood. This journalist and social activist holds fourteen honorary degrees, has written more than two dozen books, and over the years has either founded or helped to start twenty-four organizations, including a home for teenaged mothers, an AIDS hospice and the Canadian Civil Liberties Association.[47] In 1974, Callwood co-founded Nellie's, a hostel that provides services to battered women, ex-prostitutes and psychiatric patients. In the early 1980s, a black woman named Joan Johnson was given refuge at the hostel along with her three children for about a year while she sorted out immigration difficulties. Callwood used her connections to help Johnson secure a permit to remain in the country legally. Later, Johnson became a member of the hostel's collective board of directors, along with a number of other women of colour, who later formed their own caucus and came to believe that internal policy disputes over how to respond to drug addicts, for example, were connected to race issues. One journalist described matters this way:

> The situation polarized, and it wasn't pretty. It polarized around power, race, sexual preference, ideologies, personalities, written texts, spoken words, even body language—not all at once, but with the mounting force of implosion. The board split into three main factions: women with a business-as-usual approach; women of colour trying to show the workings of systemic racism at Nellie's; and their sympathizers. The staff split. When the Women of Colour Caucus—mostly heterosexual— said they would bring racism before the board, they were told by white women on staff: "Then we'll say you're homophobic."[48]

In late 1991, Johnson delivered an impassioned statement at a Nellie's board meeting in which she accused the hostel and its staff of widespread racism. Callwood, never one to mince words, responded by asking her, in essence, "Are you the same woman we helped for over a year?" This was then taken by the Women of Colour Caucus as proof that Callwood herself was a racist. She was asked to apologize and agreed to do so at the next meeting she attended because she'd violated confidentiality guidelines by revealing that Johnson had been a former client. But Callwood was still indignant about the racism accusations and it showed. Her half-hearted apology led to more accusations of racism. She left the meeting and, within days, the Women of Colour Caucus had sent out flyers to other groups in the city seeking their support. Reports another journalist:

> The hostel collective went into disarray. Chandler, the facilitator, insisted that white members write letters of apology to the women of colour for Callwood's behaviour. The letters were deemed insufficient, and they were asked to write again. And again.[49]

In March, representatives of an unrelated women-of-colour organization attended the Nellie's board meeting with a list of ten demands, one of which was that the board request Callwood's resignation and bar her from the premises as well as from participating in any of the hostel's committees. The request was repeated later in the month. On May 1, Callwood resigned voluntarily. She says, "The accusation that I am a racist was common currency at subsequent [to February] board meetings. It also appears in letters and proclamations widely distributed by the women of color."[50]

When *Toronto Life* magazine published an article about the matter that was sympathetic to Callwood, its offices were picketed by protesters who insisted that the article, too, constituted a racist attack on women of colour.[51] For someone like Callwood, now seventy, who has devoted her life's energy to propelling Canadian society in the direction of more enlightened views on a wide range of social issues, these events have been particularly painful. "Except for deaths in my family," she says, "this is the worst thing that has ever happened to me."[52] Her sterling reputation has been besmirched by feminists who claim to be fighting racism, who say they want to improve the world, but who instead appear to have used such accusations as a handy weapon in an old-fashioned power struggle.

In the '90s, charges of racism have become another way to stifle criticism and dissent in the manner that journalist Amy Friedman described earlier: she was expected to *be silent* in the face of another woman's feelings that she is oppressed. Callwood's sin was that she refused to remain silent when accusations she considered unfounded were made against the hostel and its staff. The lesson hasn't been lost on many Toronto feminists: disagree with what women of colour are saying and you, too, risk being branded a racist. No matter how many hours you've poured into good causes, such people may feel no compunction whatever about slandering your good name on the flimsiest of grounds.

I'm not the first person to observe that some of the feminists at Nellie's seemed more interested in race politics than in the health of the hostel itself—or the well-being of the women it exists to serve.

Unfortunately, this is no isolated tale. Similar difficulties have reduced New York City's Women's Action Committee to a shadow of its former self after some members accused others of being homophobic because they questioned the amount of time and energy being devoted to lesbian concerns. In Denfeld's words:

[T]heir paralyzing "antihierarchical" stance,
combined with...allowing extremist factions to
silence debate, saw the organization's meetings
degenerate into vicious insider attacks and
ineffectiveness, and their membership plummeted
from a claimed eighteen hundred members to a
handful of women.[53]

It seems everywhere one turns, there's a similar story. In
its May/June 1995 issue, Ms. magazine provided space to
articles written by three young feminists, one of whom was
a black, twenty-five-year-old graduate student in women's
studies named Tiya Miles. She was part of a group that
began a campus feminist publication in 1991, called The
Rag, at Atlanta's Emory University. Two years later, it had
collapsed due to internal squabbling. Writes Miles:

Class conflicts piggybacked racial discord. In other
meetings that semester, a black woman, who had
taken a year off to work so she could pay for the
rest of her education, expressed resentment at what
she viewed as the insensitivity of wealthy white
women. A few Rag parents had donated hundreds
of dollars to the magazine, and one staff member
had offered her family's summer house as a retreat
site. The black woman, with no funds or house to
offer, felt that her worth and strength as a group
member were diminished by those women's
economic power.[54]

In her book, Sommers describes parallel problems
encountered by the National Women's Studies Association
in the United States. She describes its 1992 conference
held in Austin, Texas, as opening with a speaker who
recounted:

...a brief history of the "narratives of pain" within the NWSA. She reported that ten years ago, the organization "almost came apart over outcries by our lesbian sisters that we had failed adequately to listen to their many voices." Five years ago, sisters in the Jewish caucus had wept at their own "sense of invisibility." Three years later the Disability caucus threatened to quit, and the following year the women of color walked out.

Sommers continues:

> At past conferences, oppressed women had accused other women of oppressing them. Participants met in groups defined by their grievances and healing needs: Jewish women, Jewish lesbians, Asian-American women, African-American women, old women, disabled women, fat women, women whose sexuality is in transition. None of the groups proved stable. The fat group polarized into gay and straight factions, and the Jewish women discovered they were deeply divided: some accepted being Jewish; others were seeking to recover from it.

Yet another conference speaker told the five hundred gathered feminists about how her lesbian support group had split into black and white factions, which had then splintered further. In this woman's words: "Those of us in the group who had white lovers were immediately targeted.... It turned into a horrible mess.... I ended up leaving that group for self-protection."[55]

Is it any wonder that Denfeld calls the women's movement a "minefield," and that Paglia says feminism should get its own house in order before making prescriptions for the rest of society?[56]

Daphne Patai and Noretta Koertge are the authors of *Professing Feminism: Cautionary Tales from the Strange World of Women's Studies*. They are both women's studies professors and avowed feminists, and their book concurs with Paglia in this respect. They say they've gone public with their concerns about what is taking place in many women's studies programs (there are currently about six hundred of them in the United States), partly because such departments offer us a sneak preview of what the world might look like if it were dominated by feminists. It is a sad comment on the current state of affairs that the women quoted in the book have requested anonymity due to the possibility of repercussions in their professional lives. While there's a dawning realization of just how far short of the ideal things have fallen, many people are still unprepared to stand up and be counted.

One passage from the book's prologue reads:

> Again and again, women told us that they had
> long wanted to discuss their concerns but had felt
> isolated and hesitant to express opinions they
> knew could be dismissed as the experience of one
> disgruntled woman unable to thrive under the new
> feminist regime. Many of the women who were
> willing to talk with us were pained or distressed.
> No enemies of feminism lurked among them.
> Instead, we found sincere and thoughtful
> individuals, providing accounts of troubling
> experiences and disappointed hopes.[57]

The women interviewed reported the same kinds of political infighting, preoccupation with personal "feelings" and intolerance discussed above. One talked about attending a meeting where a black woman at the podium declared that she wasn't going to allow lighter-skinned black women to get away with denying their "light-skin privilege." Another told of attending a showing of a video about sexism and MTV at a campus women's centre. Viewers were informed, beforehand, that if any of them wanted to watch the video in a women-only environment, they could report to such-and-such a room. They were also advised, afterward, that there were counsellors standing by to assist anyone who had been made "uncomfortable" by what they'd just seen. Rather than a serious intellectual debate, what followed was a discussion about how people "felt" about the video.[58] A number of the women Patai and Koertge interviewed have been strong supporters of women's studies as well as instrumental in founding departments, but some have transferred back into mainstream academe, and others are on the verge of doing so as a result of these sorts of attitudes. Still others have faced criticism from their own students for emphasizing scholarship above militancy.[59] This is unfortunate, because it leaves the field more open than ever to feminists who seem to have forgotten that students are paying good money for an *academic* education—not a political indoctrination or therapy session.

Patai and Koertge report on a women's studies professor whose idea of encouraging tolerance is to say the following to her students: "Personally, I can't imagine why any woman would want to have a relationship with a man, but since some do, we have to try to respect them." Another informed fellow feminists, on an Internet women's studies mailing list, that she sees nothing wrong with disclosing her personal problems in class:

> I managed to get a few older students to give some
> personal examples. I ended with telling them
> about how I had had to come to terms with an
> excruciatingly painful past (explicitly identifying
> the problem as incest), and how until I could do

that I had no future, only an endless repetition of old patterns. And now there is joy and hope and boundless energy.

This was the third class meeting (one night a week). They all sat so still, with amazement and wonder on their faces. Afterward an older student thanked me for making myself so vulnerable. I told her I didn't feel vulnerable as I spoke. I felt loved.[60]

In late 1993, when Karen Lehrman wrote a cover story for *Mother Jones* magazine about women's studies courses, she expressed similar concerns. While being careful to say that the classes she'd sat in on had varied widely, she reported that some professors and texts seemed to be "celebrating subjectivity over objectivity, feelings over facts, instinct over logic." She also observed:

Terms like sexism, racism, and homophobia have bloated beyond all recognition, and the more politicized the campus, the more frequently they're thrown around. I heard both professors and students call Berkeley's women's studies department homophobic and racist, despite the fact that courses dealing with homosexuality and multiculturalism fill the catalog and quite a number of women of color and lesbians are affiliated with the department.[61]

In her view, many of these courses seemed to be turning students into "Angry Young Women." She says that after attending a number of them in succession, she found herself noticing, quite involuntarily, that "the sign on the women's bathroom door in the University of Iowa's library was smaller than the one on the men's room door." She also noted that while a great deal of lip-service was paid to the notion of respecting "diversity," this principle didn't appear to apply to political opinions. (A study by the Association of American Colleges found that while 30 percent of students taking women's studies courses said they are uneasy about offering dissenting opinions, only 14 percent of non-women's studies students reported similar misgivings.) She described many of the students she spoke to as "quite bright," but said they "seemed to have learned to think critically through only one lens."[62]

Susan Faludi responded to the *Mother Jones* piece with a lengthy letter to the editor, which began by noting that the story had been followed by a line that said Lehrman was "writing a book on postideological feminism." She ended by suggesting that Lehrman was afraid to question authority. Here again, we see a tendency on the part of Faludi to attack people rather than confining her response to their opinions. Pauline Bart, a feminist sociology professor known for her research on rape, included these comments in her own letter to the editor: "My best guess about Lehrman is that she is exploiting the market that provides instant stardom for women criticizing feminist endeavors. Move over Camille Paglia and Katie Roiphe!" And history professor Elizabeth Fox-Genovese wrote:

> I finished Karen Lehrman's article, with a sigh of recognition: This is, indeed, the world of women's studies that I have come to know reasonably well during the past decade. And knowing the world, I hate to think of the response the article is sure to provoke. These are not stories that we tell in public.... So the rage of insiders who will dismiss her as a traitor or, worse, an antifeminist is predictable.[63]

Lehrman's comment about women's studies students

only being able to think critically through one lens is an important one. When people ask me why my opinions aren't closer to those of other feminists, particularly ones who also hold degrees in women's studies, my response is two-pronged. First, I (like many of the women who are now expressing their reservations and concerns) used to buy into a lot of these ideas. When I was a women's studies student, I was a true believer. I didn't attend such classes for five years of my life in order to spy on the enemy. Rather, I knew that I most definitely was a feminist, I was in my early twenties, and a lot of this stuff sounded perfectly okay back then. I remember having conversations with other women at the time who thought my concentration on women's issues was absurd, and I remember thinking, smugly, that they just didn't "get it." Second, I took the tools my university education gave me—such as critical thinking skills—and applied them. My ideas about the world kept evolving. I didn't chain myself to one window sill and declare that particular view to be the *only* reality.

As Patai and Koertge point out:

> Religious fanatics are adept at thinking and speaking critically about secular society. They are not so inclined to turn their scrutiny on themselves. The skill of Women's Studies students at…ferreting out the hand of the devil patriarchy in every sin and crime of society are not an exhibition of critical thinking at a very significant level. The fact that students have abandoned received views (and have some good reasons for doing so) is no indication that they have not, at the same time, uncritically locked themselves into another framework, which is at least as deeply flawed.[64]

A growing number of women familiar with feminism—

as it is practised in the real world as well as how it is being taught in women's studies courses—are deeply troubled by what we see. We see a movement marked by extremism and arrogance, a movement that venerates fanatical personalities rather than distancing itself from them, that encourages anti-male bigotry rather than condemning it. We see a movement that has responded simplistically to the controversies surrounding repressed/recovered memories, satanic ritual abuse and multiple personality disorder; a movement willing to overlook troubling mental health care practices in the interests of advancing the political thesis that child sexual abuse is widespread. We see a movement that protests sexist myths and double standards that harm women while at the same time promoting double standards that malign men. We see leaders who think they are entitled to decide whether or not other women are feminists. We see attempts to silence criticism and dissent by calling people right-wingers, traitors, racists and homophobes; by expecting female writers to talk about women's issues in certain ways; and by insisting that feelings are more important than intelligent discussion. We see a women's movement that is splintering and fracturing according to absurd group identities, that is paying so much attention to often imaginary slights that the positive aspects of the movement are being seriously undermined.

In short, feminism in the 1990s is a mess.

PART TWO

Flinging Open New Windows

No feminist whose concern for women stems from a concern for justice in general can ever legitimately allow her only interest to be the advantage of women.

–*Janet Radcliffe Richards*[1]

CHAPTER FIVE

Enter: The Men's Movement

It should come as no surprise that a women's movement that's so ill-mannered toward its own members has also responded less than graciously to the emerging men's movement. In 1992, twenty-one feminists—from American novelist Ursula Le Guin to Zsuzsanna Budapest (who advocates solving career problems by casting spells)—contributed essays to a collection titled *Women Respond to the Men's Movement*. The editor of this project was Kay Leigh Hagan, whose 1991 *Ms.* article advised feminists who live with men to use condoms, as a physical barrier when sleeping with "the oppressor," and to get a room with a door that locks. (Evidently, none of the contributors felt the need to avoid associating themselves with Hagan's extremist views.)

The book's preface is written by Gloria Steinem, thus signalling that the opinions contained within its pages are considered more or less acceptable in mainstream feminist circles. Steinem certainly doesn't declare any of *these* women to be non-feminists. Nor does she take the precaution of saying that while some of these comments are a little over the top, the dialogue is valuable in its own right.

Without a doubt, the collection is among the most disheartening pieces of feminist literature I've read. Taken as a whole, it is condescending, derisive and arrogant in tone, as well as a display of feminine busybody-ness at its worst. On the one hand, men are repeatedly condemned for thinking they're the centre of the universe; on the other, these women insist feminists have the right to be pronouncing on the men's movement as well as dictating terms to it. Writer after writer declares that a "real" men's movement should be properly concerned not with whatever *it* decides its priorities to be but with women's issues. In the words of bell hooks (who says it's unfortunate that men haven't requested "critical feedback about the direction of the men's movement" from women), it "should merely be a segment under the larger feminist movement."[2]

Steinem begins by devoting a full page of her five-page preface to listing female victimization/male misconduct statistics. She tells us that one woman in four is sexually assaulted in her lifetime, that the "most dangerous place for a woman is not in the street but in her home," that "more than half of battering husbands also abuse their children," that 50 percent of women experience sexual harassment in the paid workplace, and that divorced men are awarded custody of their children "even when there is medical evidence" of child abuse.

She says women "are literally dying" for a men's movement, but that while they want to believe in "male change," they have "little reason to do so."[3] Let's think about this for a minute. Has the women's movement been primarily concerned with *female* change, with modifying *female* behaviour? Has it spent much time worrying about

the ways in which women have benefited from long-standing sex-role stereotypes? Since no women's group I'm aware
of sees anything wrong with requiring only young men to
register for the draft, the answer is obviously a resounding
"no." Rather, feminism has focused its attention on the
ways in which oppressive gender stereotypes have harmed
women. Early feminists didn't hold meetings in suburban
homes to tell women the reason they were miserable was
because they weren't being good enough mothers and
housekeepers. They held meetings at which women concluded there was something wrong with the system, not
with them.

So why would a men's movement not want to concentrate on issues that have harmed men? Why might the
men's movement not decide that a too-narrowly defined
male role is the problem, not men themselves? Nowhere
does Steinem mention the higher suicide rates, shorter life
spans, over-representation among leading causes of death,
higher rates of crime victimization, educational inequities,
higher occupational death rates or concentration in the
worst job classifications that tell us males aren't doing all
that well in our society. These realities don't exist for
Steinem, just as they don't exist for her *Ms.* colleague Letty
Cottin Pogrebin. Young male bodies showing up at city
morgues five times more frequently than young female bodies make no impression on her. Those are the kinds of statistics one would expect a fair-minded person writing about
men's issues to be discussing, but Steinem is adamant in her
views. She says people who consider her stats "male bash-
ing" and people who think men get a bad deal are plain
wrong. In her words, the notion that men are oppressed in
our society is "no more (and no less) true than saying white
Americans are oppressed by racism."[4]

The racism analogy is a common one in the women's
movement. Feminists routinely talk about "male

supremacy," as though it were a parallel to "white supremacy." Elsewhere in this collection, the feminist writer Starhawk says the men's movement should:

> ...be clear about the difference between spiritual malaise and oppression. Oppression is what the slave suffers; malaise is what happens to the slave owners whose personalities are warped and whose essential humanity is necessarily undermined by their position.

According to Starhawk, men suffer malaise, women are oppressed.[5] Jane Caputi and Gordene O. MacKenzie suggest a link between the right-wing racists who formed the National Association for the Advancement of White People and "much of the activity going on under the rubric of the 'men's movement.'" Rosemary Radford Ruether invites us to "imagine a parallel 'white people's movement' arising that would claim to solve racism primarily by seeing it as a problem of the wounded white psyche." Elizabeth Dodson Gray says the failure on the part of men's activists to talk about male violence against women is "like focusing on the feelings of SS guards while the ovens of genocide burn a few feet away. It is like pondering the feelings of white people while black people are being lynched just over the hill."[6] This analogy, however, is fundamentally flawed.

Under apartheid in South Africa, compared with a white person, the average black person died considerably younger and was far more likely to be homeless, imprisoned or victimized by violence. In Canada, statistics tell us that native people commit suicide at a higher rate than the rest of the population, that they have shorter life spans and are more likely to die violently, be imprisoned, suffer from alcoholism or end up on the street. We say this data demonstrates that they are *oppressed*. We look at this appalling state of affairs and insist society at large must be at least partially responsible, and that we should respond with understanding, compassion and support. In present-day America, blacks live six years fewer than do whites, on average. Blacks are also statistically more likely to die violently or to be imprisoned. We say this is because they have been and continue to be *oppressed*.

In order for the racism analogy to work for feminists, it would have to be true that *women*—not men—were dying eight years sooner than their spouses; young *females* were committing suicide at a rate five times greater than young males; *women*—not men—were suffering more from alcoholism, violence and homelessness; and *females*—not males—were twenty times more likely to end up in a prison cell. (It's true men generally earn more than women and have historically enjoyed more educational, economic and political rights, but how do these matters stack up against all the above factors in the here and now?)

Let's get a grip. A true male supremacist society would not be one in which men routinely lived significantly shorter lives. A true male supremacist society—unless it were both breathtakingly stupid and hopelessly incompetent—would have ensured long ago that women outnumbered men in all the categories we've just examined.

This is not to suggest, for one instant, that women don't have legitimate and serious concerns. (As I've argued earlier, this isn't a contest.) But let's cut the male supremacist nonsense, shall we? Moreover, if it's okay for women to focus on difficulties unique to their gender, then males are perfectly entitled to concentrate attention on the ways in which their own sex is being short-changed by the system.

Caught up in her feminist world-view, Steinem insists it's the business of women to decide which parts of the men's movement we "trust." In order to arrive at these decisions, she says we should ask ourselves whether men's groups make us "feel safer as women" and whether they are devoting time and money to "diminishing violence."[7] While there's no doubt it would be a good thing for men, themselves, if violence were curtailed in North America, in Steinem's eyes only some violence matters: she doesn't talk about the women who abuse their children or attack their spouses. And while she accuses some men's groups of supporting fathers' child custody rights even in the face of apparent sexual abuse, she commits the same sort of sin herself, only in reverse. Nowhere does she acknowledge that there are women who falsely accuse spouses of child abuse during bitter custody disputes or who deliberately poison their children's minds against their dads.

And so we're left with the idiotic situation of two groups glaring at each other over a fence, each legitimately accusing the other of wrongs and oversights. Feminists like to justify their unjust treatment of men by pointing out that males, historically, have been less than fair to women. Men's activists sometimes try to excuse their own bad behaviour by arguing that feminists have treated males poorly. But two wrongs have never made a right, and this vicious cycle is going to continue until both sides start behaving like adults and ensuring that their own conduct meets the same standards they expect from others.

Hagan's introduction to the collection isn't much better than Steinem's preface. She says the thought of men organizing on their own behalf "holds a certain curious irony" and "is so absurd as to be amusing."[8] Another writer, who tells us she's using an "ironic satirical character voice," invites us to do an exercise to get our "blood boiling" and then responds to the idea of a men's movement by asking, "Is this some kind of joke about laxatives or something?" She wonders whether men are learning how "to stop worrying about the size of their dicks" in their wilderness retreats and then refers to them as "a bunch of boys playing games with the cultures of people they don't know how to live next door to."[9] (How do you suppose women would respond to a man who wondered whether they were learning to stop worrying about the size of their breasts at feminist events?)

Starhawk declares that "something is wrong with men, and the prospect of men getting together to fix it themselves is a happy one." She then adds, "On the other hand, our history with men doesn't generate much trust that, left to themselves, they will actually get it right."[10] While she says there are men she loves and respects, that doesn't stop her from characterizing the lot of them as inferior beings in need of repair.

Now I'd like to draw my own race analogy. In less tolerant times, people would make comments such as: "You really have to meet Joe. I tell you, you'd never know he's a Jew. He's not like the others." Or they'd say: "Mary's such a sweet girl. You practically forget she's coloured." These statements demonstrate racist attitudes. People who are not prepared to recognize the humanity of an entire group, who make exceptions on an individual basis but consider the group as a whole to be inferior in some way, are racists.

But is this so different from the way feminists constantly talk about men? We, too, are willing to make exceptions for individual males, but we say things about them as a group that we'd never dream of saying about anyone else. Can you imagine the uproar if I wrote, in one of my newspaper columns, that while I love and respect the occasional Chinese person living in my neighbourhood, I'm pleased they're getting together to "fix" themselves because they're really badly in need of it? Can you imagine if I then added insult to injury by saying: "But you know, I'm not certain they're capable of 'getting it right' if left to their own devices"?

I assure you that if such comments were to make it past my editor and into the morning paper, I'd no longer have a job. And yet this sort of bigotry toward men is the order of the day among contemporary feminists, journalists and even among some men. "We're in trouble; men are in trouble," says John McManiman, a counsellor who works with abusive men. His quote opened an article, a full newspaper page in length, that appeared in Canada's largest daily two days prior to the fifth anniversary of the Montreal Massacre. Elsewhere in the piece, McManiman says: "It's a great thing that feminists are holding men accountable for their behavior." Another male therapist is quoted as saying: "We're taught that if we're not violent, we're not men." Only then, two-thirds of the way into the article, does the feminist writer offer this tepid disclaimer: "Yet most men don't act in obviously violent ways, most of the time."[11]

Let's return to my analogy. Can you imagine someone saying, "We're in trouble; the Chinese are in trouble. It's a good thing society is holding us accountable for our behaviour," when the problem wasn't the Chinese community in general but Asian gang violence? These would be considered ridiculous statements. As one man indignantly responded, in a letter to the editor:

> "We're in trouble; men are in trouble." Really? Which men? All men? Me included? Why? The article doesn't explain the quote…. Vilifying an entire gender for the transgressions of some of its members is neither fair nor constructive.

Regarding the statement that men are taught to behave violently, another wrote:

> …the males in my family were taught to work out their adversary tendencies in a variety of sports. My

uncles were champions in several disciplines and I had 37 amateur fights until my future wife decided not to go dancing on Saturday nights with anyone sporting one or two black eyes.

In my family, we were taught to respect women. They were our mothers, our sisters and (often) our better halves.

On another occasion, a man wrote a letter to *The Globe and Mail* that took issue with a female columnist who had made sweeping generalizations about men and housework (something which, once again, you'd never be permitted to do if you were talking about any other identifiable group. What if I were to declare that the Chinese had lower standards of hygiene than other people?). It read, in part:

> I myself have never done any of the following with any frequency: left underwear in the middle of the bedroom floor, washed dishes only when there were no clean ones left, dusted only when the mantle appeared to be sagging, chosen cleanest dirty socks as an alternative to doing laundry.
>
> Leave me and men alone for a while, or at least castigate us in a more precise way. I am not a bad person really and neither are my male friends.[12]

When *The New York Times* reviewed Marilyn French's *The War Against Women* in 1992, the top half of the page was devoted to a discussion of another book. The headlines appearing above both reviews, though, were part of the same thought. They read: "Women Have Always Hated Men" "…And With Good Reason."[13] If these are the kind of headlines that a male supremacist society produces, I'd hate to read the headlines in a matriarchal world. Are we in the habit of declaring that blacks hate white South

Africans with good reason? Or that Jews hate Germans
with good reason? Do we not, instead, insist that it is the
behaviour of some individuals, not the entire group, that is
the issue? Kind, decent, non-violent men don't deserve to
be lumped together with troubled, abusive ones any more
than mothers who love their children deserve to be lumped
together with Susan Smith, who pushed the vehicle carrying her two little boys, strapped into car seats, into a lake.
This is, quite simply, unjust.

The feminists in *Women Respond to the Men's Movement*
are not deterred by this reasoning, however. They make
statements such as: "men's relationships with others are
held in place by the abuse of power and control" and "men
are hooked on a spectrum of control that extends from not
listening to violence." Another argues that men's involvement in parenting isn't necessarily a good thing, since men
raised in a patriarchal society might simply be contaminat-
ing the nursery with their ingrained sexism.[14] Yet another
says:

> ...how do I feel about the mythopoetic men's
> movement? I feel frightened, and angry, and
> critical, and amused. I think that anything which
> is so terrifically attractive to white, middle-class
> heterosexual men...*is probably dangerous to women.*
> [my italics]

That this writer consumes paranoia with her breakfast
cereal is evident in the very first lines of her piece, in
which she blames men even for her own confused thoughts:

> It says something about the ability of the patriarchy
> to confuse women's thinking that I, who can
> usually sit down at the computer and simply state
> what is on my mind about almost any topic, have

been for the last hour forthing and backing and
deleting lines and acting as a well-trained woman
in that I cannot seem to find my voice.

A little further on, she insists that men are solely responsible for domestic violence, air and water pollution and
social program cuts.[15] Someone else complains that women
have been organizing around violence issues for twenty
years and "the only visible response during that time is that
the violence against women has increased to proportions
that can only be seen as a holocaust!" She adds: "men are
in denial about *most* women's terrifying reality: imprisoned
in the cage of the patriarchal family, with rape and murder
a *constant* threat, and no safe place to go to get away [my
italics]."[16]

Where do these people get this stuff? Where does the
venom and hostility come from? What has happened to
their sense of perspective? *Most* women are not cowering in
their homes worried about being murdered and raped every
minute of the day. Violence against women, as serious as it
is, is not a holocaust. Women and men both vote in the
United States and Canada, which means they both bear
some responsibility for social program cuts. They both drive
cars, use electricity and buy pre-packaged goods, all of
which contribute to environmental degradation.

Sophisticated political analysis isn't necessarily a strong
point in this collection, either. Says Starhawk:

If there is to be a men's movement I could trust,
I want to know what it is going to do about war.
Because, hey, guys, you could end it tomorrow, by
simply refusing to fight in it…. Why don't men rise
up and refuse to go to war?[17]

Nice theory. But isn't this as unrealistic as saying that

women should all snap their fingers and resolve never to worry about their weight, their wrinkles or their grey hair again? Isn't this like saying that if women were really concerned about the fashion, make-up, diet, cosmetic surgery and pornography industries, they could overthrow them in a day by deciding, all at once, not to help produce or buy such services and commodities?

Why does feminism expect men to be able somehow to accomplish things women can't? Women, remember, comprise the majority of voters.[18] If we were all united, we could dictate policy to our elected representatives, who'd have little choice but to do whatever it was we wanted, including putting an end to warfare. Unity amongst men is no easier to accomplish than unity amongst women is. Nevertheless, we insist, in the words of one feminist in this collection, that men should be held "directly accountable for their continued support of patriarchy," and, in the words of another, that men have "to take responsibility for the actions of their own gender."[19]

Many of these feminists see suspect motives everywhere. One refers to Robert Bly, the author of the 1990 best-seller *Iron John: A Book About Men*, as a "rather blustery old man, an arrogant showman" who has decided he's had enough of feminism and "by golly, he's going to do something about it, maybe even make a living off the project." A second says Bly's writing is "not about social change" but rather "a backlash—men clamoring to reestablish the moral authority of the patriarchs."[20] Elsewhere, co-authors quote a passage from Bly, who says that when a father and son spend time together, especially in tribal cultures, "a substance almost like food passes from the older body to the younger" and that the "younger body learns at what frequency the masculine body vibrates." Bly says this is similar to the way a fetus becomes attuned to "female frequencies" while in the womb. Although Bly—who is, after all, a poet—

appears to me to be making use of a benign physical metaphor, these women declare: "This sounds frighteningly like psychic and/or physical incest and evinces both pedophilia and a characteristic patriarchal phenomenon: homophobic eroticism."[21]

It wouldn't be fair to leave the impression that every piece in this book suffers from such problems, but the majority do. Here, once again, we are forced to acknowledge that much of mainstream feminist thought falls into the "highly questionable" category. If these are feminism's finest minds, the movement is in deep trouble.

Men are also told by these writers that they're supposed to "shut up and listen" to women. Starhawk says, "It's not that we want you to be perpetually silent, it's just that we want you occasionally to listen first before you speak. Just listen." Laura S. Brown declares that men have "to learn how to truly listen to the tears of others."[22]

But what are women doing, here? There's very little listening taking place on our side of the table. Instead, we're busily telling men that they've got the incorrect analysis, that they're overlooking what's really important, that they're doing everything wrong. These feminists are calling men whiners. These women are ridiculing the first feeble attempts of a movement struggling to breathe air into its newborn lungs. Robert Bly's book may be flawed, but how does it compare with much early feminist writing? More than a quarter of a century later, this wave of the women's movement is still producing far more heat than light.

(It is true, of course, that female socialization often demands that women pay attention to men; thus, a certain knee-jerk negative response by feminists to the notion that the world would be a better place if women listened more is understandable. But there's a difference between nodding in all the right places and making genuine attempts at understanding. There's a difference between behaving in a manner that is virtually guaranteed to flatter a man's ego and making the sort of imaginative leap required to see life from his perspective.)

Feminists like to talk about how unkind the mainstream media was to the early women's movement. We like to talk about how men sneered and condescended.[23] And what are we—who should know better—doing in our turn? Instead of behaving as we wish men had behaved toward us, we're sniping from the sidelines.

Women, as a group, have gone through an enormous consciousness-raising process. We've actively and publicly questioned the old female role, identifying those things about it which constrained and limited us. Men, as a group, have yet to re-examine the old male role in anything approaching the same manner. They have held no lively public discussions about what to keep and what to discard, about how this role continues to circumscribe men's options and behaviour. In the words of Wendy Dennis, the author of *Hot and Bothered: Sex and Love in the Nineties*:

> ...although the nineties man has certainly become more feminized through feminism, he has never (unlike his female contemporaries, whose definition of themselves has been virtually reconstructed from the ground up) undergone a collective mind-altering process of deep internal reflection, metamorphosis and transformation of his own making.[24]

Not one of the nearly two dozen contributors to *Women Respond to the Men's Movement* is able to put aside her own concerns long enough to offer men a generous, no-strings-attached blessing. No one simply wishes men well as they embark on their own journey of self-discovery. No one says, "We hope the process is as rewarding for you as it has been for us." Gloria Steinem doesn't. The editor, Kay Leigh

Hagan, doesn't. Riane Eisler comes closest when she talks about "the straitjackets of the old roles" and says that "what the women's, men's, and partnership movements are all about is exploring new frontiers of what is possible for both women and men."[25]

As a feminist, I'm ashamed of this absence of goodwill, I'm ashamed by the display of pettiness, sarcasm and self-obsession in this book. We, who have been insisting on our own right to be seen and heard, have now grown blind and deaf to the misery of others.

Nor is the disdain with which feminists respond to men's concerns limited to this collection of essays. The January/February 1995 issue of *Ms.* magazine included the following smarmy paragraph under the headline "Like a Hole in the Head":

> Students at the Boston University School of Law have formed the Men's Law Association. Its mission? To educate "the next generation of lawyers about the impact of antimale prejudices." The group says the areas of divorce law, domestic violence, and child custody are "laden with anti-male bias." The association believes itself to be the only one of its kind in the U.S. We can see why.

A few months later, the same magazine gloated: "In case you forgot, International Men's Day came and went. Looks like everyone else forgot too. All of five men showed up for the International Men's Day convention in Toronto on February 7..."[26]

In my view, if this particular phase of the men's movement had produced no more than two specific books, it would still have made an enormous contribution to our understanding of gender issues. The first is Warren Farrell's *The Myth of Male Power: Why Men are the Disposable Sex.*

The other, by British journalist David Thomas, is titled *Not Guilty: In Defence of the Modern Man.*

Warren Farrell was elected three times to the board of directors of the New York City chapter of the National Organization for Women. As a young man, he worked on feminist issues for a decade, attempting to be a translator of sorts between feminism and ordinary men, trying to explain the feminist perspective to males. He says his speaking engagements during this period were attended mostly by women, who gave him standing ovations, warmly asked how they could "clone" him and invited him to speak elsewhere, thus assuring him a degree of financial stability. But at some point, while reviewing tape recordings of workshops he'd been conducting with both genders, he started to become aware of a bias on his own part. He noticed that he hadn't been really listening to men. He writes, in the introduction:

> When women criticized men, I called it
> "insight," "assertiveness," "women's liberation,"
> "independence," or "high self-esteem." When
> men criticized women, I called it "sexism," "male
> chauvinism," "defensiveness," "rationalizing," and
> "backlash." I did it politely—but the men got the
> point. Soon the men were no longer expressing
> their feelings. Then I criticized the men for not
> expressing their feelings!

Afterward, he says, he started listening more closely. He began responding as openly and receptively to what men said as to what women said and became aware of perspectives that hadn't occurred to him before. When he started incorporating these new ideas into his speeches, he says his "standing ovations disintegrated" almost overnight. He writes:

I would not be honest if I denied that this tempted me to return to being a spokesperson only for women's perspectives. I liked writing, speaking, and doing television shows. Now it seemed that all three were in jeopardy. I quickly discovered it took far more internal security to speak on behalf of men than to speak on behalf of women. Or, more accurately, to speak on behalf of both sexes rather than on behalf of only women.[27]

No book is perfect, and Farrell's attempts at pithiness, for example, too often end up sounding inappropriately glib ("men who are retired or fired are soon expired").[28] But having long had an interest in gender issues, and considering myself an open-minded individual, I picked up this work at my local bookstore one day and spent the entire weekend saying to my husband, "Listen to this" and "Now listen to *this*."

My husband and I have had the good fortune of developing intellectually and politically in similar directions at approximately the same time. We met each other in the peace movement, when we both had objections to the testing of U.S. air force cruise missiles over Canada's north, and have demonstrated for abortion access together. I used to share the insights of my women's studies classes with him: "This is what the lecturer talked about today. Doesn't that make so much sense?" He typically responded by thinking of other examples that served to prove the point. Several years later, as I read snippets of Farrell's book out loud, as my mind was being set on fire by an equally fascinating perspective, he was telling me that much of it rang true, that Farrell was doing a good job of capturing the male experience.

When I recommend *The Myth of Male Power* to people, one of the things I stress is that Farrell relies on tried-and-

true feminist methods. One of the most effective tech-
niques that women have used to demonstrate that something is unjust is the gender switch. In this vein, we
protested that since men weren't taking an oath to "obey"
their wives during the traditional marriage ceremony, it was
outrageous that women should be required to say they'd
obey their husbands. We argued that since men didn't
adopt their wives' last names, or have their marital status
demarcated by their form of address (as in Miss and Mrs.),
there was no good reason for women to continue doing so.
We said it was unfair to call a woman who slept around a
"slut" when men were admired for similar behaviour.

Farrell does the same thing. He says it's unfair that men
are told there's never any excuse for domestic violence, but
women get to blame their violence on PMS. He says it's
unfair that the male captain of the *Exxon Valdez* oil tanker
was tried, convicted and imprisoned for his part in the oil
spill that wreaked environmental havoc in 1989, while a
female air traffic controller who failed to perform her job
properly and was thus directly responsible for the deaths of
thirty-four human beings in 1991 was shielded from prose-
cution and publicity and provided with counselling. He
says it's unfair that while our society knows better than to
make jokes about female suffering, it considers men who
have lost their jobs fair game, despite evidence that many
men are profoundly traumatized by this experience (in the
United States, unemployed males commit suicide at twice
the rate of employed ones). He points out that while our
society doesn't have as many support services for widowers
as widows, men are ten times more likely than women to
commit suicide following the death of a spouse.[29]

For me, one of Farrell's most illuminating observations
pertains to our double standard with respect to the potential for good and evil. He writes:

> Feminism suggested that God might be a "She" but
> not that the devil might also be a "she." Feminism
> articulated the shadow side of men and the light
> side of women. It neglected...to acknowledge that
> each sex has both sides *within* each individual.
> [original italics]

He also argues persuasively that society has historically
been organized in certain ways not because men deliberately designed the world in order to oppress women but
because these structures made sense at the time. He suggests thinking of human development as falling into two
categories: "Stage I" and "Stage II"—the first being survival
based and the second being the kind of life we, who live in
the industrialized world, have been privileged to enjoy
since the end of World War II:

> In Stage I, most couples were role mates: the
> woman raised the children and the man raised the
> money. In Stage II, couples increasingly desired to
> be soul mates. Why? As couples met their survival
> needs, they "upped the ante" and redefined love.
>   In Stage I, a woman called it "love" if she found
> a man who was a good provider and protector; he
> called it "love" if she was beautiful and could take
> care of a home and children. Love meant a *division*
> of labor which led to a division of female and male
> interests.[30]

According to this line of thought, it's precisely the standard
of living we now take for granted (largely the result of male
blood, sweat and tears) that freed vast numbers of women
to think about things like self-fulfilment, to start questioning whether it was right to confine women to the home
when many of them clearly have talents that can be put to

use in the public sphere. Farrell says most men haven't gone through a similar period of self-assessment yet, that they're mostly still stuck in Stage I, and that this has caused problems all around. Writes Farrell:

> Many marriages consummated in Stage I, then, were suddenly held up to Stage II standards. They failed. Marriages failed not only because the standards were higher, but because the standards were also contradictory. For a Stage I woman, a lawyer was an ideal candidate for a husband. For a Stage II woman, the lawyer, often trained to argue more than to listen, was an ideal candidate for divorce. The very qualities that led to success at work often led to failure at home.

Wendy Dennis puts it a different way. She says:

> You've got to feel for men on this count. I certainly do. Basically, they were sitting around minding their own business when the world turned upside down on them; the women in their lives marched through a door, came out the other side unrecognizable and started barking orders and telling them to hurry and catch up. Women have been reading them the riot act, in one way or another, ever since.[31]

I used to justify taking women's studies, studying female history and literature, for example, by saying that the rest of history was men's history. I used to say that the male perspective permeated everything, that all I was trying to do was reclaim a small corner—in an overwhelmingly masculine garden—to grow a few feminine vines. I still don't think that idea deserves to be repudiated altogether.

There's no disputing the fact that 85 percent of the books I studied while completing my English major in university, and an even higher percentage of my high school texts, were written by men (although I shouldn't be holding my professors responsible for the fact that, historically, most writers were men). Indeed, I remember complaining in high school that I'd had it up to here with male coming-of-age novels. But Farrell's view on such matters is compelling. He writes:

> Women's studies questions the female role; nothing questions the male role. History books *sell* to boys the *traditional* male role of hero and performer. Each history book is 500 pages of advertisements for the performer role. Each lesson tells him, "If you perform, you will get love and respect; if you fail, you will be a nothing." To a boy, history is pressure to perform, not relief from that pressure. Feminism is relief from the pressure to be confined to only the traditional female role. To a boy, then, history is...the *opposite* of women's studies. [original italics][32]

Farrell also raises a formidable challenge to feminist orthodoxy by questioning one of our most sacred cows: the assertion that rape is a manifestation of male power, and that it's not really about sex. Again and again, one encounters this feminist dogma. A booklet titled "Sexual Assault: Dispelling the Myths," published by the Ontario government, insists it's a "fact" that "studies on the profiles of rapists reveal that they are 'ordinary' and 'normal' men who sexually assault women in order to assert power and control over them." In June 1995, a doctor who works for a Women's Health Centre in British Columbia declared in a letter to the editor of *The Globe and Mail*:

> It's both welcome and refreshing to see sexual
> assault's most common myth so eloquently
> shattered. That rape is "purely and simply an act
> of violence and degradation" rather than a sexual
> act cannot be overemphasized.... [this] article
> does far more than sell newspapers; it educates
> the public.[33]

If so, Farrell asks why it is that American women between the ages of sixteen and nineteen are *eighty-four times* more likely to be raped than women over the age of fifty.[34] When feminists first came up with the idea that rape was about power, they were trying to account for the fact that frail, elderly women as well as very young children are sometimes raped. There's no denying that assaults against people in these two age categories strike us as being particularly vile, but statistically, such rapes are the exception, not the rule. Women in their teens, who come closest to meeting our society's limited ideal of what's sexually attractive, are at the highest risk of being raped. Degradation certainly seems to be an important element in this crime, but why can't we admit that sometimes—maybe even most of the time—sex is *also* part of the rape equation? What purpose are we serving by refusing to acknowledge the complexity of such issues? This is yet another instance in which it becomes clear that feminist slogans are a poor substitute for intelligent discourse.

Farrell, as he has mentioned, isn't so popular with the women's movement any more. It's true that Camille Paglia gave *The Myth of Male Power* a fabulous review in the *Washington Post* in 1993,[35] but as I've already discussed, Paglia isn't considered a "real" feminist. Many of Farrell's arguments build on those developed in his 1986 best-seller *Why Men Are the Way They Are*. In her preface to *Women Respond to the Men's Movement*, Steinem explicitly dismisses

Farrell's ideas when she maintains that men aren't oppressed. In her 1991 *Backlash*, Susan Faludi tells us about Farrell's female housekeeper and secretary (would she be happier if he'd refused to hire them because they were women?), his leather jacket, his sports car and his vanity plates before recounting the immense contribution he's made to the organized women's movement. She then says:

> But as feminism lost its media glitter, Farrell's enthusiasm seemed to fade, too. Perhaps the changes he said he had made in himself were superficial, little more than cosmetic touch-ups to enhance his stardom in the short-lived '70s liberation drama.

Faludi describes the people who have responded positively to Farrell's recent work as "antifeminist fans," and she suggests, in language we've seen her use elsewhere, that he's simply trying "to reclaim center stage." What's remarkable is that she insists (minus any supporting evidence) on her own narrow-minded interpretation, even though she's aware he's paid a high price for his unpopular views among people whose opinions he cared about. Indeed, Faludi's four-page account ends with this passage:

> "I see now that the ideologues of the feminist movement don't want to listen," [Farrell] says, returning to the subject of *Ms.*'s failure to acknowledge his [1986] book. "Gloria Steinem didn't return my phone calls, and she used to." He studies his glass some more, then says: "It affected me a lot to see my popularity waning among people who saw me as an idol. When Gloria Steinem distanced from me, that hurt."[36]

The response to *The Myth of Male Power* in the mainstream media has tended to be a hostile one. In addition to my own columns, *The Toronto Star* has printed two other pieces about the book of which I'm aware. One, by a woman, ticks off the facts that men are over-represented in dangerous occupations, are the only sex forced to fight in wars and that prostate cancer research receives less funding than breast cancer even though these two diseases kill a comparable number of people; she then says, "*Excuse me? Is this relevant* [original italics]?" If the genders were reversed, many feminists would consider these facts to be terribly relevant. Why on earth wouldn't they be? The writer says that, in a workshop she attended in Edmonton, Farrell drew an analogy between the way men are viewed in our society and the way "the Aryans began to treat the Jews during World War II." I'm definitely troubled by this—just as I am when feminists say such things. And, as has been amply demonstrated, they tend to do so on a regular basis. While the writer grudgingly admits "nobody has a monopoly on pain," it's clear that she thinks Farrell has damaged rather than improved gender relations.

The other article was a review of the book, written by the poet Tom Wayman. His opening paragraph captures the tone of the piece nicely:

> Throughout Warren Farrell's *The Myth of Male Power*, the author evidently imagines himself riding to the defence of the besieged male sex, with all guns blazing. He aims to shoot down the idea of men as oppressors of women...and he has rounded up all the statistical and anecdotal ammunition he can stuff into his bullet clips, bandoliers and saddle bags.

Wayman accuses Farrell of harbouring "rage at the women's

movement." He accuses him of working "into the book a lot of the agenda of the U.S. right wing" and says that if the book "is representative of an intellectual backlash against feminism, women have nothing to fear from this direction."

Since we're on the subject of analogies, Wayman offers one of his own. After (in my view, wrongfully) accusing Farrell of "denigrating inequities to which women are subject," he says: "This gives *The Myth of Male Power* the feel of one of those anti-Semitic tracts where the author claims he doesn't hate Jews—merely wants to point out how Jews control not only world capitalism but world communism as well."[37] These are strange times, when people who attempt to discuss how male misery is inadequately acknowledged are compared to anti-Semites, while those who tar all men with the misogynous brush are considered enlightened and progressive.

In *Not Guilty: In Defence of the Modern Man*, which also appeared in 1993, David Thomas talks about how men themselves erect some of the biggest roadblocks to a questioning of the old male role by considering it a sign of weakness or failure to acknowledge that they, too, face problems. He tells of men who refuse to see a doctor concerning their medical ailments until they are struck down by serious illnesses. He talks about the casual brutality parents have inflicted on their male children in order to "toughen them up," of the inability of fathers and sons to express their love for one another and the fear some men have of admitting that they are burdened by old emotional wounds. But Thomas is also disturbed by a certain kind of "feminist" male:

> Brought up with the traditional male stereotypes, they have at some point internalized the feminist critique of men. The result is an over-riding

> determination to prove that they are truly
> penitent, that they are more willing than any
> woman to criticize the wrongdoings of men....
> Male feminism has almost become a perverse badge
> of machismo. It's a bit like the anti-drug campaign
> that featured an addict saying, "Heroin—I can
> handle it," as he collapsed into the gutter. The
> new motto is, "Feminism—I can handle it."[38]

Thomas says the industrialized world's obsession with women deserves notice only because it conflicts so dramatically with a lack of concern about men. While conducting research for his book, he notes that, with "the zeal of the natural obsessive," he decided to count the number of entries appearing in *The New York Times* 1991 index under the subject headings "men" and "women." The grand total: men: 104; women: 679. He notes that in the London, England, telephone book, 114 listings appear under "Women," including organizations that address rape and sexual harassment. Under "Men," there are two listings, one of which is a hairdresser. He also asks why—if men are having the far better time of it that feminism insists they are—four British males commit suicide for every British female, and men live significantly shorter lives than their spouses. "The fact is," says Thomas, "people are in pain. And right now, the ones who wear trousers and stand up to piss don't seem to count for much when it comes to being healed."[39]

Thomas admits that men continue to enjoy advantages women don't. He acknowledges that a man can walk into a drinking establishment and not worry about being ogled, and that he knows he doesn't feel as vulnerable as women do while out alone at night. "But," he says, a man "lacks one vital freedom. He cannot be himself." Instead, men are under constant pressure to conform to a definition of masculinity that feels utterly foreign to many of them, clothing taboos being only the most visible manifestation of this. He writes:

> A modern woman can, like my little daughters, play any number of roles in her everyday life. Her persona is as flexible as her wardrobe. But you do not have to venture far from the beaten path of masculinity before becoming trapped in the thickets of what society sees as effeminacy or perversion. Men have to keep any internal deviations from the straight and narrow locked up within their psyches. It is no surprise that so many men, unable to express themselves in normal circumstances, turn instead to deviancy and perversion. Countless broken lives, and careers cut short by scandal, testify to the damage that is done as a result.[40]

Like Farrell, Thomas sees both sex roles as offering pluses and minuses—not the "men-all-plus, women-all-minus" world implied by so many feminists. Stephanie (whose name used to be Keith prior to a sex-change operation) observes in an interview with Thomas that males now treat her more as an accessory to the man she's with than as an individual in her own right. She also admits that, in the professional world, life might be far easier for men. But she also says:

> ...on an emotional level, life is much, much richer for a woman. Women can let down barriers and can get much closer to people. Men have to maintain barriers. As a man, you can't go and cry on a best friend's shoulder when things go wrong. The first thing he'd do is edge away if you touch him.[41]

The experience of Graham, another Thomas inter-
viewee, who has worked in a nightclub dressed as a woman
(apparently indistinguishable from the female waitresses),
suggests that while men condescend to women, they also
treat them with greater overall kindness, consideration and
courtesy. Thomas further quotes from a magazine article
written by a female journalist who spent time undercover
as a man:

> I felt cut off from other people, distanced from
> them simply by the assumptions they made about
> manhood. As a person I had a sense of pitching
> from further back, needing to be louder and
> tougher in order to be acknowledged.[42]

Similar views were expressed by BEEN THERE, in a letter that Ann Landers published in July 1994. The writer
suggested there was a link between male violence and the
fact that males are expected to keep so many of their emotions under such tight control. It read, in part:

> ...emotionally, men are at a disadvantage.
>   It is socially acceptable for women to cry,
> scream, kiss or hug other women, act flaky or flirty
> and indulge in all sorts of behavior that would cost
> a man his job, marriage and reputation. "Real men"
> aren't permitted to do any of the above. A man
> who cries, screams or hugs a member of the
> same sex is immediately suspect. If he is overly
> sympathetic, he is considered a wimp.[43]

This isn't to say that women aren't sometimes criticized for
being "too emotional." In the business world, the less emotional male model of behaviour is still considered "normal,"
while females who occasionally end up in tears are sus-

pected of "not being able to hack it." But this suggests that when the emotional restraints imposed on men begin to relax a little, women, too, will benefit.

We need a world in which both men and women are able to express more of their authentic selves. In order to get there, though, we first have to be prepared to acknowledge that society *as a whole* constricts male behaviour, because society *as a whole* has to decide to change. If women ridicule men's attempts to express their true emotions, the process is going to take a lot longer than it should.

Thomas, too, challenges the feminist assumption that disparities between the sexes always hurt women and that they are always the result of patriarchal oppression. He points out that a feminist-inspired insistence that female tennis players deserve to be paid as highly as male tennis players has led to a situation in which the women's prize money at Wimbledon is "within 10 percent of the men's." While this appears to be nothing more than a proper and just state of affairs, in reality, it's profoundly unfair—to men. There are, in fact, many more male tennis players, which means the male winner must defeat far more competitors and play far more games in order to become a contender for the championship. Thomas observes that the 1991 men's Wimbledon championship was won by Michael Stich—after he'd played a total of 257 games that year. The women's was won by Steffi Graf, who claimed the title and the prize money after playing only 128 games—half as many. Feminists rightly protest when women have to work longer hours to earn the same pay as men, but not when the opposite is true. Thomas also notes that the current state of affairs can't be justified by the revenues the sport generates, either, since more television viewers choose to watch the men's Wimbledon finals than the women's, and the men's games command higher spectator ticket prices.[44]

We all say we support equal pay for equal work, but few people are overly concerned about the fact that male fashion models are paid significantly less than female ones. This is the case even though males are already disadvantaged by being unable to supplement their income with lucrative cosmetics contracts. Four-year, $5-million deals signed by the likes of Christy Turlington with Maybelline are out of the question for male models, who, Thomas reports, earn no more than $5,000 for a show while women routinely pull down fees in the five figures. He writes: "Everyone understands that our culture is not particularly interested in looking at men who aren't actually doing something, or who haven't already established a reputation in another field."[45]

Once again, it appears that neither feminism, nor society at large, cares about double standards per se. It's difficult to escape the feeling that feminism, a movement that started out as a crusade for genuine equality, has lost its way amid the twists and turns of modern life. Rather than carefully and consistently applying principles of justice and fairness to individual situations, rather than recognizing that human affairs can't be reduced to a single, overarching formula (such as "women are always oppressed"), feminists have embraced unthinking dogmatism.

One achieves a brighter future through moral consistency—not by playing favourites. If a daughter and a son are raised in the same home by parents who consistently take the daughter's side, even when her injuries are imaginary, the son may not grow up sympathetic to the hurts of other females. Rather, he may grow up bitter and resentful that his own abrasions mattered so little.

Thomas further challenges the feminist notion that crime is solely a male problem. (Remember the Canadian Panel on Violence Against Women, which implied that the only real criminals are male?) He points out that, in

Great Britain, the segment of the population most at risk of being murdered consists of children under the age of one.[46] These murders are frequently committed by women but are classified separately as "infanticide," which then distorts the number of homicides for which women are deemed responsible. Even more disturbing is the fact that criminal charges are laid in only a small fraction (less than 15 percent) of these deaths. (In Canada, as well, children in their first year of life were disproportionately represented among homicide victims in 1993 and 1994. According to the available data, however, it appears this country has a far better record of holding perpetrators accountable than does the U.K.[47])

In Ontario, wife battering is taken very seriously, to the point where police have been issued written directives to lay criminal charges "in all incidents of wife assault." Officers are further advised that they "should not be influenced" in such situations by factors such as the "likelihood of obtaining a conviction in court."[48] Let's look at the hypothetical situation of a couple married for many years. In the course of a heated argument, the man, for the very first time, angrily grabs his wife. If the woman picks up the phone, dials 911 and says she's been assaulted, the police are going to arrive. Sometimes it doesn't matter what the man says, it's the woman who's believed. And if the man is honest enough to admit that, yes, things got out of hand and he did grab her, it's game over. He's handcuffed and, in front of his children and his neighbours, is taken out to the cruiser. At the police station he's confined to a cell. When he's able to get in touch with a lawyer (it might be the first time he's ever needed one, and so he doesn't have the first clue who to call), the lawyer will help arrange bail. But according to the authorities I checked with, prosecutors "routinely" ask for, and judges "frequently" grant, that, as a condition of bail, the man must abide by a restraining order that says he can't return to his home until the charge is dealt with (except on one occasion, accompanied by a police officer, to pick up a few things). It might take a year for the case to come to trial, during which time the man has had to find another place to live (an expense he might not be able to afford). Meanwhile, his family, friends and, perhaps, even his wife have gone into shock at what happens once the criminal justice system gets involved. He has also had to come up with thousands more dollars to cover his legal fees. And all because he grabbed another, fully-grown, adult.

But people, many of them women, who snuff out the lives of utterly helpless infants might not even get *charged* in Great Britain? Such individuals may not be called upon in a court of law to explain themselves? Writes Thomas:

> Could it be that the legal system simply finds it
> intolerable to contemplate female perpetrators?
> The notion of a mother who kills her own child
> is profoundly horrifying. These days we talk about
> post-natal depression, or baby blues, as a means of
> explaining acts which are otherwise inconceivable.
> Yet, purely by virtue of the intimacy of their
> relationship, the stress imposed on the mother and
> the amount of time that mother and child spend
> together, it would not seem unreasonable to
> suppose that the majority of small babies are killed
> by their mothers. Unfortunately…the numbers
> dry up once men stop being the bad guys.[49]

In other words, when no charges are laid, little information about such crimes makes it into the public record, and so it becomes even easier to believe that it is solely men who commit really horrific acts against other people.

Not Guilty isn't without its flaws. Its lack of footnotes

makes it difficult to verify many of Thomas's claims. And he occasionally overlooks a perfectly legitimate alternative perspective. For example, while discussing sexual harassment allegations in the U.S. Navy, he remarks that a female lieutenant complained that the person called in to investigate had asked her out and referred to her as "Sweet Cakes." Thomas says he "fears for the future of the free world if it is to be protected by naval personnel who take fright at being called Sweet Cakes."[50] But surely the lieutenant's point was that someone sent in to *investigate* allegations of sexual impropriety should know better than to conduct himself in such a manner. That said, the book has much to recommend it—and it goes a long way toward providing a male perspective on many "feminist" issues. This is important, because until there's genuine dialogue, until *both sides* are doing as much listening as talking, the chances of achieving a more just society are remote. Shouting at people, nagging them or threatening them with the coercive powers of the state are all inferior ways of solving difficult problems. Writes Thomas:

> The last thing that the world needs now is another bunch of whining, self-proclaimed victims, and no one should close this book thinking that I spend my whole time feeling miserable about being male. I have been privileged in every aspect of my life…. But that doesn't mean that I don't get angry or hurt or perplexed by some of the things that I see happening to the men around me.

He argues that, if "we are to have a healthy society, our sons need to grow up with a sense of self-confidence and self-respect."[51] To my mind, this point cannot be stressed enough. Gender harmony depends on well-adjusted human beings who believe they are valued in their own right, and that their needs and concerns are taken seriously. Many young men currently inhabit a world in which people have little good to say about maleness, and even less sympathy for masculine anguish. With male suicide and violence rates being what they are already, we continue down such a path at everyone's peril.

Wendy Dennis, who interviewed hundreds of North American women and men for her book about contemporary sex and love, observes:

> I have come to realize that women all too often have their guns out of the holster when they encounter men, and those guns are getting in the way. Women need to listen to men more often; like women, men are hurt and confused right now, and they have something valuable to say about their hurt and confusion.

Elsewhere, she notes that her research has taught her "that a sense of humor will take a woman farther with a man, both in and out of bed, than a sense of superiority, that listening will take her farther than a lecture."[52]

Why is it so difficult for feminism to admit that men have their own, perfectly legitimate, perspective on the world? That, just as no man—however hard he studies and watches—will ever completely understand the process of giving birth, women will never fully appreciate the pressures and demands involved in growing up male? We have a great deal of sympathy in our society for women who are unable either to conceive or to carry their pregnancies to term. We mourn for them, we feel they've been robbed of one of life's most important experiences. In a way, men— all men—have been condemned, if you will, to such a situation. They are always distanced, by at least one remove, from the ultimate creative act. Surely we can grieve for them, too. Surely we can give them space to reflect on what such realities mean for them as human beings?

Women have been saying that men just don't get it. But the truth is, there's a lot that we, too, don't understand. We think we've figured men out, that we know all we need to about what makes them tick. But what we know is a feminist stereotype—our vaunted knowledge represents one, single way of looking at complex individuals in a complex world. Moreover, as many of the contributions to *Women Respond to the Men's Movement* demonstrate, it is a view of men that is decidedly mean-spirited.

A colleague of mine at *The Toronto Star* is an Anglican minister whose column on religious and ethical matters appears each Sunday. His name is Tom Harpur, and on New Year's Day, 1995, he wrote about the necessity of forgiving others for their transgressions, as well as the necessity of forgiving ourselves for wrongs we've committed. He wasn't writing about gender issues, but his comments are appropriate here. He says:

> Show me a person who is at this moment holding
> some grudge or brooding over some sense of
> having been victimized by this or that person or
> circumstance of life and I'll show you an unhappy
> man or woman.

A bit later, he adds:

> It's one thing to examine one's life and conscience
> and accept blame where it is due, together with a
> decision to make amends; but it's quite another to
> indulge in exaggerated or ongoing self-flagellation
> for past mistakes. That results in misery and saps
> the energy needed for moving on.[53]

If both women and men could be guided by such principles we might, together, be able to make it over this mountain of refuse we've been slinging at each other for far too long. We might emerge at a place where the air is a little clearer. It wouldn't be a perfect world, but it would be one where we viewed ourselves, first and foremost, as individuals—responsible for deciding how our lives will proceed from here—rather than as mere "victims" and "oppressors" in a drama of someone else's design.

The mass of men lead lives of quiet desperation.

—Henry David Thoreau
Walden

CHAPTER SIX

Men and Power

In 1994, an unlikely novel made its way onto the British best-seller list—George Eliot's *Middlemarch*. First published in 1871-72 under the now famous pseudonym, the novel was the creation of a woman named Mary Ann Evans. Described by feminist Virginia Woolf as "one of the few English novels written for grown-up people,"[1] *Middlemarch* is a masterpiece of Victorian literature more commonly found on college reading lists than front-racked in local bookstores. The nine-hundred-page work's renewed popularity was sparked by a BBC television miniseries production, which PBS broadcast to North American audiences later that year.

Middlemarch's opening scene takes place in 1829. This was a time in which women were thought to be ruled by their emotions and were therefore considered too flighty and irrational to be permitted to vote or run for public office. They weren't allowed to attend universities since it was believed their ovaries would shrivel up if they directed their energies toward academic endeavours. (Decades later, they were still prohibited from practising law or sitting on juries, their ears being too sensitive to be exposed to testimony involving violence or profane language.) Although working-class women toiled long hours under dangerous conditions in mills and factories, society considered "woman" to be fragile, weak and in need of protection. This was a time when reliable contraceptives were non-existent, and many women didn't survive childbirth.

Even feminists who have little good to say about contemporary society, therefore, would be hard pressed to deny that women's lot has improved considerably since the early 1800s. The term "oppressed" applies far more accurately to women at that moment in history than it does to those of us who live in the industrialized world today.

In Eliot's novels, large expanses of human experience are denied to women on account of their gender. For example, Dorothea Brooke, the protagonist in *Middlemarch*, is a fervent, intelligent woman born into the upper class who wishes to do something useful with her life—to leave a lasting, positive impression on the world. But she is able to accomplish little more than establishing a nursery school, funding a hospital and marrying a scholar far older than herself in the belief that lending him wifely assistance will be a noble undertaking. When he refuses to respect her intelligence and allows unwarranted jealousy to poison their relationship, Dorothea finds herself trapped in a strained, painful marriage, long before divorce was permissible, with little to look forward to. (Eliot herself scandalized society by living in sin with a man still technically married to someone else.)

Despite the author's feminist sensibilities, however, what anyone who reads this novel is forced to admit is that there are many different kinds of power. Although the female characters in this book enjoy less economic and political power than the male characters, women are far from being passive victims pushed this way and that by patriarchal forces. Many of them, for instance, hold considerable sway within their own homes and over their husbands. One of the least sympathetic male characters, who behaves ruthlessly in his public life, is described as having "unvaryingly cherished" his wife. After he is disgraced in the eyes of the community, it is her reaction he most fears, and we're told he awaits it "in anguish."[2]

Many of the women in this novel also avail themselves of whatever social power they possess. Whether it's Dorothea's attempt to mend someone else's marriage, or an aunt advising her niece's suitor that prolonged flirting minus serious intentions may harm the young woman's future prospects, women are active agents both in their own and in other people's lives. Indeed, none of the female characters in *Middlemarch* can be described as "an angel, an innocent" who "floats entirely on winds that blow from elsewhere" while doing nothing herself—which is how one critic has characterized current feminist thinking about women's lack of power and responsibility.[3]

Importantly, it is the young doctor, Tertius Lydgate, who is Dorothea's male counterpart in the novel. Through him, Eliot demonstrates that she was well aware that, for all their formal rights, men were hardly omnipotent—especially in their relations with women. Lydgate is a passionate visionary, a man of science who also wishes to leave his mark on the world. He has been influenced by the latest medical theories, and he hopes, via slow and dedicated effort, to make research breakthroughs of his own.

Just as Dorothea is mistaken about what marriage to the older scholar will be like, however, Lydgate is mistaken about what sort of woman would make a suitable wife for a man of limited means and high ideals such as himself. Early in the book he consciously dismisses Dorothea as being the wrong kind of woman for him because "she did not look at things from the proper feminine angle." He considers her "too earnest" and thinks it "troublesome to talk to such women" since, in his view, they "are always wanting reasons, yet they are too ignorant to understand the merits of any question."

On the other hand, Lydgate considers Rosamond Vincy, the mayor's shallow, prissy, blond-haired daughter, more appealing. "She is grace itself," he thinks. "She is perfectly lovely and accomplished."[4] But if Lydgate is more interested in looks than brains, and in docility rather than character, Rosamond is absorbed in how her social status will be enhanced by marrying a man who wears stylish clothes and is able to speak French.

Within minutes of their first brief meeting (which takes place as a result of her contrivance), Rosamond begins fantasizing about the house she will live in when she and Lydgate marry, and the visits she'll pay to his "high-bred relatives." Rather than feeling oppressed, Rosamond is used to the power that accrues to someone whom men usually fall in love with at first sight, and she enjoys exciting jealousy among her suitors. She muses that it will be "especially delightful to enslave" a man of Lydgate's stature. Later, when she discovers "that women, even after marriage, might make conquests and enslave men," she thinks to herself:

> How delightful to make captives from the throne of
> marriage with a husband as a crown-prince by your
> side—himself in fact a subject—while the captives
> look up for ever hopeless, losing their rest probably,
> and if their appetite too, so much the better![5]

It becomes evident that Rosamond's apparent meekness

is merely an attitude she adopts because she knows it's considered attractive in females. Beneath it lies the obstinacy of the self-obsessed. The young woman reminds her doting father, who opposes her marriage to Lydgate, that she never wavers once she's set her mind on something. She then proceeds to emotionally blackmail this leader among men by suggesting she may take ill if he doesn't give her his blessing. Says Eliot's narrator:

> Mrs. Vincy's belief that Rosamond could manage
> her papa was well founded. Apart from his dinner
> and his coursing, Mr. Vincy, blustering as he was,
> had as little of his own way as if he had been a
> prime minister: the force of circumstances was
> easily too much for him, as it is for most pleasure-
> loving florid men; and the circumstance called
> Rosamond was particularly forcible by means of
> that mild persistence which, as we know, enables a
> white soft living substance to make its way in spite
> of opposing rock.

Rosamond believes that people in general, but her father and husband in particular, exist to indulge her whims. We are told "she never [thinks] of money except as something necessary which other people would always provide," and that her idea of good housekeeping consists "simply in ordering the best of everything." While she complains that Lydgate works too much after they're married, she nevertheless holds him entirely responsible when he's unable to pay the bills. When he tries to enlist her cooperation in trimming their expenses, it's clear she views the situation as a failure, on his part, to be the good provider a husband is supposed to be.

Lydgate attempts to conceal money worries from her because she is pregnant, and yet Rosamond shows no

concern for his feelings when she insists on going horse-
back riding with one of her husband's cousins in order to be
seen with the son of a baronet. Lydgate is described as
"hurt" and "utterly confounded that she had risked herself
on a strange horse" without first discussing the matter with
him—and beside himself when a repeat occurrence leads to
a miscarriage.[6] Unlike his wife, Lydgate accepts blame,
acknowledges his own foolishness and feels guilty that he
isn't able to keep Rosamond in the style to which she is
accustomed. When he instructs an agent to attempt to sub-
let their pricey residence, she countermands the order
behind his back. To his mortification, she also secretly
writes to his relatives requesting financial assistance.

Lydgate begins to gamble and take opium, apprehensive
about moving to smaller quarters with fewer amenities,
since he knows Rosamond will be miserable as a result.
Little by little, he comes to the realization that he has
joined his life to a woman who sees marriage as something
less than a partnership. He also discovers that, whatever his
earlier views on the appropriateness of wifely submission, it
is Rosamond, not he, who dominates their relationship.
The narrator tells us that Lydgate's "will was not a whit
stronger" than Rosamond's and describes one matrimonial
conflict in the following manner:

> Lydgate sat paralysed by opposing impulses: since
> no reasoning he could apply to Rosamond seemed
> likely to conquer her assent, he wanted to smash
> and grind some object on which he could at least
> produce an impression, or else to tell her brutally
> that he was master, and she must obey. But he not
> only dreaded the effect of such extremities on their
> mutual life—he had a growing dread of Rosamond's
> quiet elusive obstinacy, which would not allow
> any assertion of power to be final; and again, she

had touched him in a spot of keenest feeling by
implying she had been deluded with a false vision
of happiness in marrying him. As to saying that he
was master, it was not the fact.

A few pages later, we read, regarding Lydgate and his wife:

He had begun to have an alarmed foresight of her
irrevocable loss of love for him, and the consequent
dreariness of their life…. It would assuredly have
been a vain boast in him to say that he was her
master.

And then:

When he left her to go out again, he told himself
that it was ten times harder for her than for him:
he had a life away from home, and constant appeals
to his activity on behalf of others. He wished to
excuse everything in her if he could—but it was
inevitable that in that excusing mood he should
think of her as if she were an animal of another
and feebler species. Nevertheless she had mastered
him.[7]

Lydgate's money problems eventually implicate him in
an unsavoury affair and lead to a sullying of his good reputation—in itself, a crushing blow to this proud man. In an
attempt to placate Rosamond, he resolves to leave town
and abandon altogether his dream of conducting medical
research. Having decided that he "must do as other men
do, and think what will please the world and bring in
money," he tells Dorothea that he'll attempt to somehow
"keep [his] soul alive" in the process. During this period, in
which Lydgate feels Rosamond's sullenness and silent

reproach so acutely that he dreads even looking at her, she reassures herself that even he, the "most perverse of men, was always subdued in the long-run."

In the novel's afterword we read that:

> Lydgate's hair never became white. He died when
> he was only fifty, leaving his wife and children
> provided for by a heavy insurance on his life. He
> had gained an excellent practice…. but he always
> regarded himself as a failure: he had not done what
> he once meant to do.[8]

Lydgate's shattered dreams, his falling so far short of the goals he'd once been confident of achieving, parallel the experience of Dorothea, who, following the death of her first husband, remarries. In the afterword we read that she, too, failed to achieve her full potential:

> Many who knew her, thought it a pity that so
> substantive and rare a creature should have been
> absorbed into the life of another, and be only
> known in a certain circle as a wife and mother.
> But no one stated exactly what else that was in
> her power she ought rather to have done…

The fact that Dorothea's keen sense of moral responsibility (at one point she asks, "What do we live for, if it is not to make life less difficult to each other?"[9]) is confined to the domestic sphere means the larger world is deprived of one of its brighter lights. But while societal norms concerning the role of women are responsible for the tragic tinge to Dorothea's life, Lydgate is in turn crippled by a woman. Rosamond doesn't have the right to vote or to pursue higher education. She is physically weaker than her husband. But it is precisely because Lydgate, for all his sexism, is a decent person rather than a feminist caricature of a man, it's precisely because he cares about Rosamond's happiness and feels responsible for her well-being and because he knows that behaving violently would only push them further apart, that he abandons his own dreams, pinches back his own desires and becomes little more than a money-earner. It is Rosamond's view of what he should be that prevails, not his. Whatever contributions he might have made to medical science are firmly, if prettily, reduced to dust beneath her delicately shod feet.

For Lydgate—the educated, upper-class white male in a man's world—women are anything but passive victims. We learn that while he was a student in Paris, he fell in love with an actress, whom he met after she "accidentally" stabbed her fellow actor (and real-life husband) to death during a performance. When Lydgate follows her to another city and proposes marriage, she admits her guilt to him:

> Again Laure paused a little and then said, slowly, "*I meant to do it.*"
>
> Lydgate, strong man as he was, turned pale and trembled: moments seemed to pass before he rose and stood at a distance from her.
>
> "There was a secret, then," he said at last, even vehemently. "He was brutal to you: you hated him."
>
> "No! he wearied me; he was too fond: he would live in Paris, and not in my country; that was not agreeable to me."
>
> "Great God!" said Lydgate, in a groan of horror. "And you planned to murder him?"
>
> "I did not plan: it came to me in the play— *I meant to do it.*"
>
> Lydgate stood mute, and unconsciously pressed

his hat on while he looked at her....
   "You are a good young man," she said. "But I
do not like husbands. I will never have another."
[original italics][10]

It's more than a little ironic that Eliot was perhaps freer
to include a female character who callously murders her
spouse than female authors are today. Rather than being
respected by feminists, a writer who included such a character in a modern novel would risk being accused of perpet-
uating "myths" about women.

In addition to Dorothea, other female characters in the
novel also have their options narrowly proscribed—by their
class, their inability to meet societal definitions of what's
attractive and, significantly, by their *lack* of a husband.
(One woman, for instance, is described as being "nipped
and subdued as single women are apt to be who spend their
lives in uninterrupted subjection to their elders."[11] In this
case, the elder is a mother.) From Eliot's perspective, therefore, there were worse things than sharing one's life with
"the oppressor." By taking a quick look at the work of one
of our feminist ancestors, we see that even in the 1800s,
when women were far worse off than they are today, gender
wasn't the single defining feature of a woman's existence. It
didn't, in itself, amount to a life sentence under the thumb
of one exploitative male or another.

Moreover, being male was no guarantee that you'd do
what you wanted during your brief sojourn on this earth.
Nor was being physically larger and stronger than your
spouse a reliable indicator of who would end up walking on
eggshells in the other's presence.

Power, who exercises it and how are complex matters.
The author of *Middlemarch* would no doubt consider preposterous the Canadian Violence Against Women Panel's
declaration that "society has given the man the power over

a woman from the point of earliest acquaintance." She would likely view the suggestion, appearing in one of the essays in *Women Respond to the Men's Movement*, that women have "no power" while men have "all the power all the time all over the world"[12] an oversimplification that does more to obscure reality than to reveal it. And if such statements weren't true in the nineteenth century, they most certainly aren't true today.

Now let's fast forward to 1950s North America, just before large numbers of women began questioning why they were expected to become Mrs. *John* Doe, to live only through their husbands and children. Margaret Atwood has described this as an era in which "condoms could not legally be displayed on pharmacy shelves, where we read Kotex ads to learn how to behave at proms and always wore our gloves when we went out." She says young women were told not to "neck on the first date" if they wanted boys to respect them and were advised: "Real women are bad at math. To be fulfilled you have to have a baby. If you lead them on you'll get what you deserve."[13]

This is the world we see in *Blue Sky*, the film for which Jessica Lange won her 1994 best actress Oscar. Compared with today, 1950s North America was far less sympathetic to women. It was a world into which Carly Marshall (the character played by Lange) had trouble fitting, one in which she worried that, after her death, there'd be no trace of her left behind. But that doesn't automatically mean Carly was oppressed by her spouse. Indeed, in this drama, the passionate, somewhat unbalanced Carly is a continuing source of public and professional embarrassment for Hank, her army major husband (played by Tommy Lee Jones). In the opening scene, Carly sunbathes and then goes swimming topless, causing a stir when she's spotted by her husband's colleagues. A superior officer then demands of Hank: "What the hell are you going to do? About your wife. She's a disgrace to the army and she's endangering your job." Hank is told the incident will be noted in his file "along with all the other" ones.

Soon afterward, Hank is transferred to another base and Carly experiences a mini mental breakdown at the thought of having to start all over again in a new community—without acknowledging that the frequent moves are connected to her own problematic behaviour. As she sleeps, Hank cooks breakfast for his two daughters on the first morning in their new home while the eldest daughter insists Carly needs professional help and tells Hank he can't keep "playing baby-sitter" to his wife. He responds by defending Carly, referring to her as "spirited" and "energetic" and saying that he made a decision, long ago, simply to love her.

When Carly falls into an earlier pattern of infidelity, in an affair everyone is aware of, her husband's endurance is sorely tested. Exhausted, demoralized and betrayed once again, Hank slowly takes off his glasses and presses his fingers to his eyes. His shoulders are slack, his face is strained. He is the picture of a beaten man, of a man who has struggled to conduct himself honourably and decently, who has borne large and small humiliations with restraint, who has been a responsible parent to his children and treated his wife with compassion. But his well of inner resources has now run dry.

Blue Sky endeavours to provide us with a slice of real life, to render a reasonably accurate portrait of a fictional couple's relationship at this particular time and place in history. Although it would be foolish to claim that this marriage is typical of others in 1950s North America, the script is so solid and the acting so believable it's also difficult to dismiss it entirely as a Hollywood fabrication. The moment we're willing to admit that such a scenario is plausible is the moment we're forced to acknowledge that, even when life was far less pleasant for women than it is now, all men weren't lording it over their wives and abusing their positions of power. Patience, self-sacrifice and forbearance are human qualities, not female ones.

Nor is there any need to confine ourselves to fictional accounts to see that this is the case. In a recent essay for *Playboy* magazine, feminist Betty Friedan writes about the frustration that her bright, articulate mother experienced— and then took out on her husband—after quitting a newspaper job when she married at the age of twenty-one (since the wives of businessmen weren't supposed to work outside the home in those days):

> Nothing he did, nothing we, the children, did, was ever enough for her. And it got worse during the Depression when the business didn't make enough to feed her fantasies. We were drawn by our mother into a conspiracy against him, not to let him know if she spent money on a new outfit for herself or us. Besides, he worked late every night and all day Saturdays. On Sundays, he was really tired. Her mysterious, painful ailment (colitis, I believe) got better when his heart disease required her to run the business. And so he died in his early 60s, and she lived until 90.

Friedan says her mother swam and played golf and tennis while the only exercise her father enjoyed came during the family's annual two-week vacation. She says this helps explain why her mother's health was such that she survived not one but all three of her husbands. Friedan suggests that her own upbringing wasn't unusual and reminds us that "there is more than one kind of power in any family, and women, kept from financial power, had to retaliate by denying and manipulating the power of love."[14]

This domestic portrait also underscores another issue, though: just because men were doing something that was prohibited to women doesn't mean they were having a good time. The grass is always greener on the other side of the fence. Men who belittle the difficulty of running a household and raising children have long been the butt of jokes in our society. I remember, as a youngster, being read a storybook in which a farmer who thought his wife's job was easy changed places with her for a day only to have a child climb up on the roof and get stranded, while the goats ate the laundry and the chickens went AWOL. When the wife returned from the fields in the evening, there was no dinner on the table and her frantic husband begged her to take her job back. But I know of no parallel jokes about women who think that digging iron ore out of a rock face five thousand feet below the surface in a dark, damp mine shaft for eight hours a day is "fulfilling." Nor am I aware of any children's tales that ridicule the notion that there's anything liberating about slinging boxes in a warehouse year after year.

There were real reasons why Friedan's mother was frustrated and angry. But one of feminism's gravest mistakes has been to assume that men's experience was vastly better. Frankly, if there were only two choices—a ninety-year life span that included golf and tennis along with domestic drudgery, or a sixty-year life span filled with little more than work and worry—I know which one I'd pick.

The fact that Friedan's father received precious little peace or emotional support from the wife and kids for whom he spent his life toiling to provide suggests that male-dominated society wasn't doing men any favours by keeping women out of the paid labour force. The fact that it pursued such a course for so long seems to be more a case of reflexive support for the status quo than a deliberate plot to monopolize all the fun and power.

· But that's not how feminism has interpreted matters. Instead, we compared the condition of women who felt trapped by domestic work not to all men—including the janitors, garbage collectors, taxi drivers, dish washers and road crews—but to the men occupying the highest rungs of the ladder, and we then concluded that women were being deprived of their fair share of power. But how much power did the average man really exercise on the job? Writes Warren Farrell:

> Almost every woman had a primary role in the "female-dominated" family structure; only a small percentage of men had a primary role in the "male-dominated" governmental and religious structures. Many mothers were, in a sense, the chair of the board of a small company—their family....
> Conversely, most men were on their company's assembly line.

He adds:

> Historically, a husband spent the bulk of his day under the eye of his boss—his source of income; a wife did not spend the bulk of her day under the eye of her husband—her source of income. She had more control over her work life than he had over his.[15]

Participating in the paid work world doesn't automatically translate into power, control or satisfaction. Only a minority of individuals in our society appear to really enjoy their work. Many more would quit in an instant if they won a lottery jackpot. But they get up every morning and report for duty because, at the end of the week, they get a pay cheque that puts food on the table.

If many men would choose to do something other than the job they're currently performing, surely feminism's insistence on seeing paid work as power is flawed. When women looked across the fence at men in higher education, the workplace or the military, they saw only the positive aspects—the opportunity to learn, wield influence and win glory in ways that were denied them. But they paid too little attention to the idea that being *obliged* to do something can be as oppressive as being prohibited from doing it. In the 1994 film adaptation of Louisa May Alcott's novel *Little Women*, the March daughters are at liberty to pursue writing and painting as young adults, but their male childhood friend, Laurie, is not. Since large amounts of money have been spent educating him, he is now expected to put his nose to the grindstone and make himself useful by becoming part of the family business. In one scene in the film, after Laurie graduates from Harvard, Jo March asks him whether his grandfather is "exceedingly proud." He replies, "Exceedingly bent on locking me up in one of his offices. Why is it Amy may paint china and you can scribble away, while I must 'manfully' set my music aside?"

Some of my feminist sisters will no doubt protest that even if paid work is not, in itself, experienced as power, the economic clout that comes with earning your own money shouldn't be underestimated. There is some truth in this. But if, as David Thomas points out, one person earns most of the money while the other one spends most of it, "you do not have to be Karl Marx to conclude that the second of those two" people may not be exactly oppressed. Research suggests that, when it comes to major as well as minor household expenditures, it is women who make most of the decisions.

While there certainly are male clotheshorses, as well as men who spend large sums on what women derisively refer to as their "toys"—golf clubs, hunting rifles, power boats and so forth—the average woman also spends a great deal on her clothing, hair and toiletries on a regular basis. It is more difficult to buy gifts for men than for women because our society is used to pampering women. You can give them perfume, bubble bath, cosmetics, jewellery, candies, chocolates and flowers. Few of these, however, are considered appropriate for men. Farrell reports on a U.S. study in which "floor space...offering male versus female items in shopping malls and boutiques" was measured. The result: "seven times as much floor space was devoted to female personal items as to male personal items." Additionally, the most valuable, high-traffic space was devoted to women's items.[16]

Some men *do* use the money they earn as a means of control within their families, but objectionable behaviour on the part of some men doesn't translate into widespread economic power for all men. Even the belief that an abusive husband's superior earning power ensures that his wife won't leave him is mitigated these days by the existence of welfare. While alternatives to staying in an abusive or otherwise seriously troubled relationship may not be altogether pleasant, they exist nonetheless.

Some critics will say that if women go to so much bother and expense about their appearance it's only because males expect it and sometimes demand it. But this can only be partially true. If the woman in the "Dear Abby" column who has exiled her spouse to the garage for fear of harming him during one of her rages gets her hair set and her nails manicured every week, it's difficult to argue that she's doing so to please her husband rather than to indulge herself. When Carly, in *Blue Sky*, makes her husband and children nearly miss a plane while she gets a make-over at the hairdresser's, her own desire to appear glamorous is the overriding motivation—not her husband's expectations. In *Middlemarch*, Rosamond is concerned with bonnets, sashes, jewels and other finery. While this is partly because she's doing what's required of her in order to attract men and exert her sexual power, she treats it as an art and science because such matters really *do* consume her interest.

Sexual power is something feminists often try to deny because, like most things in life, it isn't constant—the balance can shift. If a car pulls up to the curb while I'm waiting alone at a bus stop at midnight and a couple of young men lean out its windows and make suggestive comments, the fact that I've caught their eye because I'm a woman makes me feel at risk rather than powerful. But if it's broad daylight and I'm in an elevator with the same group of young men while struggling with a heavy load of boxes, I know that after just a few smiles in their direction, they'll likely fall all over themselves trying to help me down the hall. I also know they'd be far less eager to assist a man in this manner. The fact that I'm a woman means that, much of the time in day-to-day life, men respond to me more positively than they would to someone of their own gender. If I'm inclined to do so, I can often turn this to my advantage.

Women frequently complain that the (idealized) female image is everywhere: staring at us from billboards, magazine racks and so forth. But there may be something equally disconcerting: being next to invisible. Racial minorities sometimes object to the fact that they don't see people similar to themselves represented in advertisements often enough; that, judging by how many ads feature only whites, nonwhites don't seem very important. Because men aren't viewed as desirable sexual objects to the same degree women are, their image appears less frequently in our society, which in turn reflects the fact that, comparatively speaking, the average male exercises far less sexual power than the average female.

A rather startling example of this imbalance, despite feminist assertions that it is men who control the sexual realm (due to the possibility that they might turn violent), appears in the May/June 1995 issue of Ms. One of the three young feminists invited to contribute to the magazine confesses that she was once "patriarchy's wet dream." Twenty-three-year-old Anastasia Higginbotham tells us that, as she has matured, she has:

> ...been transformed from masochist to feminist.
> The big hair, accompanied by moderately big breasts and a dancer's ass bundled into a squeezy purple dress, attracted all sorts of attention. I could have brought my high school to its knees on charges of sexual misconduct.... In fact, I thrived on making guys hard and then laughing in their faces at the obvious fact that they could never have me. I thought I was god's gift to men because I could play glam, sweetheart, and harlot all in one shot. I had my pick [of young men]...[17]

That this young woman can consider her pre-feminist state to have been masochistic, despite having her choice of young men and the ability to manipulate them sexually, is a good example of how thoroughly feminist dogma discourages clear thinking.

Young males are socialized to believe they aren't "real men" unless they've had intercourse. The more sex they have, the better they're supposed to feel about themselves. In other words, generally speaking, sexual success is closely tied to male self-image, in much the same way that a woman's weight frequently affects how she feels about herself.

If women are conditioned to dress in a certain manner in order to attract men, males are also conditioned to respond to such stimuli. Therefore, rather than being barbarians who rape every woman they take a fancy to, it would appear that, a great deal of the time, males are quite powerless in the face of women who "thrive" on arousing them sexually and then laugh in their faces at "the obvious fact" that they can look but won't be permitted to touch. (If America were the kind of place many feminists would have us believe, a place where males routinely seize what they want at females' expense, it wouldn't have been so "obvious" that Higginbotham was sexually unavailable. Indeed, her high school experience would likely have been dramatically different.)

To put this a different way, imagine that there's a rare, somewhat addictive elixir. Imagine that women know that, by consuming a tiny vial of this substance, we'll lose the extra ten pounds so many of us are always fretting about— effortlessly. But the only place we can get the elixir is directly from men. By some twist of fate, each of them is issued a supply of the stuff on reaching puberty. Females, being conditioned to want this substance more than our male counterparts do, are frequently on the watch for it when we're hanging out with men. We often find ourselves wondering whether we'll "score." Some males, aware of how popular these vials make them, wear one attached to their watchband. They take great pleasure in seeing the eyes of women—young and old, attractive and not so attractive, strangers and acquaintances—stray there. Sometimes, when they meet a group of women in a bar, they even remove the vial and nonchalantly hold it up to the light, twirling it around before tucking it safely away again.

Now imagine that such a man and such a woman retire to the man's apartment. The woman's mouth is dry and she's nervous because those vials have been haunting her dreams of late. Imagine that the two of them sit down on the sofa, while soft music plays in the background. The woman's fingers slowly begin moving in the direction of the vial. But while she's trying to let him know she's interested, she doesn't want her desire to be too obvious. If it turns out she's misunderstood, if all he had in mind was a drink and small talk, she'd like to be able to adjust graciously.

Her fingers move still closer and he doesn't protest. Finally, she makes contact. A few seconds later, she loosens the strap and the smooth bit of glass slips free. Trembling, she holds it in her palm. But now the moment of truth has arrived, since she needs his help, since there's a good chance the vial will shatter unless he himself removes the lid. She looks up, into his eyes. He's watching her, wondering what price she might be willing to pay.

Most of us would have no difficulty categorizing this as a situation in which the man, because he has something he knows the woman wants, is in a position of power. We'd say that he's calling the shots. If the genders were reversed, if she possessed the vial while he waited with bated breath, the "price" might have been the dinner and the movie he'd taken her to, Rolling Stones concert tickets or a diamond ring. Whatever it was, we'd say her bargaining position was a good one—that where such vials are concerned, one gender has a distinct advantage over the other.

This analogy isn't perfect, but it begins to explain the reality of the sexual power dynamic for large numbers of males. Female bodies are always on display—because women, too, think they're beautiful, but also because it's a guaranteed way to catch male attention, just as an ad featuring vials of elixir would be noticed by women. This means that men are constantly surrounded by reminders of how much they want sex, of how much they're expected to want sex and, in the experience of many of them, of what failures they are when they aren't getting it often enough. Imagine what wrecks women might be if everywhere we looked we saw men wearing vials on the street, men with vials on the television screen, men with vials in the pages of the magazine at the dentist's office. If, no matter where we turned, we were reminded that there was something we urgently desired that depended on the co-operation of a member of the opposite sex. We, too, might be tempted to commit to a lifetime of financial support in exchange for a steady supply. And we, too, might end up feeling cheated if it turned out that we'd been misled about how much elixir our new partner was actually willing to part with over the long term.

But there's even more to it than that. I used to think that television ads featuring an elegantly dressed woman draped over a car were the height of false advertising, that men had to be uncommonly stupid if they bought the idea that driving a certain kind of vehicle would get them a woman who looked like this. Only now do I realize that, in fact, the suggestion contains more than a grain of truth. Generally speaking, young men who have access to cars in high school are more popular with girls than those who don't. There are also plenty of women who *do* go gaga over sports cars. Many men know, from first-hand experience, that if they proposition women from behind the wheel of a convertible their success rate is far higher than if they do so from behind the wheel of a station wagon. But the category of woman goes up as well. If what you're interested in is the curvy blond with the floor-length fur coat and the diamond tiara, you're going to need the upscale car to drive her around in, because she's unlikely to get into your rusted-out bucket of bolts more than once. While I, personally, have long seethed at the crass use of female sexuality to sell automobiles, from the male perspective, linking sex and cars makes sense. It happens to reflect certain facts of life.

Leaving the idea of sexual power behind, let's turn our attention back to economics, to whether the traditional male role of provider translates into raw financial power or is instead accompanied by an imperative to stifle one's individuality, to assign one's hopes and dreams lower priority than the interests of the people who depend on you. As Susan Faludi points out in *Backlash*, men have long told an America-wide survey that they take this role very seriously:

> For twenty years, the Monitor's pollsters have asked its subjects to define masculinity. And for twenty years, the leading definition, ahead by a huge margin, has never changed. It isn't being a leader, athlete, lothario, decision maker, even just being "born male." It is simply this: being a "good provider for his family."

Faludi takes evidence of what might otherwise be considered admirable qualities in men—such as a profound sense of responsibility and a willingness to serve—and turns it against them. Suggesting that wanting to be a "good provider" is the same thing as needing to be "the prime breadwinner," she tells us "it is hard to imagine a force more directly threatening to fragile American manhood than the feminist drive for economic equality." But surely part of the reason being a good provider is so central to male identity is because this *matters to women*.[18]

In the film version of *Little Women*, Laurie is not only expected to become a breadwinner because that's what males do, it's clear he won't be considered husband material until then. The adult Amy March, the youngest of the four sisters, declares that she has always known she wouldn't "marry a pauper"; she considers accepting the hand of one of her suitors, whom she doesn't appear to love but whose sizable income makes him attractive. She tells Laurie, who's resisting going into the family business, that she despises his dissolute lifestyle. "You laze about, spending your family's money and courting women," she scolds, before urging him to make himself useful. As a direct consequence, he finally resolves to settle into the job that has been waiting for him, in order to prove himself "worthy" of her affection. Only afterwards does Amy accept him as her husband. (That she appears to do almost as much lazing about, while being courted by men, doesn't seem to matter.)

There's no need to depend on fiction to make the point that employment in the wider world is a prerequisite to marriage for men. Stephen Hawking is the world renowned theoretical physicist and author of the immensely successful book *A Brief History of Time*. In 1963, shortly after his twenty-first birthday, Hawking was diagnosed as having the degenerative disease ALS, also known as Lou Gehrig's disease, and advised that he probably had only a few years to live. He writes:

> There did not seem much point in working at my research because I didn't expect to live long enough to finish my Ph.D. However, as time went by, the disease seemed to slow down. I began to understand general relativity and make progress with my work. But what really made a difference was that I got engaged to a woman named Jane Wilde. This gave me something to live for, but *it also meant that I had to get a job if we were to get married.* [my italics][19]

While Hawking is a remarkable individual, he was merely conforming to societal expectations in this regard. On the other hand, it would be a rare woman who wrote that, before her husband's family and friends would give their blessing to his marriage during the 1960s, she was required to find employment first.

In a similar vein, the American writer Kurt Vonnegut talks about how his own obligation to support his family meant that, for a number of years, he was unable to quit his "goddam nightmare job" at General Electric and devote himself to his craft. It was only after accumulating the equivalent of a year's salary in a bank account from selling short stories in the late 1940s that he was able to do so in good conscience. He relates this anecdote within the context of talking about his father, observing that it was only when his dad achieved the age of sixty-five that he admitted that being an architect had "been no fun at all." Writes Vonnegut:

> I now perceive his deception, so suddenly discontinued, as having been a high order of gallantry. While my two siblings and I were growing up, he gave us the illusion that our father was jauntily content with his professional past and excited about all the tough but amusing challenges still to come. The truth was that the Great Depression and then World War II, during which almost all building stopped, came close to gutting him as an architect. From the time he was forty-five until he was sixty-one he had almost no work. In prosperous times those would have been his best years, when his evident gifts, reputation, and maturity might have caused some imaginative client to feel that Father was entitled to reach, even in Indianapolis, for greatness or, if you will, for soul-deep fun.[20]

Vonnegut tells us that his father spent much of his career taking jobs that wouldn't have caused a high school drafting class difficulty—because he needed the money to support his family.

Vonnegut's mother doesn't appear to have been fulfilled by her domestic duties, either. (Indeed, her son says the poor woman was mentally ill and that, "[l]ate at night, and always in the privacy of our own home, and never with guests present, she expressed hatred for Father as corrosive as hydrofluoric acid."[21]) But the point is that whether she was miserable or content tells us *nothing* about how much satisfaction her husband derived from the sex role he'd been assigned. To his credit, Kurt Vonnegut, Sr. made the best of a bad situation with grace and dignity. Rather than allowing his professional disappointment and frustration to contaminate their young lives, he spent decades hiding the true state of affairs from his children.

That men still face immense pressure to be breadwinners even in the '90s is illustrated by the answer Ann Landers gave to GROWING UNEASY in 1994. This letter-writer told Ann she'd been living with a "very attractive, intelligent, charming, affable, humorous, loving" and thoughtful man (who was also good in bed) for almost a year, and intended to marry him. The couple were childless and planned to remain so. "Greg" was also described as being supportive of the woman and her career, as well as someone who shared "in the cooking and cleaning." But UNEASY was uncomfortable about the fact that while she herself earned an above-average wage, her partner was unemployed—partly because his profession was "saturated with qualified people" who couldn't find work, but partly, she suspected, because he lacked ambition. "Is Greg a lazy parasite, exchanging sex and emotional security for an easy life?" she asked Ann. "Should I give him the boot and look for someone who can support me if I choose not to work?"

Ann told UNEASY that she was an "enabler" who had "made Greg so comfortable for so long that he sees no reason to try to support himself." She said the woman should insist Greg get "some kind of job—even part time—as a matter of self-respect." Ann made no comment about the fact that UNEASY still thought *she* should have the option of choosing "not to work." Indeed, the main reason Greg appeared unsuitable to UNEASY was because life with him would prevent her from exercising a choice she wasn't comfortable with when it happened in reverse.

This is one of those situations in which it becomes clear that while the number of avenues open to women have (thankfully) expanded in recent years, men remain stuck in the past. Some women think they should have the choice to work outside the home or not, depending on how they happen to feel. They think they're entitled to be supported by men. Which means men are still expected to get up every morning and report for duty. In Warren Farrell's words:

> Today, when the successful single woman meets the successful single man, they appear to be equals. But should they marry and consider children, she almost invariably considers three options:
>
> *Option #1:* Work full time
> *Option #2:* Mother full time
> *Option #3:* Some combination of working and
> mothering
>
> He considers three "slightly different" options:
>
> *Option #1:* Work full time
> *Option #2:* Work full time
> *Option #3:* Work full time[22]

Calling her a "female chauvinist oink oink," Ann's male readers didn't hesitate to draw her attention to the double standard she'd applied in this case. While one of the six letters she published blamed feminism for doing women "more harm than good," others simply implored her to be fairer in her treatment of both sexes. "If women are now allowed to get *out* of the kitchen, why shouldn't men be allowed to get *in* [original italics]?" asked one. Ann responded by saying that the men had "made a pretty good case for themselves."[23]

There's no need for any hard rules here, of course, since no one formula is going to work for everyone. I've personally spent the past several years developing my freelance writing career, earning less money along the way than I might have if I'd been employed as a receptionist, for instance. The comfortable life I've enjoyed has been disproportionately the result of my husband's labour. I've also known couples where the roles were reversed—where a woman supported a man throughout medical school or while he matured as a painter. For people with children, there are compelling arguments in favour of one parent staying at home, particularly during the early years. The important thing is that both parties are happy with whatever arrangement they choose.

But just as women were entitled to feel resentment when society expected them to quit their jobs when they got married (or pregnant), men can be forgiven for feeling something similar when we expect them to settle for one option instead of our three. Sometimes it appears that we feminists want all the positive things life has to offer, minus any risk or responsibility. We want to pursue a career, but we also want a financial cushion (in the form of a husband) to fall back on in case we make the wrong decisions. We want to be treated as seriously as men in the workplace, even in those cases where we don't bring the same commitment and focus to our jobs that they do. (When not working for a living isn't an option, the incentive to persevere and excel is much stronger.) We want the option of contributing financially to our households, but like UNEASY, we shy away from assuming sole responsibility for the mortgage payments.

In the short term, while this unequal state of affairs

continues, it wouldn't do any harm for women to be a little more appreciative of what the traditional male role has demanded from men—as well as given to them. Over the longer haul, we should endeavour to ask ourselves difficult questions. For example, why does a woman who is now divorced and perfectly capable of working insist that she has a right to stay home with her kids and live off support payments from her ex? While her presence at home might have been a mutual decision made by the couple, when the couple splits up, that arrangement surely becomes null and void. No doubt she would *prefer* to be home (survey after survey tells us that many mothers in the workplace would), but so, too, might many men. Why do these women feel more entitled to pursue their desires? Why aren't *they* called "lazy parasites"?

When it comes to work, some men feel trapped in a "damned if you do, damned if you don't" situation. On the one hand, they feel a great deal of pressure to support their families to the best of their ability. On the other, they are often criticized for paying too little attention to their wives and children, for being preoccupied with work. In this latter instance, they're often further accused of being obsessed with material gain, of being greedy and one-dimensional. In my view, this is another example of how feminists have jumped to the worst possible conclusions when it comes to male behaviour.

There's no doubt that women who stay at home with young children while their husbands work long hours often find the experience stressful and demoralizing. There's no question that many men still aren't doing their fair share of the household chores. There's no question that many males are seriously flawed, self-centred human beings who routinely leave the wife at home with the kids in order to go out with the boys. But let's assume that most men are honest and decent. If large numbers of people think that being a good provider is the essence of being a man, then men who shift into overdrive at the workplace after their children are born may not so much be pursuing their own satisfaction as demonstrating their love. Rather than merely trying to escape the chaos that children often bring to a home, they may be endeavouring to be as successful and as secure as possible in order to give shelter and comfort to these young lives. The terrible irony is that, by performing his designated role, a man is distanced from the very people he's working to support. The better provider he is, the less time he's likely able to spend with his kids, the less opportunity he has to get to know them or to learn how to communicate with them.

I remember my paternal grandfather as a quiet, gentle soul. My grandmother was a knitter, a quilter, a creative mind. She always had six different projects on the go, and visiting her was an adventure. She could turn an egg crate and lengths of coloured yarn into the most amazing crafts. But other than pulling fresh carrots from the garden, there was little my grandfather could give us, as youngsters, that interested us. We had less in common with him than we did with my grandmother and so less to talk about. Which is why it was he who would load us into his panel truck and take us to the store for a treat. Spending money on us was one of the ways he expressed his love. Earning it, even when that meant walking miles to and from his blue-collar job in waist-deep snow, was how he showed his family of eight kids that he cared for them. Rather than being about power and self-gratification, work was about duty and responsibility for my grandfather.

Indeed, when it comes to children, men often feel far less powerful than many feminists imagine. The women's movement has done a good job of articulating the notion that women who discover they're pregnant sometimes aren't prepared for motherhood. We've argued that parenting is too serious a matter to be embarked on by people who aren't wholly committed to the task, that every child should be a wanted child. And, because it's the woman's body that goes wonky for nine months, we've decided that the ultimate decision about whether or not to carry a pregnancy to term should be hers. But where does this leave men? Where does it leave the man who is ecstatic to find his partner is pregnant, is suddenly thrilled at the thought of being a dad, but discovers that she wants an abortion—which she then proceeds to have? Why has feminism chosen to deny the pain experienced by such a man? Conversely, why is there no recognition of the *powerlessness* of men who don't want children (who may even have been deliberately misled by a sexual partner into becoming a father) but are told that it's her decision, and that although his feelings don't count, he's still going to be held financially responsible for this new life for the next twenty years? Why does feminism not condemn women who, years later, get in touch with the father and demand retroactive support for a child whose very existence they've kept a secret, thus denying him any opportunity to be involved in the youngster's upbringing?

On three occasions in early 1995, Ann Landers published letters from individuals facing these kinds of situations. The first was from a woman whose husband was contacted by someone he'd had a one-night stand with fourteen years earlier. The child, whose paternity was confirmed by blood tests, was now thirteen. The next letter was from the girlfriend of a man suddenly informed that a woman he'd gone out with briefly in 1973 had borne their son—who was now twenty-one. The other was from a man who, nine years previously, at the age of eighteen, had inadvertently impregnated a woman he'd been dating. He claimed that although he'd "ordered" her to have an abortion, or to put the child up for adoption, she had refused.

He now expressed outrage that while he's legally compelled to pay support, she refuses to work to support herself.[24]

I'm not suggesting that men should be able to veto an abortion, or, alternatively, that they should be able to force a woman to have one. What I am saying, though, is that this is another example of how we've refused to recognize the possibility of other legitimate perspectives. Instead, our response has usually amounted to a declaration that a man who is unprepared to deal with such matters should "keep his dick in his pants." This, of course, is as callous as telling a woman seeking an abortion that if she didn't want to get pregnant she should have kept her legs crossed.

Life is full of moral dilemmas in which none of the available solutions seem particularly adequate. But even if we aren't able to give men more power or rights in such circumstances, the least we can do is acknowledge their point of view—thus treating them with more sensitivity and respect.

Let's suppose that both parties welcome the news of a pregnancy and that they're living together in a heterosexual family unit. Partly because the child grew to term in her body, and partly because her socialization has probably given her more direct experience with infants, the woman is likely to spend larger chunks of time with the baby after it's born. This will be even more true if she breastfeeds. Rather than leaving a man feeling powerful, this state of affairs may cause him to feel he's being shunted off to the periphery. In the rueful words of a cab driver I hired one evening, "Since she came, it's been 'baby this, baby that.' The house is upside down. Now everything revolves around the baby." While this man's other remarks made it clear that he was intensely proud of his first child, a fourteen-month-old daughter, he still needed time to adjust to the changes she'd wrought in his life. Whether he succeeds in this adjustment will depend a great deal on whether his wife encourages and welcomes his participation, or whether she impatiently dismisses his attempts to be more than a meal ticket to his daughter.

Moreover, should the marriage falter at some later date, once again the man is likely to feel anything but powerful. While feminists have rightfully protested the sexist attitudes of lawyers and judges in the courtroom, we haven't talked much about how sexism sometimes works in our favour, how old-fashioned notions about mothers and children sometimes lead to a bias against men.

It's true that some men aren't interested in their children after a marriage breakdown, but others have been full participants in their children's lives from the beginning. These guys attend childbirth classes, assist in the delivery room, get up for 3:00 a.m. feedings, pace the floor for hours at a stretch with colicky babies, change diapers and walk around with infant carriers strapped to their chests. It is yet another example of feminism's mean-spiritedness that we remain unwilling to give these men the credit they're due. Says Marilyn French in her 1992 *The War Against Women*:

> Presenting themselves in a new role, as caring
> fathers, *an image built not on men's actual behavior
> but by media presentations* of ideal fathers, men
> increasingly seek custody of children after divorce
> or children they fathered outside marriage.... If
> fathers wanted closeness with their children, one
> would sympathize, but few men seeking custody are
> prepared to care for their children themselves...
> [my italics]

French goes on to say that she knows fathers aren't so much interested in their children as they are in power struggles with the women in their lives. Based on the conclusions of Canadian feminist Susan Crean, published in a 1988 book about male custody, French declares "that there is no evidence that men as a group are any more interested in or willing to deliver twenty-four-hour child care than they ever were."[25] But it's individual males, not "men as a group," who seek custody of their children after a marriage breakdown. Individuals deserve to be judged on their own merits. Ms. editor Letty Cottin Pogrebin tells us:

> Today, in courtrooms and news stories, the fairy
> tale single daddy serves as a subliminal propaganda
> tool for "father's rights" advocates who battle for
> child custody in order to punish their ex-wives.[26]

Another feminist, writing in *Women Respond to the Men's Movement*, says:

> ...once feminists began fighting for equal pay and
> for the right to abortion, the backlash was on. If
> women wanted the right to leave men or take
> men's jobs away from them, then men, and the
> women who support them, would simply repossess
> women's children.

She goes on to say that:

> Divorcing fathers increasingly use the threat of a
> custody battle as an economic bargaining chip.
> And it works. He gets the house, the car, and the
> boat; she gets the kids, and, if she's lucky, minimal
> child support.[27]

These statements are true some of the time. Some men *are* driven by anger, vengeance and malice. Some go to extreme lengths in an attempt to make the lives of their ex-wives miserable—including suing for custody of children they don't really care about or threatening violence. It would be dishonest to deny this. But it is equally dishonest to suggest that only men behave this way. Women also pursue custody for less than noble reasons, ranging from the relatively benign expectation that no decent mother would "abandon" her children to motives as angry, vengeful and malicious as any man's.

One of the most heartbreaking testimonials I've listened to came from a man whose wife is a chronic alcoholic barely capable of taking care of herself, never mind kids. Because she knows he cares a great deal about their two young children while having lost all patience with her, she's fighting him tooth and nail regarding custody. This has included making allegations of physical abuse against him, which, at least until the matter is resolved in court, has resulted in his being able to see his children for only a few hours a week. This man is no "fairy tale." He's flesh and blood. He has been the primary caregiver and is genuinely afraid for his kids' safety during the time they spend alone with their mother.

Just as contemporary feminism denies that this man exists, so do older (often male) judges and lawyers. They don't believe the bond between a child and its father is as strong as the one that exists between mother and child. Products of a more sexist time, they sincerely feel that women are better than men at some things and men are better than women at others. While feminism has made it politically incorrect for such people to voice the last part of this notion too loudly or publicly, it has tended to reinforce the first part when it's been in women's interest. Which means that when custody battles end up in court, men sometimes face a bias that leaves them feeling less than powerful.

Indeed, while feminists claim that men frequently win court custody battles, these figures—which range from 50 to 80 percent—are significantly skewed. Since everyone knows that anti-male bias exists with respect to some matters, particularly in certain jurisdictions dominated by certain judges, lawyers often advise men that unless they can prove the mother's a heroin addict or a prostitute, they might as well not waste their time and money trying to get custody. Other men are cautioned that, due to their lower chance of success, they should consider such a course of action carefully, since ugly custody battles can further traumatize the children involved and make an already strained adult relationship even more difficult.

When men decide not to attempt to secure sole or joint custody of their children after a marriage breakdown, feminism uses this as proof that they don't care about their kids as much as women do. When they do go to court and do win custody, feminism insists this is a women's rights issue, that men are trying to take "women's" children away from them.

Then there's the whole matter of access and visiting rights. While women properly complain about men who miss their support payments, non-custodial fathers just as rightly complain about women who flagrantly violate court-ordered visitation agreements. And while society is only beginning to acknowledge that this second state of affairs can be as detrimental to children's well-being as the first, feminists continue to pretend it isn't important (or that every mother who contravenes an access agreement is genuinely concerned about child abuse).

While feminism—backed up by the highest levels of the Canadian government—now goes around declaring that men are always in positions of power, both art and real life demand that we question such a view. George Eliot, our feminist foremother, knew that numerous factors determine whether individuals flourish or atrophy as human beings. She didn't make the mistake of thinking that just because women's lives were restricted as a result of their sex role, men's weren't too; that just because females were worse off than males in some respects, men must be having a grand time. She didn't assume that the only kinds of power that matter are those involving paid employment and electoral politics.

Rather, she knew that men sometimes work themselves literally to death in order to provide for their families, and that even women who are physically weaker and smaller than their husbands are capable of emotional manipulation. She knew that fathers often find that having children invests them with as much vulnerability and responsibility as it does power.

And if Eliot knew all of this, 125 years ago, what's our excuse?

The desire to explore the limits of power and submission is not a *male* compulsion but a human one.

—*Erica Jong*[1]

CHAPTER SEVEN

Our Secret Garden

The man, whose name is Warrick, is six-foot-three with broad shoulders and rippling muscles. He is naked except for a towel draped over his hips, and he is flat on his back on a bed. Iron cuffs attached to lengths of chain encircle his wrists and ankles.

Rowena, the woman, is young and slender, with waist-length blond hair. She stands over him and shakes her head when his eyes implore her to remove his gag. She strips the towel from him and tries to climb astride his body, but he struggles violently and she falls back. She tries again, and this time his resistance is so strenuous that the entire bed moves along the floor, and his wrists and ankles become smeared with blood. "You stupid man," she says to him. "Why cause yourself pain over something you cannot prevent?"

She removes her clothing and tells him that, while he may fight her, it will do him no good. She begins to caress

240

him and sweat breaks out on his brow as, despite the outrage he feels, his body begins to respond to her. The sight of
her breasts swaying above him, the sound of her panting,
and the feel of her hair on his skin all arouse him. He wages
a bitter internal battle as she slides his erect penis into her
vagina. He continues to struggle and strain. But all his
willpower, all his conscious effort, is not enough. Finally,
she brings him to orgasm.

A servant is sent to minister to Warrick's injuries, to
bathe him, feed him and help him with his bodily functions
while he remains chained. The next night, his struggles
start his wounds bleeding again as Rowena visits him three
times, coaxing an ejaculation from him on each occasion.
The following evening, she returns another three times.
She examines him closely, remarks on his body, uses him.
Despite the fury that burns in his eyes, he is powerless to
stop her. Not once is he permitted to speak to her. Later,
Rowena will recall how exhilarating it was to have him
completely at her mercy.

On the fourth day, he is released, given a set of clothes
and threatened with death should he ever show his face in
the vicinity again. But the year is 1152, and Warrick, kidnapped from an inn by bumblers unaware of his identity, is
an English lord who does return—with his army. He orders
Rowena transported to his castle and locked in the dungeon. Before he leaves, he sets fire to the bed on which he
had been confined and gathers up the chains.

After spending three weeks in the dungeon, Rowena is
taken to Warrick's room. He threatens to beat her if she
faints and informs her he intends to repay her in kind.
After warning her never to interrupt when he's speaking to
her, he orders her to strip. He assures her that, should he
not find her sufficiently arousing, there's nothing stopping
him from having as many as ten of his men rape her while
he looks on. As she undresses, she watches him positioning

the chains and pleads with him, promising not to resist. But to no avail. She lies down in the centre of the bed and he orders her to spread her legs. She's told to spread them wider, and he then chains each to a post. He secures her wrists and pushes a gag into her mouth.

Gradually her trepidation subsides as he begins to coax a sexual response from her. He caresses her gently, persistently. She begins to arch against him. His touch becomes rougher. When he enters her, her eyes fly open to see the triumph in his. "Now you know how it feels to have no control of a traitorous body," Warrick says to her. "You made me want this, despite my fury, so I have made you want it, despite your fear."[2] Soon she is screaming in orgasm. Afterward, she thinks it inconceivable that she found anything pleasurable in such an experience.

Hours later, Warrick returns to the room where Rowena has remained bound and gagged. When she closes her eyes to block him out, he orders her to look at him. "Whenever you are in my presence, wench," he says, "you will look at me unless I tell you otherwise. Do not make me repeat it."[3] She is forced to do so as a servant feeds her and attends to her other needs, but she manages to look through him rather than at him. He punishes her by having intercourse with her again.

The next morning, he takes her before she is fully awake. Twice more he returns. The following day, it's the same. On the fourth, she is released from the chains, but Warrick has a reputation for exacting revenge in excess of the crimes committed against him. Rowena, who belongs to the upper class, is now dressed in the clothing of a servant. She is told that she is to refer to him as "my lord" and will be whipped if she fails to comply. She is now his personal attendant, required to wait on him during meals in the dining hall, clean his room and launder his clothes.

She is ordered to prepare Warrick's bath and told to

undress him. When she recoils against removing his lower garments, he threatens to chain her to the bed again, and so she sinks to her knees as commanded. "'Tis quite satisfying, seeing you in that humbled position," he says. "Mayhap I will have you serve me at table just so."[4]

She is forced to wash and then dry him. "On your knees again," he says. "And take care, wench, that you do not miss a single drop of moisture. Do I catch a chill because of your negligence, I *will* beat you for it." While she is performing these tasks, however, it becomes clear they are both sexually aroused. When she balks, he tells her it's his right to have sex with his servants "at any time, in any place."[5] He drags her to the bed and uses his superior strength to keep her there. Then he kisses and caresses her relentlessly until, overcome with sexual hunger, she shames herself by obeying his command to beg him to take her.

Afterward, Warrick taunts her by reminding her of her capitulation and she thinks, "All the power was his. He had control over her body, control over her emotions, control over everything she did. She could not even get angry without his leave, for he knew well enough how to frighten the anger out of her."[6] He pulls her onto his lap in the dining hall and, in front of everyone, touches her intimately and then orders her to wait for him in his bed. He humiliates her by giving his daughters the fine gowns that had once belonged to her. He tells her she is stupid. Even when she comes to him willingly, he restrains her hands during love-making.

The above narrative isn't found in a pornographic video produced by chauvinists and then rented from seedy triple-X outlets by male sex offenders. Nor has it been stopped at the border and examined by customs agents before being allowed into Canada, despite its blatant domination and submission theme. Rather, all of the above takes place in a romance novel written by a woman for other women. It appears in Johanna Lindsey's 1991 *Prisoner of My Desire*.

According to the inside back cover of *Surrender My Love* (a 1994 novel in which the heroine is fitted with specially fashioned shackles and tethered to a wall in the hero's bedroom), Lindsey is one of the "most successful authors of historical romance," with over 40 million copies in print.[7] Each of her more than two dozen books has been a U.S. national best-seller. A number of them incorporate similar ideas. Her first, *Captive Bride* (originally published in 1977), is about a young woman who turns down a marriage proposal by an Arabian sheik she's just met, only to be kidnapped by him and brought to his isolated desert camp. Imprisoned within his tent, she's told, "You're mine now, Tina. The sooner you realize that, the better it will be for you." He informs her that she has missed her chance to marry him and will, instead, be his slave.[8] Despite her protests, he carries her to his bed. He pins her arms above her head and rips the clothing from her body. Then he lets her go, saying he will not rape her. But he promises that, when the time comes, her desire will match his. She tries to escape into the desert, but he chases after her. He threatens to tie her to the bed and says she deserves to be beaten. Laying her over the back of his horse, he smacks her bottom when she struggles.

Later, he takes her to the outdoor bathing pool and makes it clear that if she wishes to use it, she will have to disrobe in front of him. On another occasion, when she challenges his orders in the presence of others, he tells her: "I'm your master, and you belong to me. If you'd like me to find a whip and bare your back in public, I'll be happy to oblige you. Otherwise, return to my tent."[9] He brings her books but says she must kiss him if she wishes to read them. She complies and feels the stirrings of sexual desire. That night, she refuses to remove her clothing and so he does, forcibly. Gently, he kisses and caresses her, inserting his knee between her legs. Reads the novel: "Her mind cried out for him to stop, but her body demanded that he go on.... She hated her body for betraying her, but she wanted him."[10] After receiving her consent, he takes her virginity. The next night, she fights him and he strips her again. He pins her to the bed and caresses her before she succumbs and asks him to make love to her.

Repeatedly, the sheik threatens to punish her for defiant behaviour. She physically struggles against him night after night until "her passions [overcome] her resistance and [sweep] her away."[11] On one occasion, while not making love, he demands that she admit that she enjoys having sex with him. On another, he spanks her bare bottom. On a third, when he is especially angry with her, he pushes her onto the floor:

> His lips seared hers painfully, silencing her screams
> as he entered her viciously. Her mind was beyond
> reason as her body accepted his like a wild animal,
> and the pain turned to violent waves of ecstatic
> pleasure.

We read that the sheik gets into the habit of having sex with her in the morning "before she awoke fully and knew what was happening."[12] When she is abducted by a rival tribe, however, she realizes that she is in love with her original captor.

In *Secret Fire*, published in 1987, the heroine is spotted on the street by a Russian prince visiting London, England, in the 1840s. He instructs his servant to arrange for her to warm his bed that evening, but her disinterest in the task prompts the servant to pull her into a carriage and to administer a powerful aphrodisiac. As it begins to work, she fails to understand what is happening. By the time the prince comes to her room, she is writhing on the bed.

He caresses her, bringing her to orgasm. During the brief respite, before her sexual tension builds again, she tries to pull away, but he pins her to the mattress. When he offers to make love to her, she refuses, so he waits patiently until she says, "I can't bear it anymore. Alexandrov, do what you will, please, anything—just do it now." She achieves orgasm after orgasm:

> As long as she obeyed his every command, he was there to soothe and relieve and give her hour after hour of the most incredible ecstasy, with his hands, his mouth, his body. All he asked in return was that she allow him to play with her, to caress her as he would.[13]

In the morning, the heroine is furious and insists that the servant's actions be brought to the attention of the authorities. As a result, the prince decides to take her with him when he sets sail for Russia. She tries to jump overboard, but he stops her. Although the two are highly attracted to one another, she resists his further advances during the voyage.

She is taken to one of his country estates and humiliated before the servants by being dragged by him into the house and installed in the bedroom adjoining his own. Despite his promise never to give her the aphrodisiac again, he orders it administered to her food and then waits for her to be reduced to a state of sexual frenzy. Another passionate night follows, and she knows that she loves him. Part of her is "pleased that he could be so desperate to have her" that he would drug her.[14]

Not all romance novels are the same, of course. Within this genre of formula fiction, the variety is impressive. There are slim works that take place in contemporary, if frequently exotic, settings. There are thicker historical romances—often referred to as "bodice rippers"—and futuristic romances involving alien planets and species. In comparison to Lindsey's books, the approach to sex in many of them is decidedly staid. But even acknowledging such variations, sex is a mainstay of much of the escapist fiction large numbers of women now enjoy reading. Bare backs and chests, as well as exposed bosoms and thighs, appear on the covers of many of these books. Moreover, sexual power struggles, in which the central female character often plays the submissive, are common.

These power struggles are frequently used to "sell" such works. For example, in Amanda Quick's 1994 *Mistress* (a *New York Times* best-seller), the preview inside the paperback edition has the hero "caging" the heroine between his arms and a piece of sculpture during a dispute, and behaving in a sexually domineering manner.[15] The tantalizing tidbit at the front of Mary Lou Rich's 1993 *Bandit's Kiss* has the virginal heroine being undressed and caressed. When she protests, telling the hero he can't continue, he replies, "But I can."[16] The back cover of Karen Robards's 1985 *To Love a Man* (recently referred to as a "classic" by *Romantic Times* magazine) reads, in part:

> Sam would make her his captive, his woman,
> taunting her, teasing her, treating her no better
> than a slave. He would take her when and where
> he chose, hurting her pride even as he healed her
> wounds. She would love him, hate him, fight him,
> need him...[17]

Highlighted phrases on other jackets declare: "She was his captive in the burning sands—at the mercy of his every desire" and "He took the proud vixen as his prisoner and swore she would serve."[18]

It's no exaggeration to say there's a whole sub-category

of romance fiction in which male sexual dominance and female sexual submissiveness is a major theme. Titles such as *Sweet Silken Bondage*, *Captive Chains*, *No Choice But Surrender*, *Creole Captive*, *Passion's Prisoner*, *Bound by Ecstasy*, *Defiant Captive*, *Enslaved*, *Ravished* and *Fires of Surrender* make this undeniable.

In Catherine Hart's 1993 *Silken Savage*, Tanya, the heroine, is kidnapped in a raid by Cheyenne warriors in the American Old West. On arrival at the Indian camp, a leather collar and leash are fitted around her neck. She is pushed from the horse and required to run beside it as a taunting crowd gathers to grab at her. A searing-hot brand is removed from the fire and applied to her thigh, permanently scarring her and marking her as Panther's property. During the night, she escapes, but he catches her and returns her to the teepee, where he beats her.

Tanya is led everywhere on the leash. With each passing night, Panther forces her into closer intimacy. At first he merely insists that their bodies touch. Then he begins to caress her before falling asleep. Kisses and whispers follow. Eventually, she begins to respond to him sexually. On one occasion, he brings her to orgasm with his fingers.

The next morning, Tanya is filled with "self-loathing" but is unable to keep her eyes off Panther, who smiles to himself and decides that he has succeeded in ensuring that she will be "willing and eager."[19] That evening, he orders her to undress him and loosen his braids. He caresses her and, before commencing intercourse, makes her admit she wants him. Fifty pages and some time later, we read:

> She sensed Panther's need to master her and
> succumbed to him willingly. She made no protest
> when he locked her arms over her head and held
> them there, nor when he spread her legs wide and
> anchored them with the weight of his own.[20]

It isn't uncommon in these novels for women not only to be subjected to rough sex but to find it enjoyable. *Allegheny Captive*, written by Caroline Bourne, contains a scene involving a drunk, emotionally distraught hero who ignores the heroine's struggles as he tears violently at her clothing and then has intercourse with her. We read:

> When, at last, glimmering lights filled her brain and her body in one delightful burst of energy, she forgot that his actions might be construed as rape. If he had done it again, oh, so much more slowly, she would not have fought him, not even a little.
>   His possession of her was the most erotic and wildly wonderful experience she had ever imagined...[21]

In *Slave of My Heart*, the hero encounters the heroine after she has run away from him. He angrily accuses her, in essence, of being a whore and attacks her from behind. Although the language isn't specific enough for the reader to be certain, the suggestion is that he then sodomizes her. Furious and in pain, she feels her own desire awaken nonetheless.[22]

Even when the heroine is far from being an innocent, even when she doesn't need the hero to introduce her to the pleasures of the flesh, sexual power struggles remain an important element. This is the case in Susan Johnson's 1994 novel *Pure Sin*. Flora and the hero, Adam, have intercourse within minutes of their first meeting—on page twelve. But as in many other romances, both protagonists are proud, obstinate and short-tempered, thus setting the stage for a continual battle of wills. Frustrated by his inability to win other skirmishes, and aware of how much Flora desires him, Adam strives to gain the upper hand in the sexual arena.

On one occasion, she arrives at his hotel room at two in the morning. He reclines in a chair and tells her to undress in front of him. She removes her blouse and he orders her to caress her breasts. He asks her whether or not she's wet and tells her to raise her skirt and insert her own fingers in order to prove it. We read that she does so "because she desperately wanted him and because she realized too she would have him only if she was obedient to his wishes." Crudely, he asks her whether she's come to his room "to get fucked" and makes her answer.[23] He chastises her for having traversed the hallway in revealing clothing and asks her who else she's slept with since he's last seen her. When she says it's been thirty-three days and that she's had sex with no one else, he's pleased and tells her all she has to do is remove her skirt. Naked, while he remains fully clothed, she does as she's told and raises her foot, resting it near him on his chair. He looks at her open thighs and caresses her while she pleads with him to take her. He pulls her onto his lap and slides his penis into her but then holds her still. He makes her plead some more. He commands her to lift her breasts to his lips, telling her she isn't allowed to be too vocal in her response or she'll disturb the hotel guests in nearby rooms:

> "Now the other one," he said with that authority
> in his voice that intoxicated her libido, as if she
> had no control over her body, as if he possessed her,
> owned her, mind and soul. "You've been so quiet,
> you deserve a reward....
>   "Bring it closer." He rested his head against the
> back of the chair and waited for her to lean forward
> to offer him the breast that always brought her to
> climax.[24]

Holding her hips immobile, Adam asks whether she is

about to achieve an orgasm. "I asked you a question," he repeats. In the morning he tells her he thinks he'll keep her naked so she can "service" him any time.[25]

Where sex is concerned, contemporary feminist thinking often has much in common with old-fashioned beliefs. Pamphlets about date rape, for example, leave the distinct impression that—unlike men—women are never aggressive about pursuing sex and don't get swept away by desire. In Katie Roiphe's words, such thinking seems to start from "our grandmothers' assumption: men want sex, women don't."

The feminist anti-pornography position is just another version of this. It says that while men like certain kinds of sexual activity, women don't. Specifically, while men enjoy raunchy, politically incorrect fornication, women like soft-focus, syrupy sweet, egalitarian love-making. While men find the idea of some kinds of violence sexually arousing, women do not; while men are titillated by the notion of dominating or being dominated in the bedroom, women aren't; while men think that, under certain circumstances, pain can be pleasurable, women don't.

In the words of the Canadian Panel on Violence Against Women, erotica (good) can be distinguished from pornography (bad) "by examining the issues of power." The report maintains that erotica "portrays or describes people in situations of mutual respect and pleasure," while porn "relies on the depiction of domination and unequal power relationships through the degradation and humiliation of human beings."[26]

As we've seen earlier, feminism has been heavily influenced by people such as Catharine MacKinnon, who insists that "[p]ornography, in the feminist view, is a form of forced sex."[27] According to the Violence Panel, pornography is one of a number of under-acknowledged "forms of violence" against women. This report says that while

"Canadian feminists have been working toward recognition of this strong link between pornography and violence, harm and degradation of women and children," "civil libertarians and some arts groups" equate anti-porn measures with censorship (the implication being that no feminists have concerns about censorship, and that one cannot be both a feminist and a civil libertarian).[28]

The feminist anti-pornography lobby has been so adamant in this respect that many people now believe it's been proven beyond a shadow of a doubt that there's a direct connection between porn and rape. It hasn't, and there isn't. If you put a group of young men in a room and show them videos containing violent sexual material, their adrenaline levels will increase and they will demonstrate a propensity to behave more aggressively than usual. But *anything* that causes higher adrenaline levels will produce the same result—including twenty minutes on an exercise bicycle, or watching violent material with no sexual content whatsoever. Unless we're prepared to ban exercise bicycles, jogging and large numbers of mainstream films, there's no reason to scapegoat porn.[29]

Other people consider the fact that sexually explicit material has been found in the home of serial rapists—or that a few of these criminals have declared, in a new twist on "the devil made me do it" defence, that porn caused their horrific behaviour—to be evidence of a link between crime and porn. But that overlooks the millions of people who use pornography and don't turn into rapists. It also ignores the fact that some criminals blame the Bible for inspiring their crimes. If we're going to hold porn responsible, there can be no reason not to indict the Holy Book as well.[30]

According to feminist anti-porn activists there's only one way to interpret a photograph depicting a woman restrained and gagged. The notion that it might be harmless sexual entertainment, produced and consumed by consenting adults who understand the difference between fantasy and coercion, doesn't even make it into the discussion. Rather, such an image is viewed as part of a training manual for misogynists who, according the Violence Report, force their wives or girlfriends into similar poses once such ideas have been implanted in their heads.[31] (In *Only Words*, a collection of anti-porn lectures, MacKinnon says that permitting men to view porn is like telling a trained guard dog to "kill."[32])

Such thinking extends beyond feminist circles. In what is known as the Butler decision, the Supreme Court of Canada ruled in 1992 that pornographic materials that place women "in positions of subordination, servile submission or humiliation" violate "the principles of equality and dignity of all human beings." It further proclaimed that "[c]onsent cannot save materials that otherwise contain degrading or dehumanizing scenes" since, in its opinion, "[s]ometimes the very appearance of consent makes the depicted acts even more degrading or dehumanizing."[33]

Referring to the findings of the controversial American Meese Commission investigation into pornography, among others, the court said that since "a substantial body of opinion" considers such material to be harmful to women, it isn't necessary to actually prove this. In the court's view, not just feminists but the Canadian public in general considers this sort of porn dangerous.[34] As a result, such material (when it appears in gay publications, men's magazines or explicit videos—but not elsewhere, apparently) is illegal in this country.

In order to come to such a decision, though, Canada's highest judicial body first had to arrive at a moralistic judgment. There's no law against tying up another consenting adult and having sex with them. There's no law against role-playing sexual fantasies in which one partner kisses the other's feet. Therefore, when the court called depictions of these perfectly lawful activities "degrading" and "dehumanizing," it was making a statement about what kinds of sex it thinks are healthy and what kinds it thinks are pathological—in the same way that some people still declare gay sex to be "abnormal."

Next, the court accepted the argument put forward by the feminist Legal Education Action Fund (whose brief was co-authored by MacKinnon) that this is an issue of *male* freedom of speech versus *female* safety.[35] In the name of promoting female equality, then, the court chose to believe that men and women are fundamentally different with respect to what turns us on—a profoundly sexist doctrine.

Such ideas should give any thinking woman pause, because underlying them is the notion that no self-respecting female would have the slightest interest in sexual fantasies that involve power struggles. The court seems convinced that no healthy woman would fantasize about chaining a gorgeous man to the bed and having her way with him for seventy-two hours. It clearly cannot conceive of any woman in her right mind day-dreaming about being kidnapped by a tall, dark and handsome stranger who finds her so alluring he can't keep his hands off her, who is so overcome by desire that he rips the clothes from her body, pins her down and drives her wild with sexual pleasure.

Not long ago, "pure" women—the sort that men brought home to their mothers—were expected to view sex as nothing more than an unpleasant duty. Those who acknowledged their own libidos were considered aberrant. In 1858, for example, a British surgeon named Isaac Baker Brown introduced clitoridectomies as a "cure" for female masturbation. While nineteenth-century medical and religious authorities also condemned male masturbation, girls weren't simply warned that such activity would cause them to go insane; there was concern they'd end up in brothels.[36]

Today, women are being told—by mainstream feminism and the Supreme Court of Canada—that "good" girls aren't interested in sexual fantasies that involve domination, submission or bondage. We're told that only men (violent, nasty ones) get turned on by such things. We're told that we shouldn't look at these sorts of images, think these sorts of thoughts or participate in these sorts of activities, since they lead to a wide range of social evils. We're told that, if our sexuality isn't as strait-laced as the court assumes it to be, we should feel ashamed, dirty, perverted, abnormal.

But the truth is that women *do* find porn—kinky or otherwise—arousing. In 1987, *Time* magazine estimated that women were renting as much as 40 percent of X-rated videos.[37] A British women's magazine readership poll published in 1993 found that 83 percent of women acknowledged being aroused by porn, while a joint *Details* and *Mademoiselle* readership survey that same year determined that 21 percent of female respondents enjoyed explicit videotapes and that one in four had been tied up during sex.[38] More to the point, no one remotely familiar with the sort of contemporary women's romance fiction I've described above can possibly deny that plenty of women are interested in sexual fantasy material that involves overt or implied bondage. Despite what anti-porn feminists would like to believe, many women are also turned on by scenarios in which females are kidnapped and threatened with rape.

Let's be clear about this: *female* consumers are the reason the $855-million (U.S.) per year romance industry exists.[39] While men purchase most of the material we normally think of when we talk about pornography (such as *Playboy*, *Penthouse* and explicit videos), and while we may quibble over who reads other types of erotic literature, there's no question that women buy the vast majority of romance novels. If domination and submission held no allure whatsoever for women, if every last one of us was interested only in unmistakably consensual sexual fantasies, the kinds of novels I've described wouldn't be readily available in every general interest bookstore.

Formula fiction publishers publish what sells; although the writing is often more than competent, no one is pretending these are literary masterpieces. Rather, romances are a commodity, and commodities that have no appeal in the marketplace are pushed aside by those that do. Whatever else one might say about this genre, readers have a great deal of choice with respect to what kinds of books they buy and which authors they choose to support or avoid. How women have been exercising these choices tells us something important about female sexuality—if only we were honest enough to acknowledge it.

In a 1991 article published in Ms., Gloria Steinem describes a typical scene in a movie, involving the hero (who possesses an air of authority) and the heroine (who's beautiful).

> At first, she resists. He uses just enough strength
> to be a real man, but not quite enough to be a
> bad guy. She guards her virginity—or in a modern
> movie, the psychic virginity of her independence—
> with words, with the language of her body arching
> away, with her fists pushing against him.
> Then he kisses her—and suddenly, everything
> changes. Her body softens, her fists unclench.
> The camera focuses on the ritual image: her hands
> sliding around his neck in total surrender.[40]

Steinem tells us that, as "a little girl watching versions of this scene in Saturday matinees," she remembers feeling "betrayed." She says she was left wondering why the heroine was "giving in to a man who behaved like a bully."

Initially, she assumed that these "dominant/submissive scenes" were an accurate reflection of adult reality. Later, she says, she came to realize that "even a little aggression was a sexual turnoff," but she still assumed that most women disagreed. She writes:

> Only when I was past 30 and feminism had
> arrived in my life did I finally stop believing movie
> dialogue and listen to what real women said. I
> discovered that most of them felt endangered by
> domination, as I did; that the few who found it
> sexual often had grown up with attention, love,
> sex, and violence so intertwined that they believed
> you couldn't get one without the others.[41]

This is Steinem's rendition of the "healthy women aren't interested in sexual domination fantasies" argument. Now, I'm not saying anyone should be second-guessing Steinem about her *own* sexuality. I'm sure such fantasies do nothing for her, just as they don't appeal to many other women. What disturbs me is that she takes things a step further, that she then declares her own sexual response to be normal and suggests that women who are aroused by such scenes were probably abused as children. According to Steinem, these "resistance to surrender" scenes are *male* fantasies, which serve to justify real-life violence against girls and women. She spends the remainder of the article linking childhood sexual abuse to former Hollywood sex goddesses and the people who exploited them during their careers.

When discussing these issues, Steinem refuses to acknowledge the all-important distinction between fantasy and reality. Indeed, it's astounding that she's more concerned about imaginary female characters in films than she is about the real-life multiple personality patients who are being drugged, strapped down and urged to admit to experiencing sexual invasions that may or may not have happened. But be that as it may, Hollywood is in the business of producing escapist entertainment, first and foremost. It's understandable that, as a child, Steinem failed to appreciate that a heroine who melts after being kissed by the hero is acknowledging the power of sexual passion, of lust. For an adult male viewer, the idea that a woman might find his kiss so devastating that all other reservations she has suddenly disappear is a potent one. For a female viewer, who is conflicted about whether she likes or is supposed to like sex, the notion that a mere kiss might banish all her doubts is equally powerful. This is the kind of passionate response many people yearn to experience, as well as invoke.

That it took Steinem more than thirty years to realize that "movie dialogue" doesn't necessarily depict real life is unfortunate. What she still doesn't seem to understand, though, is that there's an enormous difference between the *idea* of domination and submission and the real thing. The readers and writers of contemporary romance novels, however, do understand this difference. Indeed, one might say that the unspoken rule in this kind of fiction is: context, context, context. In *Heart's Surrender*, a 1994 novel by Kathleen Morgan, Rissa is among a group of women captured by a small band of Cat People, an alien (but still humanoid) species living on a fictional planet. Rissa is selected as a mate for the leader who, early in the novel, thinks:

> As furious as Rissa could make him, he knew he couldn't raise a hand against her.
> Cat Men never struck their females. The few that ever did were severely punished, their mates given to another. And now that females, in their scarcity, were an even more precious resource, no

> one could dare be permitted to harm one. Even
> one such as Rissa, who dearly needed a lesson in
> respect, not to mention obedience.[42]

Although male sexual dominance and female sexual submission is an unmistakable theme in this novel, the threat
of Rissa suffering vicious, ugly violence at the hands of the
hero is explicitly ruled out early on. It's the *idea* of the sexual power struggle, the *suggestion* of violence that appeals to
readers of such books.

Indeed, as this story progresses, it becomes evident that
the hero, despite his aggressive posturing, is not only strong
and handsome but honourable and kind. Rissa is eventually
reunited with her father (whom she hasn't seen since she
was a child), only to find that he treats her with far less
affection and respect than her "savage" Cat Man lover. The
fact that her kidnapper ends up looking good by comparison gives Rissa permission to love him unashamedly—just
as the often convoluted plot lines in these novels give
female readers permission to fantasize about things they
know shouldn't appeal to them. After all, in real life we're
aware that one is more likely to be forcibly abducted by a
physically unappealing sicko than by a heart-throb who
turns out to be a well-balanced, decent guy.

Again and again, authors signal to readers that only certain kinds of violence, in certain situations, are being eroti-
cized. In *Silken Savage*, when the heroine is branded and
beaten, she still receives far better treatment than the other
women who are captured along with her (they're raped and
assaulted even before arriving at the Cheyenne camp).
This larger context, therefore, allows her to view her particular kidnapper as a worthy love interest.

In Heather Graham's 1989 *A Pirate's Pleasure*, set in the
early 1700s, Skye's ship is boarded by pirates. An accomplished swordswoman, she kills one of the men who tries to

abduct her, before the leader—described as "a small, sinewy man" with an "evil leer" and "yellowed, rotting teeth"— gives instructions that she isn't to be harmed. "If she's as feisty beneath the covers, I want her alive!" he says. Since such a scenario veers too close to a real rape situation, the ship is promptly rammed by another, under the command of a different pirate. Known as the Silver Hawk, he's dressed stylishly, is tall, "whipcord lean and hard-muscled." It is Hawk who, after besting her with a sword, plants one "foot on either side of Skye, catching the tattered remnants of her once-beautiful gown and strands of her golden hair beneath his boots" and takes her prisoner. But despite his overbearing manner, sexually charged taunting, inappropriate caresses and the fact that he forcibly undresses her, Hawk doesn't rape her—even though we're left with no doubt that the first pirate would have done so. When they finally have sex, on page 159, she runs into his arms and invites it.[43]

Hawk, like other heroes in this genre, is an exceptional man: in addition to exuding an animal magnetism, he is smart, self-assured, kind, rich, powerful and titled. Just as very few women possess the perfect bodies one finds in magazine centrefolds that appeal to a primarily male market, few men walking the earth can possibly compete with the fantasy males one encounters in such romances. Most real men aren't independently wealthy, and we all know that brains and brawn don't necessarily come in the same package. In this sense, women appear to be even more demanding than men when it comes to their sexual fantasies; merely having fabulous pectorals isn't quite enough to enchant these heroines.

In *Beloved Bondage*, a 1993 book by Katharine Kincaid set in ancient Rome, the hero is a slave who is purchased by the female protagonist and told that he must be "submissive and obedient." He has "the body of a giant" and is "truly the most magnificent male specimen" she's ever seen. Though neither rich nor powerful when she first meets him, he is loyal and trustworthy. Significantly, before she orders him to take off his clothes and have sex with her, she first assesses the quality of his mind. They discuss politics and philosophy and we read that, as "they debated back and forth, she could not remember ever having been so mentally stimulated, so excited."[44]

Most importantly, what the men in all these novels have going for them is their skill in bed. They are irresistible because they have the ability to both awaken and satisfy a heroine's deepest sexual longings. These books are about female desire as a powerful force in its own right, as something that has the ability to overcome fear and shatter social convention. It doesn't matter that she's there against her will, that he's insufferably arrogant or that he's using sex as a weapon in a power struggle between them; the lust she feels is so overwhelming, sex with him is so good, that thinking has been replaced by feeling. In one novel, we read:

> ...he knew how to make love. He knew how to move: how fast; how deep, how slow; how hard. He knew how to kiss a woman's mouth and the tender warmth behind her ear; how to suckle her nipples and draw his tongue lightly over the curve of her breast or the pouty fullness of her lips. He knew when to lift her hips to meet his plunging invasion, when to be gentle and when not to be. He understood the delicate balance between violence and pleasure, between harshness and tenderness. He was accomplished at bringing a woman to climax simply by caressing her or talking to her. He was very good.[45]

The world of the romance novel is a place where female readers are freed from the pressures and expectations of society, religion and family. It's a place where disapproval and responsibility fall away, as female characters abandon themselves to lust and indulge their senses. This world is attractive precisely because it conflicts so profoundly with the real one, in which dirty diapers, financial worries and indifferent sex are far more common experiences.

Moreover, in this world the people are every bit as glamorous as the ones who inhabit Hollywood movies and the pages of fashion magazines. These are fantasies not only about meeting handsome princes but (often) about being breathtakingly beautiful as well. In *The Beauty Myth*, Naomi Wolf argues that society exerts great pressure on women to expend large amounts of time, energy and money on their appearance. Even if she pushes this idea rather far, there's still something to it. And for those of us who don't look like fashion models, this state of affairs can be rather demoralizing.

In romance novels, readers get to fantasize about what it would be like to be so attractive that men view you as a "prize" to be sought after, fought over and worth breaking laws to get their hands on. Readers experience, vicariously, the thrill of being so desirable that otherwise emotionally distant heroes astonish long-time friends with their obsession for you, their clouded judgment, their loss of self-control while in your presence. The notion that a man as perfect as these heroes are would have to struggle to keep his sexual hunger in check whenever he looks at you, would even be interested in you in the first place when other beautiful women are continually throwing themselves at him, is a highly gratifying one. Why wouldn't such fantasies be appealing?

I am hardly the first person to observe that a fantasy situation in which a woman is, to some degree, forced into having sex (with the right man) has the allure of absolving her of responsibility. If romance readers remain embarrassed by or afraid of sexual pleasure on some level (since sex is, after all, "filthy" and sinful, and desire should always be kept under tight control), or if they, simply because they're women, associate sex with worry about pregnancy, bad reputations or violence, such fantasies are a way of pushing all that aside. If a woman can reply to all those whispers in her head, "But it's not my fault, I tried to resist, honest," she is then freed to play the wanton.

In *Revolution from Within*, Steinem says that "[r]omance itself serves a larger political purpose by offering at least a temporary reward for gender roles and threatening rebels with loneliness and rejection.... It privatizes our hopes and distracts us from making social changes." She goes on to compare romance to ancient Rome's bread and circuses, saying it's a way of keeping "the masses happy."[46] (In a similar vein, MacKinnon declares that some women "eroticize dominance and submission" as a means of coping with a hostile world, since "it beats feeling forced."[47]) But just as there are usually more than two windows in a castle, there are also other points of view. Even if romance novels had started out as a male plot to convince women to buy into marriage by making a presumably bad deal seem attractive, after nearly thirty years of feminist influence (in the best sense of that term) the genre has changed.

Being the child of two avid readers, I consumed both romance novels and westerns from an early age. And I can attest to the fact that while sexually domineering heroes, as well as heroines who turn to jelly after a single kiss, appeared in female formula fiction when I was an adolescent, such books have become more sexually explicit and significantly kinkier over time. The heroines in such novels have always been spunky, courageous, resourceful, smart, articulate and headstrong—in other words, anything but submissive outside the bedroom. They often challenge the authority figures in their life and, in the numerous novels set in the Old West, frequently stand up to anti-Indian racial prejudice. But an increasing emphasis is now being placed on female sexual satisfaction.

If romance novels are simply a means of "selling" unequal gender relations to women, of convincing us that men are swell even when they oppress us, why are the heroes so unlike real men? Surely one could argue more persuasively that such novels are a recipe for dissatisfaction, that they encourage women to expect the unlikely, to yearn for the improbable in their relations with the opposite sex. And while it's one thing to suggest, as old Hollywood movies do, that a mere kiss can transform resistance into surrender, it's another matter altogether to bring in chains and gags, repeated sexual encounters and extended flesh-on-flesh seductions. In earlier years, women weren't really supposed to want sex, but they would respond to "the right man." Here, women end up wanting sex badly enough to beg men for it—even men they fear or are angry with.

Ironically, a woman who genuinely pleads for sex is a woman who acknowledges that she is capable of feeling desire as powerfully as any man. This is a fascinating inversion of the old order, in which women disburse sex strategically and in small doses while men do the courting and the begging. We aren't overly surprised when the chained Warrick responds to Rowena's caresses. Conventional wisdom tells us that men—particularly young, virile ones—always want sex. The fact that Warrick is able, in turn, to get Rowena so utterly and completely aroused that nothing else matters to her might look like just another male power grab, but it actually represents a profound repudiation of long-standing sexual double standards. Here, female desire is a vigorous, dizzying force too potent to be fenced in and parcelled out at will by even the most determined of heroines.

Considering that thousands of women have told Ann Landers they prefer hugging and kissing to intercourse, and that nearly four out of ten Canadian women prefer chocolate to sex, it appears that many people's sexual experiences have been less than mind-blowing.[48] That women's formula fiction now includes heroes who are not only rich and handsome but are also sexual dynamos who typically spend a great deal of time ensuring that the heroine experiences nothing less than absolute bliss suggests that women's own fantasies and longings, rather than a male conspiracy, are responsible for the content of these books. And while many women no doubt find such fiction highly unappealing, others clearly enjoy it—thus making it impossible to claim, as so many people have in recent years, that sexual material that features dominance, submission, bondage, humiliation or rape fantasies is the product of sick male minds.

Romance novels are an important element of "female culture," and their contents have remained a dirty little secret for far too long. The truth of the matter is that women are in no position to be casting stones at male porn for featuring unrealistic objects of desire, or for mixing sex with issues of power. If women can chain men to beds in romance novels, why can't the reverse be depicted in *Playboy*? If women can freely purchase fantasy material in which heroes ravish heroines, why can't men look at photo spreads portraying the same thing? What anti-porn feminists don't want to talk about is the fact that romance novels contain at least as much politically incorrect sex as does male pornography.

In addition to all the other evils male porn is supposedly responsible for, feminists also like to accuse it of fanning racism. That some male consumers—who may or may not be white—have an interest in sexual fantasy material featuring more than just white women is considered evidence of racial bigotry. Reads the Canadian Panel on Violence

Against Women report:

> There is very little published material on the role
> of racism in pornography, or on the links between
> pornography and racism. Yet in magazines and
> videos, women of color are often featured as
> "exotic." Mainstream men's magazines such as
> *Playboy* and *Penthouse* frequently publish photo
> features which degrade women of colour and feed
> and build upon ideas perhaps already existing in
> the mind of the viewer.[49]

As vaguely worded as it is, this statement is more than sufficient to telegraph the feminist "party line" regarding porn
and race, to make it clear that non-white models are generally considered a bad thing.

Yet this may be a case of "damned if you do and damned
if you don't"; if male porn only featured white women,
would feminists not be criticizing it for considering only
white women sexy? Moreover, there is no shortage of
"exotic" heroes in romance fiction. Relationships between
white women and native Indian men are so common that
there's a Reviewers' Choice Award for Best Indian Series.
Many of the other heroes are also "half-breeds," whose
Indian blood is said to be responsible for their tall, dark and
handsome appearance, their mysteriousness, as well as the
fact that they're considered "untamed" and more than a little dangerous. Nor do women in such novels limit themselves to lusting after men alone. As has been mentioned,
in futuristic romance novels, heroes belonging to other
species are sometimes considered appealing because, among
other things, they're believed to be more sexually skilled
than mere human males.

In addition to the evidence available in the romance
section of your bookstore, there is another reason, too, to

be suspicious of the notion that women have no interest in anything other than the kind of straightforward sex most of us imagine our parents having—landmark erotic writing is also being authored by women. *Story of O*, which first appeared in France in 1954, was written by journalist Dominique Aury under the pseudonym Pauline Reage.[50] It's a fictional account of a woman who becomes a sex slave and is frequently whipped, humiliated and abused by (mostly) male lovers and strangers. Rather than rebelling against such treatment, O revels in it, striving to be utterly submissive.

Elizabeth McNeill's *9 1/2 Weeks: A Memoir of a Love Affair* appeared in 1978. We're told that McNeill is a pseudonym for the "New York career woman" who experienced these events. The book begins, "The first time we were in bed together he held my hands pinned down above my head. I liked it. I liked him." The intense, obsessive, extreme relationship that follows includes blindfolding, bondage, spectacular sex, beatings, and public humiliation—all of which end when she suffers a mental breakdown. The book remains popular and has engendered a movie, suggesting that large numbers of people find such ideas arousing.

But it is perhaps the *Beauty* trilogy, by American author Anne Rice, first published under the pseudonym A.N. Roquelaure between 1983 and 1985, that demonstrates most clearly that the female erotic imagination is as varied as the male one. The first book, *The Claiming of Sleeping Beauty*, based roughly on the fairy tale in which the entire castle falls asleep for a hundred years, begins with the prince taking fifteen-year-old Beauty's virginity prior to kissing her awake. What follows is a novel of "tenderness and cruelty," in which Beauty is one of a number of young men and women required to complete a term of sexual servitude in the kingdom of a powerful queen. Tormented by female as well as male masters, the slaves are routinely slapped, spanked, paddled and lashed in these novels, which feature both heterosexual and homosexual sex. They are required to perform demeaning tasks and are subjected to ritual humiliations.

Women have been dealt a full share of all those qualities that make us human—the ones we are proudest of as well as those that most disturb us. Each individual possesses these qualities, although they may differ in strength from person to person and are affected by the way other tendencies combine and interact within our psyches. That there are people—both male and female—who are left stone cold by the above sorts of explicit material is beyond dispute. Noting the enormous variety of sexual responses among individuals, anti-censorship feminist Carole Vance has formulated what she calls her "One-Third Rule." She says: "show any personally favored erotic image to a group of women, and one-third will find it disgusting, one-third will find it ridiculous, and one-third will find it hot."[51]

Among those who are turned on by such material, there is infinite variety as well. Many people are titillated by specific elements and repulsed by others. Some individuals are so discomfited by their positive response that they're barely able to admit to it. Others happily imagine, read about or look at drawings, photos and videos of dominance and submission scenes, but stop there. Some enjoy play-acting these sorts of scenarios with consenting adult partners, while others push things even further by participating in activities that approximate the real thing—as the author of *9 1/2 Weeks* did. As well, there are a minority of individuals who step over the line from legal to illegal activity, who force unwilling sexual partners, or children, into taking part in this sort of activity. It is at this point that such behaviour becomes morally objectionable, that the term "violence" becomes appropriate.

Although raised as a Roman Catholic, I abandoned the Church during my teen years because I wasn't prepared to accept its view that I should feel guilty about impure thoughts as well as actual deeds. While murder is a terrible crime, I don't view murder mystery writers—who think about these matters a great deal—as having sinned. Nor do I believe that an actor who goes through the motions of killing someone is guilty of any transgression. There is a difference between thinking about something and actually doing it. There is a difference between fantasy, play or pretence and the real thing. In the words of one of the men interviewed by Wendy Dennis for *Hot and Bothered: Sex and Love in the Nineties*:

> ...I find the *idea* of overpowering a woman sexually and taking her against her will extremely erotic. That's rape, and I would never dream of acting on that desire in reality because rape is vicious and horrible. There's a difference, though, between having an erotic desire and acting on it. A fantasy is a pretend story...[52]

Dennis begins the first chapter of her book with the following: "I won't divulge *all* the dirty details of my sexual fantasies here, just a few choice tidbits. I will confess up front, however, that they're not even marginally politically correct [original italics]." She goes on to explain that, over the years, she's had difficulty reconciling the content of her submissive fantasies with the modern, assertive woman she knows herself to be. "In the juiciest variations, I willingly submit while Mongol hordes of broad-shouldered, masterful, slavering men do unspeakable things to my body," she writes. After interviewing hundreds of people in cities across the United States and Canada, Dennis reports that what we humans find sexually arousing runs the gamut:

...what's "interesting" to some is conventional
beyond words to others. If I tell you, for instance,
that some couples revitalize their sex lives by
lighting candles in the bedroom and taking baths
together, some of you are going to think that's baby
stuff. If I tell you that some couples watch porn
regularly, or make their own dirty movies, or make
dirty movies with other couples and watch them
together, some of you are going to say that's
disgusting while others will say, "Yeah, tried
that...what else have you got?"[53]

When Dennis asked people specifically about their sexual
fantasies, she found no less variety:

I heard female fantasies that involved a woman
masturbating in a roomful of guys, being tenderly
caressed by two adoring men, being the only
woman on a plane hijacked by Iranian terrorists
and being savagely "taken" by them in the cockpit,
having her pussy licked by a German shepherd,
seducing an uninitiated teenage boy who was hired
to clean out the garage, servicing a hundred guys in
a hotel room, all of them eating beer and pretzels
and waiting for their turn...[54]

"I assure you," she hastens to add, that the people "having
these fantasies are solid citizens and contributing, produc-
tive members of society."

As a rebellious teen, I was also disinclined to feel guilty
about being sexually active before I was married just
because the Catholic Church said I should. There are a
great many things in this world that are unjust or otherwise
unacceptable, that are worth getting upset about, but
(assuming that people take precautions against disease and

are responsible about birth control) in my view sex isn't one of them. We all do enough things in our lives that we should rightly feel ashamed of, there's no need to add consensual sex that harms no one to the list—regardless of how bizarre it might be.

Some of us like spicy food and exotic flavours, while others prefer simpler fare. Similarly, people who abhor horseradish no doubt find the slogan on the label of one brand that talks about enjoying "tears of happiness" incomprehensible. Why would anyone want to eat food that practically curls your hair, they might ask? How could it possibly be a pleasurable experience? I suspect the answers to such questions have much in common with why some people enjoy being spanked or fantasize about having another person at their mercy in a sexual context.

Such ideas inform my opinions about sexually explicit material—whether it be a men's magazine, an X-rated video, a steamy romance novel or an image transmitted across the Internet. There's nothing wrong with loving chocolate, but people who are so addicted to the stuff that they resort to robbing store shelves or assaulting others have a problem. Nevertheless, we don't get confused and start thinking that chocolate is, in itself, evil. And yet, when it comes to sexually explicit material, it's amazing how easily we can be led to believe that it, itself, is the problem. That if we just get rid of it, or regulate it tightly enough, if we force *Penthouse* to insert enough black circles and rectangles in its comic strips, drawings and photographic spreads, and compel it to cover up or remove altogether enough select words and sentences before we allow it into Canada (as is routinely the case these days), we've accomplished something. Yes, there are rapists out there. Yes, there are people who inflict real violence on others in sexual contexts, and who coerce others into posing for porn. But it's their *criminal behaviour* that's the issue—not sex or porn itself.

One of the reasons anti-pornography feminists have been so successful, and their arguments seem so convincing, is that while we are a sexually permissive culture in many ways, large numbers of people still view sex as a dangerous, hedonistic force. Even those of us who no longer consider oral sex, masturbation, premarital intercourse or homosexuality sinful often still harbour residual feelings of guilt, shame and disgust. Feminism has tapped into these sentiments.

That this is the case becomes evident when one considers what feminists have not attempted to demonize: alcohol. Diana Russell, one of the violence-against-women researchers whose work is frequently cited by feminists, admits that her findings (as well as those of others) suggest that alcohol is a factor in a significant percentage of rapes and wife assaults.[55] Linda Fairstein, a Manhattan sex-crimes prosecutor and the author of a recent book about sexual violence, estimates that alcohol plays a role in up to 70 percent of date rapes.[56] How accurate these stats are isn't as important as the fact that alcohol turns up far more often in such research than porn does. And yet, feminists have not mounted large-scale campaigns against drinking. They haven't produced emotionally manipulative documentaries such as the National Film Board of Canada's *Not a Love Story* or travelled from campus to campus talking about how alcohol's real purpose is the subjugation and degradation of half the population.

Why? Because North Americans have heard—and rejected—similar arguments before, and because the issue of drinking isn't clouded by nearly the same knee-jerk emotion that accompanies discussions about sex. History teaches us about the Prohibition era and how futile it was to try to outlaw a product that millions of ordinary, otherwise law-abiding citizens were interested in consuming.

Attempting to restrict the adult population's access to alcohol only ended up enriching the coffers of organized crime. Moreover, because we're able to think more clearly about alcohol than about sex, it's clear that, since most people who consume alcohol don't metamorphose into rapists, this chemical substance isn't the determining factor.

That feminists have insisted porn, rather than imbibing, is a violence-against-women issue represents a willingness, on the part of these activists, to play on people's deep-seated guilt and shame about sex in order to advance their political agenda. In a revealing moment, MacKinnon, speaking at a conference in 1987, said of feminists such as herself:

> To change the norm, we looked for a vulnerable
> place in the system. We looked for something that
> could be made to work for us, something we could
> use. We took whatever we could get our hands
> on, and when it wasn't there, we invented. We
> invented a sex equality law against pornography
> on women's terms.[57]

The effectiveness of the feminist anti-porn campaign reveals how vulnerable our fundamental freedoms are when pitted against ideological fervour. Significantly, the feminist anti-porn ordinance MacKinnon helped draft contains no exemption for works having artistic merit, even though this is a usual feature of anti-obscenity laws. MacKinnon has asked, "[I]f a woman is subjected, why should it matter that the work has other value?" In 1994, Andrea Dworkin—the ordinance's co-author—admitted in *Ms.* that, "It's very hard to look at a picture of a woman's body and not see it with the perception that her body is being exploited."[58] A year earlier, such thinking led one group of lesbian feminists to attempt to suppress a magazine produced by

another group of lesbian feminists on the grounds that the
cover was degrading. As Nadine Strossen warns in her
impressive book *Defending Pornography*:

> If the procensorship feminists had their way,
> pornography would be equally unattainable for
> women and men, for gays and straights. Those
> concerned about the rights of lesbians, gays, and
> bisexuals should not delude themselves that the
> feminist antipornography juggernaut would not
> ride roughshod over their preferred sexual materials
> along with everyone else's.[59]

In other words, in the name of improving women's
lives, anti-porn feminists have demonstrated disdain not
only for men's civil rights (which is unjust in itself) but for
women's, as well. Putting their views into practice would
leave virtually every visual representation of women now
appearing in mainstream women's magazines, as well as in
many feminist ones, open to suppression. Because the
Dworkin/MacKinnon ordinance applies to "pictures and/or
words," the kinds of romance novels discussed in this chapter would most certainly fall under its rubric. Since the law
prohibits the exhibition of women's body parts such as
"breasts and buttocks," exercise videos and even feminist
works such as *Our Bodies, Ourselves* (whose authors campaigned against the ordinance prior to it being temporarily
enacted in Minneapolis in 1986)[60] might well be prohibited. Such a law could potentially cripple much television
and film, gut libraries and ransack art galleries (how many
paintings by the Old Masters do you suppose would receive
the Feminist Purity stamp of approval?).

In my view, this sounds an awful lot like a totalitarian
state, in which—in the words of Isaiah Berlin—people
whose "eyes are fixed upon some ultimate golden future"

sacrifice much of what their fellow citizens hold dear to their own particular brand of fanaticism.

During the years I marched and picketed for abortion access, one of the more enduring slogans was the one that said: Keep Your Laws Off My Body. The idea was that the decision about whether or not to carry a pregnancy to term was a personal, individual matter. It's still my fervent belief that (barring exceptional circumstances, such as a considerably advanced pregnancy) neither the church nor the state has any business interfering with women's difficult choices in this regard.

I consider the issue of pornography to be a similarly personal, individual matter. I don't think it's any of my concern what kind of sexually explicit material my neighbour reads or looks at (and, according to the "One-Third Rule," he or she is likely to be unimpressed by what I'm viewing). While I support legislation outlawing sexual interference with children and feel that it's more than reasonable to limit access to sexually explicit material to adults, I think we should endeavour to keep laws off our fantasies as well as off our art.

Instead, we should commit ourselves to reinforcing the difference between pretence and reality, between play and the real thing. We should ensure that our children understand that the stunts they see on television aren't humanly possible, that even movie stars require special lighting and airbrushing to look the way they do, that physical violence is rarely appropriate and that other people should be treated with respect both in and out of the bedroom. Patiently and consistently, we should teach them to value substance over style.

Porn is a challenge for many couples, since what appeals to one person may be a total turnoff for the other. Large numbers of women, for example, say their self-confidence is undermined by the knowledge that their mates are ogling the flawless bodies that appear in men's magazines. Everyone has a right, of course, to decide what they will and will not tolerate in their own homes. However, a woman tempted to censor her spouse's fantasy life could ask herself how she'd respond if her husband demanded that she stop reading romance novels (or murder mysteries). She might consider how she'd react if he asked her not to bring home any more interior decorating magazines, since he feels inadequate knowing she's day-dreaming about houses and furnishing that he feels unable to provide for her. In the words of Christie Hefner, the daughter of Hugh Hefner and now the CEO of Playboy Enterprises Inc., "Men are very visual in their sexual lives. That doesn't make them bad, it just makes them different" from many women.[61]

Here, as elsewhere, tolerance and flexibility may be the best policy.

How brittle, fragile and aggrieved we have become.

–Editorial
The Globe and Mail[1]

CHAPTER EIGHT

Sex, Lies and Court Transcripts

In the heart of Toronto, in office space leased by the Ontario government, in the files of an august and official body are gathered a selection of pornographic magazines bearing titles such as *Couples in Heat, D-Cup, Hot Shots* and *Tight Cheeks*. They have been purchased with taxpayers' money, photographed and duly examined—all in an effort to force three mom-and-pop convenience stores to stop selling them.

In January 1988, teacher Pat Findlay and psychologist Marty McKay approached the operators of three stores in their Toronto neighbourhood and asked them to discontinue the sale of pornography, including mainstream titles such as *Playboy* and *Penthouse*. According to documents filed by the two women, one of the owners refused their request, the second "became very defensive and hostile and refused," while the third "became very hostile and started shouting at us, advising us that the magazines were there for men to buy and were none of our business."

Undaunted, the women returned two weeks later. On this occasion, the owner of Mike's Smoke and Gifts again declined to listen to them, the cashier at Jug Mart picked up the phone and began to call the police (prompting the women to leave since "his manner was threatening and he was not willing to hear our complaint"), while the person behind the counter at Four Star Variety "again became hostile and shouted" at Findlay and McKay. The two feminists say they followed up by writing to each of the stores in question, once again asking them to stop selling such material.[2]

Findlay and McKay have every right to hold negative opinions about pornography. They have every right to lobby their elected representatives and to attempt to persuade others of their views. These women were entitled to communicate their opinions to the businesses in question and, having been unsuccessful at convincing them to adopt another course of action, had the right to vote with their feet, to do their shopping elsewhere.

For their part, the stores were selling perfectly legal publications, many of which would have been inspected by Canada Customs prior to being allowed into the country. Furthermore, the stores were in compliance with a municipal by-law that stipulates that adult magazines must be displayed five feet above the floor, behind barriers that reveal little more than the publications' titles.[3] Having been informed that two of their customers found such magazines offensive, the proprietors had a choice: either act on these concerns or disregard them. They were well within their own rights to pick the latter option.

But matters didn't stop there. The women then filed formal complaints with the Ontario Human Rights Commission, alleging that they were being discriminated against on the basis of their sex. Findlay and McKay contended that the mere presence of such publications creates "an environment which is hostile to and discriminates against women." They claimed that, "because of their stereotypical and demeaning portrayal of women, the display and sale of these magazines creates a negative environment for [us] as well as for other women."[4]

McKay would later tell the media that porn makes her feel like a second-class citizen, that she symbolically identifies with the models in these magazines, and she doesn't think she should have to walk by such publications when coming in for a loaf of bread. Findlay would express frustration that, after having been informed that the magazines were "harmful," the store owners persisted in selling them anyway.[5]

This matter has consumed inordinate amounts of time and money. Human rights officers have visited the stores and photographed the magazine racks. They have purchased and examined copies of these publications. By-law enforcement personnel have been interviewed. Two different investigative reports have been written and distributed.[6] A number of legal opinions have been solicited. In January 1993, a relatively rare three-person board of inquiry was appointed to preside over a human rights hearing that was expected to stretch on for weeks. The store owners, all of Korean extraction, who work long hours at their family-run businesses, were advised that if they or their lawyers failed to show up for the proceedings they would "not be entitled to any further notice" of what transpired.[7]

Press releases were issued and newspaper ads were purchased informing the public of the inquiry.[8] In response, nearly three dozen groups and individuals applied for intervenor status, including various feminist anti-porn organizations, the Canadian Civil Liberties Association and Canadians for Decency (the majority of them were allowed to make written submissions at the end of the hearing). A judge was interrupted during a party one evening by lawyers seeking a ruling on whether the board was within its rights to ban the publication of Findlay and McKay's names in the media (he decided they weren't entitled to anonymity).[9] The total cost to taxpayers is estimated to be in excess of half a million dollars. How much the store owners, as well as a periodical distributors' group that came to the defence of one of them, have been obliged to spend on legal fees remains unknown.

In October 1994, two of the three people on the board of inquiry decided it couldn't continue hearing the case, but only because of a technicality. By not attempting to negotiate a settlement between the parties prior to turning the matter over to the board, the Human Rights Commission was found to have violated its own guidelines. What's disturbing is that the board unanimously rejected preliminary arguments that the Commission was overstepping its mandate by taking such complaints seriously in the first place.[10]

The Ontario Human Rights Code was established to give people who suffer sexual harassment on the job—or are denied employment, accommodation or goods and services as a result of their race, creed, gender, marital status, disability and so forth—somewhere to turn. Indeed, as one of the board members has conceded, this case isn't your run-of-the-mill human rights matter. Rather, it represents an attempt to "expand the existing jurisprudence to include the concept of a 'poisoned or hostile environment' in the provision of services," and it is "based on a ground not specifically set out in the Code."[11]

In other words, the selling of pornographic magazines in corner stores isn't on the list of behaviours that the Code clearly and expressly forbids. Nor is this a situation in which such behaviour has already been found to be a legitimate human rights issue by earlier boards of inquiry. Rather, this is a test case, in which people are trying to use mechanisms that were intended to address very real, tangible instances of harassment and discrimination (such as a woman being denied a promotion because she refused to sleep with her boss, or someone being denied an apartment because he or she is black) to determine where legal goods can be bought and sold. Moreover, this is a case that has received large amounts of attention at the same time that other, more obviously appropriate human rights complaints continue to be backlogged at the Commission.[12]

The fact that these complaints have been treated with such gravity provides an indication of the thoroughness with which feminist thought has permeated the highest levels of our society. But this matter also demonstrates how well-intentioned activists can, if they're not careful, end up making the world less just rather than more so. What these complaints suggest about feminist ideas regarding politics, insults, discrimination and sex is also deeply troubling.

In this instance, three convenience stores out of an estimated 4,500 retailers of adult material in the province were singled out for a highly stressful, time-consuming and potentially expensive legal ordeal—for no other reason than because they had the misfortune to be located close to where Findlay and McKay live. (A report prepared by the Commission found that there were, indeed, other stores in the area that didn't stock porn, which these women could have frequented instead. The *Toronto Sun* noted that a retailer across the street from one of the three stores "opens earlier, stays open later and sells no skin magazines at all."[13]) Once these women filed their complaints, the vast resources and intimidating authority of the state were arrayed against a few small, law-abiding entrepreneurs. At the time of this writing, nearly eight years after their filing, the saga continues as the Human Rights

Commission, having been unsuccessful in mediating a settlement between the complainants and Four Star Variety, considers whether to call a second board of inquiry.

(As of March 1995, McKay was saying she'd be satisfied if Four Star restricted its sale of pornographic magazines to no more than three titles, while Findlay was insisting that such publications should not be displayed at all but kept "under the counter" so that patrons had to ask for them. Four Star rejected these terms, since such restrictions wouldn't apply to its competitors and afforded no protection against someone filing a future Human Rights complaint over the few remaining publications. The other two stores have now come to some arrangement with the women, but the Human Rights Commission has declined to release details.[14])

Responding on behalf of his parents, the co-owners of Four Star Variety, Peter Kwon calls Findlay and McKay's paperwork one-sided. He alleges that the women went behind the counter without permission, "aggressively seeking the store's vendor permit," behaved rudely and tried to intimidate his mother by threatening to call the police. He says he believes Findlay and McKay are "on a crusade to decide what society should or should not read," something he finds disturbing in a democratic country.[15] While Findlay and McKay weren't required to hire lawyers when they filed their complaint and ran no risk of being hit with a $10,000 fine should the decision go against them, the same cannot be said for the store owners.[16]

What conclusions, though, are those of us who believe there's more than one kind of injustice in the world supposed to draw here? First, two established, middle-class women choose to make a statement about pornography, not to a large milk-store chain but to the working-class proprietors of family-run businesses—all the while refusing to acknowledge that the sale of this material might be a significant factor in whether or not these people earn a living from one month to the next. When that didn't work, the women then took steps to subject the store owners, some of whom have a limited command of the English language, to a bureaucratic nightmare that has stretched on for the better part of a decade. Next, they have the audacity to insist that they themselves have a "right to privacy," that the media shouldn't be allowed to report their names.

In 1993, a Commission lawyer told the board that "the claimants feel that they at this point are on trial for having voiced a complaint," adding that Findlay "and her two children and husband have been shouted out of one of the stores and indeed feels that publication of her name may increase this kind of treatment." Reva Landau, acting on behalf of McKay, said of the psychologist:

> ...my client is in a profession where she deals with
> other people, and the other people she deals with
> might react very negatively to the knowledge that
> she had been involved in this kind of case. I do not
> mean that they will take away their business and
> she will suffer financially, I mean it would create a
> very unpleasant atmosphere.[17]

But who says taking a political stand should be a "pleasant" experience, insulated from all risk, consequence or inconvenience? Changing people's attitudes, or the direction of public policy, shouldn't be easy. Demonstrating against capital punishment or nuclear weapons or for abortion access often isn't "pleasant" either—especially when one is confronted by equally passionate protesters on the other side of the debate. But surely this is the price one pays for having moral convictions.

Findlay and McKay, though, seem to be saying that while they believe pornography is harmful to women, they

should be able to protest it without disturbing the calm of
their own lives. Don't get me wrong. These women deserve
to be protected from criminal behaviour like everyone else.
It would be unacceptable for anyone to assault them, for
example, or to commit vandalism against their property.
But why should they be shielded from the opinions of fellow citizens who disagree with them, or who think their
own actions raise difficult questions? Why should they
think they're entitled to a "pleasant" life when they pre-
meditatively and of their own free will chose to set into
motion a series of events that have caused other people a
great deal of grief?

Surely there were other ways Findlay and McKay could
have protested against pornography. Surely these mom-
and-pop stores have a right to earn a modest living in the
same manner that those across town do without being per-
secuted by governmental bodies that can afford to view the
question of the availability of porn as an intellectual exercise. Surely the discomfort two women feel while being
exposed to little more than the titles of such magazines during the few minutes they're in a store they needn't be shopping at anyway should be balanced against the views of
numerous other customers who regularly purchase porn
there. (Incidentally, in Ontario, a human rights board of
inquiry doesn't enjoy the same far-reaching authority as a
court. Any ruling it makes applies only to the specific store
against which a complaint has been filed. Therefore, in
order to enforce a ban on porn in *all* corner stores in the
province, a complaint against each of the thousands of
individual stores would have to be filed with, and investi-
gated by, the Human Rights Commission. It's difficult to
imagine a more inefficient, costly and ungainly mechanism
than the one Findlay and McKay chose to make use of in
their campaign against porn.)

But just as Findlay and McKay think they have a right

to a "pleasant" time even while they're making other people's lives miserable, underlying their assertion that the
mere presence of porn creates a "hostile" and "negative"
environment is the idea that women have a right to go
through life without ever being offended, insulted or
uncomfortable. Says who?

The first investigator's report prepared by the
Commission observed that some of the adult material being
stocked by these stores was in "bad taste," and added,
"Although many women have come to ignore the magazines in question, those women who acknowledge or examine them, will *probably feel insulted* by at least some of them
[my italics]." In a newspaper opinion column, Landau
(McKay's representative at the hearing) has written:

> The argument is over which is more important:
> the right of men to have quick access in residential
> neighborhoods to magazines that degrade women
> or the right of women to buy milk for themselves
> or their families in the "convenience store" most
> "convenient" to them without being *insulted.*
>
> Men are not *insulted* when they buy milk: Why
> should women be? [my italics][18]

Let's take this one step at a time. First of all, being in
bad taste, or offensive, isn't the same thing as being dis-
criminatory. I personally think much of the marketing of
children's penny candy these days—such as the plastic nose
containing a confection called S.N.O.T.—qualifies as
downright disgusting. But that doesn't mean anyone is
being discriminated against.

Second, who gave Findlay, McKay and Landau the right
to speak for all women? Many women *are* genuinely
offended by the pornographic material available at their
corner store. So, too, are many men. But this is a matter

that doesn't break down neatly along gender lines. Furthermore, some of us are equally offended and insulted by Findlay and McKay's arrogance in claiming that they know what women think about this matter, that they're in a position to pronounce on how women feel. Even those women who consider porn to be offensive can still be opposed to the tactics they've adopted in response.

Third, who says men aren't equally insulted by copies of *Playgirl* when they buy milk at these stores—a publication whose presence on these very same shelves both the complainants and the human rights investigators managed to avoid even mentioning?

Fourth, why should adult magazines be the only things a person might find disturbing? Do vegetarians get to argue that luncheon meat in convenience store coolers creates a hostile shopping environment for them? Do people who are trying to stop smoking, or those struggling with compulsive gambling, get to say they shouldn't be exposed to tobacco and lottery tickets whenever they drop by for a soda pop? Do diabetics get to argue that a large percentage of the items available in your typical corner store pose a very real health hazard (forget poisoned "atmosphere") to them and therefore should be removed? Surely it's obvious where we'll end up once we start down such a path.

Fifth, if these publications are offensive "because of their stereotypical and demeaning depiction of women," why did Findlay and McKay restrict their complaint to sex magazines? I could show you covers of *Cosmopolitan* that are as revealing as many that have appeared on *Playboy*, in addition to being equally stereotypical in their portrayal of women. If we're talking about the casual exposure one gets to such material when lining up at the cash register, why is a copy of *Penthouse* that's mostly hidden behind a barrier worse than the cover of *People* featuring Hollywood actresses falling out of their dresses? (To its credit, the second report prepared by the Human Rights Commission acknowledges this point.[19])

Finally, if the Human Rights Commission is required to respond every time someone feels offended, why not look beyond the corner store? If I were to file a complaint every time I feel something insults my intelligence, the government would be spending a lot of time investigating laundry detergent advertising on television.

We all know it's impossible to please everyone. Since even my closest friends are sometimes appalled by material I consider harmless or even hysterically funny, how much is going to be left over after we all register our gripes with the authorities? This book will undoubtedly offend some people. Should it be kept out of stores and libraries so as not to contribute to a "negative" and "hostile" environment for establishment feminists?

Let's backtrack for a minute to the issue of sex, to the fact that the only magazines Findlay and McKay complained about were publications that, whatever else one might think of them, are honest enough to admit up front that they are about sex. Unlike *Cosmopolitan*, or *Sports Illustrated*'s swimsuit issues, for example, these magazines aren't coy about the fact that they view female bodies as sex objects. What appears to have offended Findlay and McKay, then, wasn't so much *sexism* on the magazine rack but sex itself. They didn't zero in on all kinds of stereotypical portrayals of women, only those appearing in sex magazines. And even then, they didn't target all sex magazines, only those aimed at a predominantly male audience.

Hiding behind the issue of how women as a group presumably feel about porn in their convenience store, therefore, appears to be another matter: feminist hostility toward men and male sexuality. When we think back to Catharine MacKinnon's contention that all heterosexual sex equals rape, and to the fact that mainstream feminism has not taken pains to distance itself from such ideas, these views aren't surprising. MacKinnon's long-time colleague, Andrea Dworkin, is equally hostile. According to Dworkin, intercourse with men is bad for women because:

> It requires an aborting of creativity and strength,
> a refusal of responsibility and freedom: a bitter
> personal death. It means remaining the victim,
> forever annihilating all self-respect.[20]

Elsewhere, Dworkin insists that "intercourse remains a means or the means of physiologically making a woman inferior,"[21] and still elsewhere, she claims that women who enjoy sex with men are "collaborators, more base in their collaboration than other collaborators have ever been, experiencing pleasure in their own inferiority, calling intercourse freedom."[22] Dworkin is known for insisting that marriage is "a legal license to rape" and that, in a situation involving "seduction, the rapist bothers to buy a bottle of wine."[23]

Mainstream North American feminism continues to embrace Dworkin. Despite her offensive views, Ms. has actively solicited and published her work in recent years.[24] And in 1991, when the Canadian Mental Health Association sponsored a conference titled Women in a Violent Society, attended by 1,200 delegates including prosecutors, defence lawyers and social workers, Dworkin was a key-note speaker who received a standing ovation when she entered the hall in Banff, Alberta. Her controversial suggestion on that occasion was that battered wives should kill their abusers since governments and the courts don't seem to be responding effectively to such situations. Michele Landsberg, the Canadian feminist newspaper columnist who used to be one of my heroes, said of Dworkin, commenting on that speech:

> In case you haven't read Dworkin, and have
> accepted the male descriptions of her as crazed
> and dangerous, she is indeed a radical theorist.
> Her searing analyses of sex, porn and violence are
> deeply disturbing and brilliantly argued.
>   You don't have to agree with all her conclusions
> to be galvanized by her.[25]

Well, I don't need to be male, either, to feel uncomfortable when Dworkin, in her book *Pornography: Men Possessing Women*, describes pregnancy thus:

> Pregnancy is confirmation that the woman has
> been fucked: it is confirmation that she is a cunt....
> The display marks her as a whore. Her belly is her
> sex. Her belly is proof that she has been used. Her
> belly is his phallic triumph.

Dworkin continues, saying that doctors have added sex to pregnancy itself, in the form of the caesarean section, which she refers to as "a surgical fuck." A little further along, she says:

> Modern childbirth...comes from the metaphysics
> of male sexual domination; she is a whore, there
> to be used, the uterus of the whore entered directly
> by the new rapist, the surgeon, the vagina saved to
> serve the husband.[26]

I don't have to be male to think of Dworkin as dangerous if feminists who are making decisions about people's lives—in their capacity as lawyers and social workers—are prepared to give her a standing ovation when she walks into a room.

Landsberg insists it isn't necessary to agree with everything Dworkin says. This sounds all very tolerant and admirable. But as we've seen earlier, feminist tolerance turns out to be a rather selective notion. Any movement that is willing to excuse Dworkin her excesses but won't excuse Madonna or Camille Paglia theirs is a movement more interested in covering up for its friends than it is in ensuring moral consistency.

The Ms. "rage" issue contains an entirely positive review of British lesbian Sheila Jeffreys's book, *Anticlimax: A Feminist Perspective on the Sexual Revolution.*[27] Jeffreys, writing with a hostility toward sex, men and male sexuality that equals MacKinnon's and Dworkin's, considers the loosening of conservative notions toward sex that occurred during the 1960s and '70s part of a patriarchal plot to keep women down. In this book, which Ms. calls "remarkable," she takes issue with those who believe that experiencing sexual pleasure with men is a good thing for women. For example, she criticizes the views of two other feminists for applauding middle-class British women in the late nineteenth century who were able to reject the Victorian notion of the pure, asexual woman and achieve orgasms. Jeffreys's characterization of nineteenth-century female middle-class life, the sort of life Rosamond Vincy leads in Eliot's *Middlemarch*, is worth noting. In a 1987 speech, she said:

> These middle-class women were in relationships
> which were unregenerately patriarchal, in which
> men had all the power. These women were probably
> simply being used as spitoons in the act of sexual
> intercourse. Was orgasm in such a situation some-
> thing positive, empowering, something that meant
> resistance to patriarchal oppression?

Jeffreys argued that rather than being feminist pioneers, such women had simply learned to take "'pleasure' in their own subordination." She also declared:

> We have got to understand that sexual response
> for women and orgasm for women is not necessarily
> pleasurable and positive. It can be a very real
> problem. It can be an accommodation of our
> oppression. It can be the eroticizing of our
> subordination. We need to appreciate that the
> word pleasure is often used for what we experience
> as humiliation and betrayal.[28]

The theories of people like MacKinnon, Dworkin and Jeffreys—their belief that male sexuality is, in and of itself, a destructive force that turns women into victims—help explain much current feminist thinking about such issues as sexual harassment and assault. (MacKinnon, it should be noted, made history as a sexual harassment lawyer prior to taking up the anti-porn cause.) The terms "poisoned/negative/hostile environment" associated with the Ontario convenience store porn complaints derive from sexual harassment theory. And while there are many legitimate cases of sexual harassment, it's also true that contemporary feminism has contributed to a situation in which the idea of sexual harassment is being pushed to extremes, in which virtually anything that makes some women feel "uncomfortable" is said to be intolerable discrimination that the authorities must step in and do something about.

These days, charges of sexual harassment aren't limited to instances in which a person is threatened with retribution in a work environment for refusing to perform sexual services, or those in which someone persistently continues to make inappropriate sexual remarks long after they've been told such remarks are unwelcome. Rather, hostile environments are created by photos of wives dressed in bathing suits displayed on men's desks. In 1993 a graduate teaching assistant at the University of Nebraska was compelled to remove such a photo.[29]

Sexual harassment has been alleged when professors discuss nude images in photography courses. In 1993, fine arts professor Don Evans was charged with sexual harassment at Tennessee's Vanderbilt University when a female student complained about his use of such images. The institution has since instructed all professors to warn students about sexually explicit material at the beginning of each course.[30]

Sexual harassment has been seen to occur when professors use examples from the Talmud, the Jewish law book, in class. In 1994, a female student complained about a professor who referred to the story of a man who fell off a roof, landed on a woman and inadvertently had intercourse with her. Although the professor had used this example for thirty years when discussing moral issues such as guilt and responsibility, the Chicago Theological Seminary which employed him responded to the complaint by formally reprimanding him and distributing a memo to every student and faculty member, informing them that he had engaged in sexual harassment.[31]

Sexual harassment takes place when children call each other names and tease one another about body development in schoolyards. During the 1991-92 school year, more than one thousand elementary school kids were suspended or expelled under Minneapolis's Hostile Environment Sexual Harassment Program.[32]

Sexual harassment happens when professors and students feel "uncomfortable" about reproductions of famous paintings in their classrooms. Pennsylvania State University agreed to remove Francisco de Goya's The Nude Maja, in 1992, after an English professor complained that, hanging at the front of her classroom, it embarrassed her and some of her female students. The professor refused the institution's offer to relocate the class, and was only satisfied when the painting was banished from campus altogether.[33]

Sexual harassment is alleged when customers read *Playboy* in diners. In 1991, a California waitress refused to serve a journalist who was doing so on the grounds that his behaviour qualified as sexual harassment in the workplace. As Nadine Strossen, the president of the American Civil Liberties Union, asks in *Defending Pornography*:

> Suppose a customer had been reading a newsletter
> from the National Organization for Women or
> from Planned Parenthood, and the waitress was
> a Catholic who believed that abortion is murder.
> Should she be permitted to deny service to the
> customer on the ground that this reading material
> constituted religious harassment...[34]

Guidelines put in place in order to ensure that everyone has the right to be served in a restaurant regardless of their sex or the colour of their skin are now being manipulated by people who want to use their own rights as an excuse to trample on other people's. If the Ontario convenience stores, for example, had signs on their doors saying "No women allowed," or if male professors on U.S. campuses routinely "joked" that only those female students proficient at oral sex would receive an A, human rights or sexual harassment complaints might well be in order. But rather than ensuring that we all have as many options and opportunities as possible, rather than pursuing "a climate of understanding and mutual respect" (as is the stated intention of Ontario's Human Rights Code), the complainants in these kinds of cases are insisting that their right to feel "comfortable" supersedes other people's rights to free expression and freedom of choice.

Another issue, though, is this: what sort of messages are

being sent by and to women with respect to such complaints? Let me give you another example. I have a friend who is attractive, athletic, blond and friendly—in essence, many men's dream girl. A couple of years ago she attended a staff meeting at the government-run institution where she works. A fellow (male) employee she'd never spoken to before asked her whether she "was as nice as she looked." Afterward, my friend was approached by another (male) staff member who suggested she consider filing a sexual harassment complaint based on this single comment. Being a feminist with a sense of perspective, my friend laughed out loud at such a suggestion and that was the end of the matter. But it might not have been. Had she responded differently, a great deal of official attention and a large stack of paperwork might well have been devoted to investigating a remark that, while perhaps a bit oafish, was a long way from being a misogynous diatribe on the one hand or an overtly sexual threat on the other. Nevertheless, here she was, being urged by a male co-worker to consider herself grievously wounded.

What view of male sexuality are women being encouraged to embrace when the definition of sexual harassment gets pushed to such extremes? How are women supposed to feel about their own hardiness and their chances of success in the wider world when governments declare that the terrible thing known as sexual harassment includes: staring, suggestive looks, sexual remarks, teasing, insults, subtle sexual hints or comments about one's body?[35] What message are we sending young girls when feminists refer to boys who try to lift up skirts in the school yard as "gender terrorists"?[36] Is this how we produce strong, capable women equipped to overcome life's obstacles, or is it how we end up with pampered, helpless whiners? How can people such as Findlay and McKay think they're doing women a favour by suggesting that our sensibilities are so delicate that society has to shield us from porn in our local convenience store? Feminism has spent decades trying to lay to rest the Shrinking Violet and Nervous Nellie stereotypes. We don't need women reviving them again in the name of protecting us from insults. To quote the U.S. group Feminists for Free Expression concerning a similar matter: "It is ironic that just as women are finally making inroads into such male-exclusive venues as handling a skyscraper construction crane, a hostile corporate takeover attempt, and an Air Force fighter plane, we are being told we cannot handle dirty pictures, and certainly that we would never enjoy them."[37]

Paglia has a point when she says that what troubles her "about the 'hostile workplace' category of sexual harassment policy is that women are being returned to their old status of delicate flowers who must be protected from assault by male lechers."[38] When Katie Roiphe talks about the images of "men as hunters and women as hunted" evoked by much of the discussion surrounding sexual harassment, she's touching on the same subject. Concerning the Minnesota seven-year-old whose mother initiated sex harassment charges against boys on her daughter's school bus, Roiphe observes: "The idea of boys as a sexual threat, girls as vulnerable, now takes root early and stubbornly. These are not the facts of life they are learning, but a way of interpreting them."[39]

What we seem to have lost sight of in our urgency to ensure female safety is the ability to make intelligent distinctions. The feminist "continuum theory," which maintains that remarks about a woman's appearance are connected to violent rape, that they are both symptoms of the cancer that is woman-hatred and must be dealt with harshly, is largely responsible for this inability to distinguish minor incidents from major ones. In the words of the Canadian Panel on Violence Against Women, "violence must be understood as a continuum that ranges from verbal insults through physical blows to murder."[40] There may be something to the argument that all of these things are, on some level, connected. As theories go, this one seems relatively straightforward and innocuous. But being *connected* to something is not the same as being *as bad as*. As John Fekete has noted, "[s]team and ice may both be composed of water molecules in a continuum of transformations, but if we lose the distinction between hot and cold" we're likely either to drown or get burned.[41] When people forget this, when they declare that there should be "zero tolerance" for any kind of suspect behaviour (as the Canadian Violence Panel does),[42] relations between males and females are likely to be aggravated rather than improved.

. The tendency to interpret sexual harassment so broadly that anything that makes women uncomfortable becomes an offence is paralleled by our current approach to rape. In 1993, I attended a court case in Toronto in which three thirteen-year-old boys (whose names cannot be published under Canada's Young Offenders Act) were accused of sexual assault, a term that encompasses offences up to and including brutal violence and penetration. On at least one of their trial dates, court documents indicated that this was a case of "gang rape." In reality, however, one of the two female complainants—who were both schoolmates of the accused—alleged that one of the boys had touched her breasts while a number of the young people had been roughhousing. The other complainant alleged that, on a separate occasion, a second boy had grabbed her arm in the school hallway so that the third could *try* to kiss her (everyone agreed he didn't succeed).

After the girls mentioned these incidents to a teacher, they were brought to the attention of the school principal, who advised the girls' parents to report them to the police. Charges were laid. The girls apparently received a certain amount of moral support from their elementary school teachers, some of whom appear to have behaved less than warmly toward the boys. Before the matter wound its way through the court system, the young people graduated from elementary school and began high school, where the social stigma associated with the charges followed the boys. At a certain point, one of the girls complained that the presence of an accused in one of her classes made her uncomfortable. In the interests of treating victims of sexual assault sympathetically, the boy was required to take another course.

Eventually, after five adolescents and five sets of parents had shown up a handful of times in court over a period of months, after the police officer who had laid the charges had spent hour upon hour in court as well, after the young people had all testified, after three legal aid lawyers had made their arguments, the boys were acquitted of all charges by a judge still capable of telling the difference between normal (if arguably objectionable) adolescent behaviour and rape. This costly affair could have been avoided had the teacher, the principal, the girls' parents, the police officer or the prosecutor exercised some discretion and common sense—not one of them did. All of them appear to have been blinded by zero-tolerance thinking. None of them was willing to risk being accused of not taking "sexual assault" seriously. Parents of the boys insist matters could have been resolved if they'd merely been contacted by the school and the boys had been given an opportunity to apologize. Two of the three defence lawyers claim they suggested to the female prosecutor, on several occasions, that the boys be allowed to sign peace bonds that would have brought matters to a speedy conclusion. Independently of one another, however, they told me she'd responded by declaring the young males to be "rapists in training."

It's unclear what kinds of attitudes about sex, women

and rape these three young men will be taking with them into adulthood as a result of this experience, but they may be very different ones from those that feminism might have hoped to instil. Perhaps the fact that the boys were acquitted will, with time, blunt their bitterness and confusion. But should any of them ever be accused of such an offence again, this matter might return to haunt them. Conversely, if either of these two young women—who were encouraged by the adults around them and by the kid-glove treatment they received in the courtroom to consider themselves rape victims—should ever be genuinely and seriously assaulted, they're already going to have a black mark against them. In the eyes of some people, they've already "cried wolf" once.

Surely we can do better than this. Surely we're able to detect the puritanical, reactionary nature of zero-tolerance thinking. Zero tolerance was Ronald Reagan's response to illicit drugs. During the 1980s, the United States increased spending on anti-drug measures by 1,300 percent and, over a twelve-year period (1982-94), the number of people incarcerated in U.S. prisons doubled.[43] Despite this, you'd be hard pressed to find many people who'd say the authorities are any closer to stamping out illegal substances now than they were in the 1970s. Those individuals who have stopped using soft drugs in the interim have likely done so not because they've been genuinely convinced that drugs are morally reprehensible but because it's a safer course of action. In other words, all this coercive state power might have inspired fear but there's little evidence that it has necessarily changed people's attitudes and beliefs.

Zero tolerance says that everyone who smokes marijuana ends up becoming a heroin addict, that people who start off drinking beer will become alcoholics, that every fertilized human egg is an expression of God's will and cannot be interfered with even when a mother's life is in danger. It is an approach to the world that is absolute, inflexible and unforgiving.

Although zero tolerance represents a flawed way of dealing with complex social problems, currently we're tilting more and more in that direction. When Ohio's Antioch College introduced a sexual offence policy in 1992 that requires students to ask for express verbal consent before kissing someone, and before proceeding to the next "level of sexual intimacy" and then to the next, a number of U.S. commentators reacted with ridicule and scorn.[44] Little did they realize that federal sexual assault legislation passed that same year in Canada (after consultations with, among others, Catharine MacKinnon) has enshrined similar ideas into this country's Criminal Code.[45] Dubbed the "no means no" law, this legislation was hailed by feminists but criticized by lawyers, who argued that it's inappropriate to use criminal sanctions to effect changes in sexual etiquette. In the words of one spokesperson for the Canadian Bar Association, "I'm not sure that we want to put people into jail to educate them."[46] The following passage, which appeared in a front page article in *The Globe and Mail* during May 1995, describes matters three years after this law came into force:

> Crown lawyer [prosecutor] Marc Garson likes to tell university students the story of a young man and a woman who were kissing when the man stuck his hand under the woman's shirt and touched her breast.
>
> The woman pushed his hand away and the two eventually parted without further incident. But the woman, a high-school student, told her parents. They reported the man to the police, who charged the man with sexual assault under Canada's no-means-no law of 1992.

> "The defence lawyer was saying, 'This is a
> joke,'" Mr. Garson, an assistant Crown attorney in
> Sudbury, told 50 employees of Ontario university
> residences at a conference this week…
>   But there was no laughter when the man was
> convicted and put on probation.

The piece continues:

> The law means much more than no means no:
> Even without a formal no, tears or physical
> resist-ance, a sexual act may be considered an
> assault. It's up to those who initiate the acts to
> show that they took reasonable steps to determine
> whether the other person consented.[47]

Despite the prominence given to this story, there has
been little public outcry. Few people seem to care that
young Canadian men are being burdened with criminal
records, are facing life with the label of "convicted rapist"
hanging around their necks, for doing things that it's difficult to believe any sane person could view as sexual assault.
Garson, who's only thirty-two himself, isn't perturbed by
this state of affairs. On the contrary, he told the newspaper,
"The government [has done] a tremendous job of finally
offering protection to women."

But at what cost? And how could we have possibly
arrived at this point? How can we be living in a society in
which governments fund pamphlets that advise young men
that if they've ever convinced a woman to have intercourse with them by, among other things, "begging," then
they have "had sex through pressure, coercion or force"
and that this is against the law?[48] Such a notion would be
outrageously funny if real people's lives and reputations
weren't at stake. How is it that, in the 1990s, anti-date-rape

"education" campaigns take as their starting point the notion that while males want sex, females apparently don't? Judging by such literature, women spend all their time being threatened, cajoled and mistreated by men rather than doing any pursuing, initiating or enjoying themselves. Writes Roiphe:

> With titles like "Friends Raping Friends: Could
> It Happen to You?" date-rape pamphlets call
> into question all relationships between men and
> women. Beyond just warning students about rape,
> this movement produces its own images of sexual
> behavior, in which men exert pressure and women
> resist. By defining the dangerous date in these
> terms—with this type of male and this type of
> female, and their different types of expectations—
> these pamphlets promote their own perspective
> on how men and women feel about sex: men are
> lascivious, women are innocent.[49]

Rape is a very serious matter. It's one that I, as a feminist and long-time advocate of female self-defence courses, consider an important women's issue. But laws that transform the most minor sexual misstep into a criminal offence are unjust. Laws that assume that sexual interaction can be sanitized of all ambiguity, misunderstanding, confusion or unpleasantness are the height of foolishness. Laws that take it for granted that men are more likely to be brutes rather than merely awkward, vulnerable, imperfect human beings are morally objectionable.

Such laws, however, are the logical result of much feminist thinking on such issues. In 1988, for example, the Ms. Foundation published a book titled *I Never Called It Rape: The Ms. Report on Recognizing, Fighting and Surviving Date and Acquaintance Rape.* Based on the results of a study of more than six thousand male and female undergraduates on thirty-two U.S. college campuses, the book claims that "[o]ne in four female respondents had had an experience that met the legal definition of rape or attempted rape."[50] This number has since been quoted *ad nauseam* by people who suggest we are in the midst of a date rape epidemic. But there are some disturbing addenda to this statistic that often don't get reported. According to the book:

- "Only 27 percent of the women whose sexual assault met the legal definition of rape thought of themselves as rape victims." (p. 26)
- "42 percent of the women who were raped said they had sex again with the men who assaulted them." (p. 63)

Let's think about this for a minute. The researchers specifically ask 3,187 young women whether they've ever been raped. A small minority of them—less than 3 percent—say "yes." The researchers then reply, in effect, "Ah, but we're smarter than you. What you think happened doesn't count. Although we weren't there, we know better than you what really took place. And, based on other information you've given us, we've decided that four times as many of you—or 10.3 percent—are actually rape victims." (This approach is, of course, contrary to Ms.'s current declaration that "anyone who has experienced something is more expert in it than the experts.")

If I punch my younger brother in the shoulder the next time I see him, I'll technically commit an assault that fits the legal definition of that offence. If he is of a mind to pursue matters, I could be charged and convicted. The point being, therefore, that whether or not something meets the legal definition of rape may not be the best indication of the precise nature of the incident. Despite this, however, the Ms. study chose to disregard the views of the women who were actually present in favour of this strict legal interpretation. Indeed, it wants us to believe that 42 percent of those it classified as rape victims were stupid enough to have sex with their rapist again. In a 1991 letter to the editor of the *Wall Street Journal*, Mary Koss, the study's primary researcher, tried to clarify this incredible notion:

> The observation that 42% of the women had sex again with the man who perpetrated the rape requires explanation. The rape victims in the national study were young, sexually inexperienced women; almost half were virgins at the time of the assault. Thus they lacked familiarity with what consensual intercourse should be like. Even though most of them said "no" repeatedly, tried to reason with the offender, and physically struggled, many victims reacted to the first rape with self-blame and thought that if they tried harder to be clear they could influence the man's behavior. Only after the second rape did they realize that the problem was the man, not themselves. Afterward, 87% of the victims ended the relationship with the man who raped them.[51]

It may well be that many of the men under discussion far exceeded the bounds of civilized behaviour and deserve to be considered rapists, but it's worth observing that Koss's explanation invokes a flagrant double standard. She asks us to believe that these young women were so sexually inexperienced, so lacking in adequate information about what "consensual intercourse should be like," that they didn't even recognize rape when it happened to them. If that's the case, why can't the presumably young, sexually inexperienced men with whom these women were having relations be assumed to be equally ignorant? If a woman can be raped and not realize it, why can a man not commit rape without realizing it? And if this is what's actually going on, what's the point of declaring these men criminals rather than treating them as ill-informed young people in desperate need of education? Criminals they become, however, when incidents that might have been written off as bad sexual experiences get reclassified as rape, when women who "never called it rape" begin doing so at Ms.'s urging.

A further demonstration of the way our definitions of sexual assault have been stretched almost beyond recognition was provided by the lap-dancing controversy that raged in Toronto during the summer of 1995. While strip clubs featuring female dancers used to have "no touching" policies enforced by bouncers, in recent years the market has changed. The clientele of such establishments apparently lost interest in stage shows and table dancers once they were offered the option of having performers dance literally on their laps—the nominal price per song seemingly negotiable according to just what the customer was willing to pay for the privilege of touching. Those women who were willing to take off their clothes for a living but weren't prepared to permit strange men to grope them were understandably upset. They took their complaints to the media and soon municipal politicians jumped into the fray, eventually passing a by-law banning lap-dancing. Whether or not you believe it's appropriate to legislate sexual behaviour between consenting adults is a separate issue. For the purposes of this discussion, what's significant is that Jack Layton, one of the municipal councillors opposed to lap-dancing—and a long-time campaigner against male violence—publicly declared that dancers who were unhappy about doing such work were being *sexually assaulted*.[52]

According to this argument, it didn't matter that these

women were showing up for work of their own accord rather than finding another job. It didn't matter that they were approaching customers, performing certain services and accepting money in exchange. It didn't matter that they were spending that money and, the next day, returning to work again. Rather than being viewed as adults who had made conscious, if difficult, decisions about whether or not to abandon the lucrative sex industry when their job description changed, male politicians on white horses were insisting these women were damsels in distress who were being raped.

It does no one any good to trivialize real rape in such a manner. Indeed, it could be argued that hyperbole of this sort could eventually contribute to a situation in which the public reacts with automatic suspicion, rather than support, to sexual assault allegations. But there's yet an additional reason to be concerned. In order for there to be a sexual assault, there has to be an assailant. If going into a club, giving a woman ten dollars and caressing her breasts while she dances for you makes you a rapist, surely men have reason to feel both confused and defensive about such matters.

Yet another aspect of our current situation is the business of lies. This applies both to anti-date-rape dogma as well as to the notion that women don't lie about sexual assault. One of the most popular slogans in recent years is the one that maintains that "No means no." If only this were the case. In 1990, Paglia raised hackles when she declared:

> ...[contemporary feminism] has shut itself off from [Freud's] ideas of ambiguity, contradiction, conflict, ambivalence. Its simplistic psychology is illustrated by the new cliché of the date-rape furor: "'No' always means 'no.'" Will we ever graduate from the Girl Scouts? "No" has always been, and always will

be, part of the dangerous, alluring courtship ritual
of sex and seduction...[53]

In Vancouver, a judge found himself picketed by angry feminists in 1991 when he observed, in the context of acquit-
ting a man of sexual assault, that "at times 'no' may mean
'maybe' or 'wait awhile.'"[54]

Such views are, of course, regarded as heresy by the contemporary women's movement. In a chapter addressed to
men, *I Never Called It Rape* tells us:

> "No" means "no." Forget all the times your friends
> told you that all women say "no" when they mean
> "yes." It's not true.
>
> When a woman says "no" that means "no."
> Stop. She does not want to go further. Do not try
> to cajole her or argue with her. And do not ignore
> her...
>
> If a woman says "no" and really means "yes, but
> you have to convince me," then you don't want to
> be with her anyway. She's playing a game and it's
> a game that nobody wins. Forget about "losing an
> opportunity." Just walk away.[55]

The book deserves credit for its willingness to include this
last paragraph. And, in fairness, the chapter addressed
specifically to women tells them that they must clearly
communicate with their sexual partners since "most men
are not psychic," and further advises them: "When you say
'no,' be sure that you mean 'no.'" Yet female readers aren't
explicitly informed that it's dishonest and dangerous to
"play games" with men.[56] Pamphlets about date rape routinely tell men it's a "myth that women say 'no' when they
really mean 'yes.'" I've yet to see one aimed at women,
however, that urges them to speak up about flaky female

behaviour that contributes to such beliefs.[57]

Let there be no mistake. Any man who doesn't take "no" for an answer is playing with fire and shouldn't be surprised to find himself hauled into court. There are a great many women who, when they say "no," do indeed mean it. But few people living in the real world can deny that human beings don't always say what's exactly on their minds. Because they're often in a position of power when it comes to sex, many women expect the guy to work for it. This can take the form of requiring him to say the things she wants to hear—such as telling her she's attractive, that he's missed her, that he loves her, that she turns him on, that he really really needs her and so forth. Furthermore, people do change their minds. If a woman is entitled to withdraw her "yes," to back out of a sexual situation that's suddenly become too weird, for instance, why should she not also have the right to say "yes" after she's already said "no"? When this happens, the man who has stuck around learns that, feminist dogma to the contrary, "no" can, in fact, mean "wait awhile."

Then there's the notion, touched on earlier in this book, that women don't lie about being raped. In this vein, *I Never Called It Rape* tells us:

> In acquaintance rapes, it is especially likely that
> myths about rape and the continuing belief that
> women lie about rape to "punish" men for broken
> relationships or [to] win attention for themselves
> greatly influence police decisions to declare some
> cases "unfounded." Although better education
> about rape is changing these attitudes, old ideas
> still die hard.[58]

In 1991, Michele Landsberg declared in one of her *Toronto Star* columns that "[w]omen don't falsely report rape, precisely because the courts are so relentlessly biased and the trial process so grueling."[59] If only this were true.

Two of my female friends are criminal lawyers practising in downtown Toronto. They're also feminists who have no sympathy for real rapists. But they both routinely represent clients who are falsely accused of sexual assault by girl-friends trying to get back at them after relationships break down. Rikki Klieman is a U.S. attorney who prosecuted rape and other sex crimes during the 1970s. In 1983, *Time* magazine named her one of the country's top five female trial lawyers. Currently, she spends much of her profes-sional life defending men she feels have been falsely accused of rape.[60] No amount of official feminist naysaying can change the fact that these women have encountered false rape allegations first-hand. They know these cases exist. The rest of us can bury our heads in the sand, or we can acknowledge that, often, the real world isn't the way we'd like it to be.

According to Statistics Canada, 14 percent of sexual assault complaints in this country are classified as unfounded by police.[61] That's one in seven. How many of the allegations that make it to court end in acquittal—not because the justice system is sexist but because it seems clear the complainant is lying—is unknown. Incidentally, only 8 percent (one in twelve) of non-sexual assaults are classed as unfounded by the police, thus contradicting the notion that there's no difference between the rate of false allegations associated with sexual assault versus other kinds of crimes.

In 1994, researcher Eugene Kanin published the results of a study of false rape allegations reported to a single police agency in a small midwestern U.S. community between 1978 and 1987. He cautions that his study involves only forty-five cases and so cannot be accurately extrapolated to other populations. (He also notes, however, that "nothing peculiar exists about this city's population composition to suggest that an unusual incidence or patterning of false rape allegations would occur.") At any rate, it's worth observing that, over this nine-year period, a full 41 percent of the forcible rapes reported to police were classified as false after each of these complainants later admitted that she'd lied. Luckily for the men involved: "These women were not inclined to put up a steadfast defense of their victimization, let alone pursue it into the courtroom. Recantation overwhelmingly came early and relatively easily." Reads the report a few lines later:

> We know that false convictions occur, but this study only tells us that these false accusers were weeded out during the early stages of investigation. However encouraging this result may be, we cannot claim that false charging does not incur suffering for the accused. Merely to be a rape suspect, even for a day or two, translates into psychological and social trauma.[62]

Kanin found that over half these women lied about being raped because they needed "to provide a plausible explanation for some suddenly foreseen, unfortunate consequence of a consensual encounter, usually sexual, with a male acquaintance." For example, the wife of a man who'd had a vasectomy was worried that she might become pregnant by her lover when his condom broke, and therefore fabricated a tale of being raped. A further 27 percent of the complainants brought false rape charges out of revenge—because they were rejected by men, either initially or afterwards, following a relationship with them. Another 18 percent made up stories about being raped in order to get attention.[63] While these findings should be taken with a grain of salt, they suggest that when feminism tries to say that women never lie about rape, it is merely attempting to replace old patriarchal stereotypes ("a woman can run faster with her skirt up than a man can with his trousers down") with equally flawed feminist ones. This isn't progress.

I fervently believe that we should strive for a world in which women are able to live their lives without being sexually harassed by their supervisors, bosses, superintendents and professors. I believe women should live free of the threat and fear of sexual assault—from strangers, acquaintances, relatives, roommates, dates and spouses. But I also believe women are a lot tougher and more capable of standing on their own two feet than contemporary feminism gives them credit for. It disturbs me that female self-defence training as a regular part of high school physical education programs is such a hard sell among, of all people, feminists. Instead, feminism often seems to take the approach that it's everyone else's responsibility—men, business, government—to fix things, to protect us. In 1992, one of my newspaper columns pointed out that while a recent federal government report had advocated media literacy training in schools in order to combat violence against women, it made no mention of self-defence instruction. In response, a letter to the editor declared that "[w]omen are fed up with being blamed for being attacked"; its female author claimed that this was exactly what I was doing by arguing that women "are responsible for the prevention of violence perpetrated against" them.[64] According to such reasoning, however, none of us should bother applying sunblock, either, since it's industry and government that are responsible for the depletion of the ozone layer. But who ends up on the operating table with skin cancer?

I don't think we women should be encouraging each other to run to the authorities every time we see or hear something that offends us. I think we should learn to tell the difference between real cases of sexual harassment and rape on the one hand and crude, oafish and insensitive behaviour on the other. Moreover, if the choice is between the dainty, spineless creatures that much of contemporary feminism seems to suggest women are and the assertive self-reliance advocated by some of the dissident feminists... well, there's just no contest. Writes Roiphe:

> Instead of learning that men have no right to do these terrible things to us, we should be learning to deal with individuals with strength and confidence. If someone bothers us, we should be able to put him in his place without crying into our pillow or screaming for help or counseling. If someone stares at us, or talks dirty, or charges neutral conversation with sexual innuendo, we should not be pushed to the verge of a nervous breakdown.[65]

Adds Paglia:

> A male student makes a vulgar remark about your breasts? Don't slink off to whimper and simper with other campus shrinking violets. Deal with it. On the spot. Say, "Shut up, you jerk! And crawl back to the barnyard where you belong!" In general, women who project this take-charge attitude toward life get harassed less often.[66]

It is imperative that our society take a hard look at where establishment feminism is now leading us. This task can't be left in the hands of experts or academics. This isn't a debate about obscure, arcane points of law or theory. Rather, these issues matter to flesh-and-blood people in the flesh-and-blood world.

The women's movement has been responsible for a

great deal of positive, reasonable, sensible change, but that doesn't alter the fact that shoddy feminist thinking is now adversely affecting real human lives. Women, as well as men, are being accused of cannibalism by daughters who—with the aid of feminist therapists—have come to believe they were ritually abused while still in diapers. Women, as well as men, are having their reputations smeared by feminists who think nothing of calling those with whom they disagree sexists, racists, homophobes and right-wingers. Women, as well as men, are affected when young males take their own lives at alarming rates and older ones die younger than their spouses (these men are, after all, women's sons, husbands, fathers, brothers and friends). Women, as well as men, are affected when our society encourages females to see themselves as besieged victims-waiting-to-happen. Women, as well as men, lose when frank discussions about female sexuality are discouraged. Women, as well as men, have their lives turned upside down when a family member is charged with sexual assault for *trying* to kiss someone.

Mainstream North American feminism has gone badly off the rails. It's time that honest, decent people started saying so.

We have fallen into the belief that morality can be ascribed to groups. But groups cannot be moral or immoral: "women" are not more or less moral than "men".... Morality is an attribute only of persons. Individuals can suffer because of the group they are perceived to belong to, and they can benefit by identifying consciously with a group, but no one is a better person simply by virtue of belonging to a group. Groups are essentially imaginary. Souls are real, and they can be saved, or lost, only one at a time.

–*Louis Menand*[1]

The Western world is full of people who've been through this experience of being, when young, a member of a group of raving bigots and lunatics, and have emerged from it.

–*Doris Lessing*[2]

Epilogue: Approaching Tomorrow

When my mother was born in 1945, the year World War II ended, women had held the right to vote in Canadian federal elections for fewer than three decades. It had been only five years since women living in Quebec were permitted to cast ballots at provincial polls, and seventeen since the Supreme Court had declared that women weren't "persons" and so could not be appointed to the Senate. (This ruling was overturned by the British government the following year.)

When my mother was six years old, Canada elected its first female mayor. My mother was ten before women were no longer required to quit their federal public service jobs when they got married, and twelve before the first female federal cabinet minister was chosen. As a young woman, my mother had never heard of rape crisis centres or battered women's shelters, because none existed then. If she had gone to university she would have encountered male professors who felt free to tell overtly sexist jokes in class, and who declared certain essay topics "too difficult" for female students to attempt.[3] During job interviews, she would have been advised that, since she wasn't a male with a family to support, she had less chance of being hired. Were she a "stewardess," she would have known that she was expected to resign at age thirty-two, since youth was considered a necessary employment qualification.

In 1969, when this country's Criminal Code was amended so that it was no longer illegal to disseminate information about birth control, my mother was twenty-four years old and had already delivered two children. She was twenty-seven, and I was nine, before another amendment ensured that women couldn't be disqualified from jury duty in criminal cases due to their sex. When I was eleven the Royal Canadian Mounted Police accepted its first female officer, and when I was fifteen Air Canada hired its first female pilot. It was only when I was nineteen that the Supreme Court acquired its first woman judge. In the United States, there has yet to be a female president or vice-president.[4]

From a historical perspective, then, the idea that women are men's intellectual and political equals is still a recent one. Within the lifetimes of people who are currently in their eighties, women won not only the vote but everything else that came afterwards. Seen against a backdrop of thousands of years of human history, the changes that have occurred in these few brief decades are nothing short of astonishing. It's time we acknowledged that they are also a testament to the good faith and goodwill of men.

In the face of contemporary feminism's anger, self-obsession, extremism and arrogance, it's easy to forget that women of my generation wouldn't be enjoying the wide range of opportunities we now take for granted if older white males had been strongly opposed to such an idea. It's easy to forget that it was *male* politicians, elected solely by *male* voters, who extended the franchise to women. If most men early in this century had viewed their wives and daughters as hopelessly inferior beings, if most men had considered females to be merely sex objects and baby machines, if the vast majority of men had been truly unwilling to share political power, we'd be living in a very different society right now.

It might well be a society in which information about birth control would still be illegal and where females, rather than being professors, politicians and doctors, would be treated the way they often are in historical romance novels—as domestic possessions expected to be "constantly and immediately [sexually] accessible."[5] Considering that men wielded all the political and most of the economic power until recently, and that they tend to be physically larger and stronger than women, if feminists such as Catharine MacKinnon are correct about most men's propensity to sexually exploit women, there's little reason why North American females wouldn't currently hold a status far closer to that of slaves.

It's time we started asking a few obvious questions. If men are primarily violent brutes who believe they have a right to hurt and control women, why aren't females still considered the legal property of men? Why aren't there laws that confine women to their homes? Why aren't there others that make it impossible for women to work, drive cars or even talk on the telephone to each other? Alternatively, why aren't there rules that say all of the dirtiest, most dangerous jobs in society must be performed by women? If men are really waging an "unremitting war" against women, as Marilyn French insists, why would *male*-dominated legislatures have passed laws against such things as wife battering? Let's be blunt, here. When males conduct real wars they kill hundreds of thousands of their opponents in rather short periods of time, often treating the prisoners with shocking barbarity. If North American men were really waging war on women, they wouldn't be messing around with cutting funds to rape crisis centres. There are far more efficient ways to accomplish such an objective.

The fact that we live in a vastly different society suggests that, despite the very real sadism and violence of some men, most have been far more interested in doing the right thing than in jealously guarding or expanding male privilege. Without denying all the legitimate criticisms of male-dominated thinking, it should also be acknowledged that ideas such as equality, justice, reason and fair play are also the product of this system of thought. It was these ideas that inspired men to give women voting and other rights when they need not have done so. I don't mean, here, to denigrate the contribution of women such as the suffragettes, but merely to point out that had men not been willing to listen to reason, had they refused to be persuaded by appeals to their sense of justice, the struggle for the female vote might still be going on today. It's worth remembering that, despite widespread lobbying and organizing, it required a protracted and bloody civil war before black slavery was abolished in the United States, before some men were willing to give up those particular powers and privileges.

One of the biggest mistakes of feminism has been the systematic belabouring of the worst-case scenario while at the same time routinely discounting the best case. A visitor from another planet whose information came from feminist sources might be forgiven for thinking that the "average man" was a rapist, child molester or wife abuser. This is because the women's movement is often silent about the hundreds of thousands of volunteer firemen who regularly put their brawn and their courage at the service of the community, about the men who've gone out of their way to mentor female employees, and about the male doctors who often still live with great personal risk because they perform abortions. When such men are acknowledged by feminists, they get credit for being good human beings, not good *men*.

Yes, males have traditionally been associated with qualities such as aggression, but we've forgotten that they have also been associated with ideas such as honour. A real gentleman was expected to keep his word, for example, because the knowledge that he had conducted himself honourably was one of the things that mattered most to him. Among the many definitions my dictionary gives for honour is the one that reads: "a strong sense of what is right; keen moral judgment." Honour is about doing the moral thing, even when it may be to your own disadvantage. A handful of the older white males I have had the pleasure of meeting over the past few years have practically exuded this quality. Among them have been lawyers, journalists, a judge and a doctor—in other words, men of some power and influence. These are the kinds of men who were responsible for the passage of human rights codes, laws against child abuse, the establishment of social assistance programs for the needy and (in Canada) the outlawing of the death penalty. These are the men who, for all their blemishes, are largely responsible for the kind of society we live in today. Although far from perfect, it remains the envy of most other parts of the world.

While feminism has overlooked the notion of honour in its discussion of the traditional male, in truth this is a quality more of us would do well to cultivate. In 1987, calling for a return of what she considered an earlier, more pure stage of the women's movement (one uncontaminated by the presence of "liberals"), Catharine MacKinnon declared: "This was a movement that took women's side in everything. Of everything, it asked the question: 'Is it good for women?'"[6]

Is it good for women? That is the standard that many feminists now use to assess ideas. That is the question they apparently deem most worth asking. Not: Is it just? Not: Does it treat human beings who don't happen to be female unfairly or cruelly? Not: Is it morally defensible? If men at the turn of the century had considered *Is it good for men?* the primary question, MacKinnon wouldn't be a lawyer today. If our male-dominated legislatures were currently making decisions according to what was good for men, there's no way on earth MacKinnon would be permitted to teach or speak at publicly funded institutions, to publish books or to influence legal history.

A system of thought that is based on consistently taking the side of a particular group of citizens at the expense of others is one that begins to approach totalitarianism. Such thinking is symptomatic of people who believe that the current situation is so grim, and that our institutions are so tainted and corrupt, that everything must be rebuilt from the ground up if the group it cares about is to be treated better. Says MacKinnon:

> ...this movement believed in change. It intended
> to transform language, community, the life of the
> spirit and the body and the mind, the definition
> of physicality and intelligence, the meaning of
> left and right, right and wrong, and the shape and
> nature of power.
> It was not all roses, this movement we had.
> But it did mean to change the face of the earth.[7]

Anyone who thinks I'm overreacting by calling attention to the similarities between what is considered acceptable mainstream feminist thought and other grandiose schemes that started out intending to build a better world but ended up slaughtering millions of human beings and confining

critics to death camps, prisons and insane asylums is invited
to ponder another of MacKinnon's remarks on this occasion. Speaking to the more than eight hundred individuals
assembled at the New York University Law School, she
began her closing paragraph by drawing a deadly parallel:
"there are more people at this conference than it took
Bolsheviks to topple the czar,"[8] she told them.

According to contemporary North American feminism
men, "especially straight white ones, live in a gender-neutral universe" which "is a lot better than the sex-specific
universe women live in."[9] If this book accomplishes nothing else, I hope it has succeeded in demonstrating that this
is utter nonsense. If men inhabited a gender-neutral universe, they wouldn't find themselves arrested or assaulted
for wearing clothing that women wear freely. Rather, there
are still large tracts of emotional territory and self-expres-
sion that are largely forbidden to men in our society *because
they are male*. If men's lives were "a lot better" than
women's, they wouldn't be killing themselves at four times
the rate of females overall, and dying seven years younger
than their wives, on average. They wouldn't be the majority of the homeless, the majority of those in prison and the
majority of murder victims.

As I've argued earlier, this isn't a contest. It's childish to
waste time and energy arguing about which sex is worse off.
Just because water can take the form of a placid, silent
pond doesn't mean it can't also take the form of a flowing,
gurgling stream. Just because women have been disadvantaged by long-standing stereotypes about female inferiority,
weakness and over-emotionalism doesn't mean that males
haven't been damaged and scarred by the sex role to which
they've been expected to conform. This isn't a case of
either/or. Both can be, and are, true at the same time.

Like the princess in the fairy tale, many feminists have
merely exchanged one limited way of looking at the world

for another. We've rejected one brand of dogma (men are the ultimate example of everything admirable) only to adopt a new one (men are brutish swine). In other words, feminists have made more than a few mistakes. Surely, though, we're adult enough, surely the women's movement is mature enough, that we can acknowledge our errors and move on.

A century ago, it may have made a certain amount of sense to split society along clear gender lines. Biology should not be destiny, but one has to admit that, at times, practical considerations have been difficult to ignore. When much paid work required the application of physical strength, when reliable birth control was non-existent and since only women have babies and breastfeed, sending men out to work in the wider world while expecting women to maintain the home made a certain amount of sense.

Over the past several decades, though, justifying old-fashioned gender roles has become more difficult. Feminism has done a good job of challenging those roles from a female perspective, of arguing that many of the restrictions placed on women were unreasonable and unjust. Some parts of the emerging men's movement have now begun to re-examine the old roles from a male perspective. Men have begun to demand good reasons for our society's insistence on such things as clothing taboos. They've begun to ask why women are free to choose between paid work and staying at home with the children, while men are supposed to continue bringing home the bacon.

This process of re-examination is an absolutely necessary next step. The old feminist analysis of sex roles was a good start, but it's no longer adequate. Instead, it's time for us to acknowledge that there are other legitimate perspectives, and that no single theory can account for everything. It's time we stopped obsessing about "women's rights" and started thinking more broadly—about "gender issues," about how both girls *and* boys are short-changed by the process that begins in the nursery with pink and blue colour coding.

We also need to learn to lighten up a little. Rather than reacting in predictable, knee-jerk ways, we need to remember to bite our tongues once in a while, to try harder to be more patient with and charitable toward one another, to give each other the benefit of the doubt more often. We need to make sincere efforts to understand other people's point of view.

We also have to beware of merely getting stuck at yet another window, of seeing evidence of sex bias—whether against women or men—everywhere we look. My brother's fiancée used to waitress at a major Toronto hotel. One day, she sat a female customer at a particular table in the dining room in an effort to ensure that each of her co-workers had approximately the same number of patrons to attend to. The next time she walked by, she was waylaid by the unhappy woman who was sure she'd only been shown to this table (which was closer to the door than some others) because she was female. On another occasion, my brother's fiancée was obliged to inform a male diner that the Eggs Benedict he'd ordered for breakfast were no longer available; it was late in the morning and the kitchen had run out of hollandaise sauce. The man responded by declaring that he was certain that if he were a woman, she'd be making more of an effort to bring him what he wanted. In truth, gender had nothing to do with either of these situations, but that didn't stop both these diners from convincing themselves otherwise.

With the new century fast approaching, this is an opportune time to end the accusations, the finger-pointing and the mud-slinging between men and women, to declare an armistice, if you will. Our sojourn on this earth is too brief to permit it to become twisted by feminist theories that appear to have far less to do with living, breathing human beings than with stereotype and caricature. Vaclav Havel, the renowned Czechoslovakian playwright who, under the dark days of communism, spent nearly five years in prison for daring to say that there were other ways of looking at the world than the government-sanctioned one, has long warned of the danger of political jargon and theory being used to prevent us from seeing life as it is. In 1965, he began a speech titled "Evasive Thinking" by talking about how parts of a decaying building had come loose and fallen on the head of a pedestrian, killing her. He spoke of how a certain journalist had attempted to deflect public concern over this event by suggesting that there were larger, more important issues—such as the prospects of mankind—worthy of people's attention.

But then a second incident occurred, and another person was killed. In Havel's words:

> As it had done many times before, the public again
> showed more intelligence and humanity than the
> writer, for it had understood that the so-called
> prospects of mankind are nothing but an empty
> platitude if they distract us from our particular
> worry about who might be killed by a third window
> ledge, and what will happen should it fall on a
> group of nursery-school children out for a walk.[10]

A little further on, Havel spoke specifically about the danger of allowing politically charged language to obscure clear thinking:

> We need only to use the magic word "dispropor-
> tion," and something unforgivably half-baked is
> suddenly not only excused but may even be raised
> to the level of an historical necessity. Sadism need

only be cloaked in the grandiose notion of
[responding to] an "offense against socialist
legality" and suddenly it ceases to appear to us
in such an evil light. It's enough to call a fallen
window a "local matter," and criticism of the way
buildings are maintained "municipal criticism"
and we immediately feel that nothing so terrible
has happened.[11]

We in North America are currently at great risk of
allowing words and terms such as "patriarchy," "male privilege," "female oppression," "male supremacy," "the exploitation of women" and "equality" to blind us in precisely the
manner Havel describes. Just because women remain "disproportionately" represented in some areas of our society
doesn't mean that everything we might do in the name of
alleviating that situation is sensible. Just because someone
claims that a certain policy, law or protest action is in the
interests of "female equality" doesn't make it so. Sexual
assault laws designed to protect women that have the effect
of leaving young men with criminal records for innocuous
behaviour are still evil—no matter how much people want
to blather on about the larger issue of patriarchy.

We have to see past words and phrases that, while they
may be well-intentioned, serve to distract us from real people, real suffering—real life. We need to remember that
there is a crucial difference between a feminism that
informs one's opinions and a feminism that *dictates* how one
should think. There's nothing wrong with habitually considering the implications of certain questions from a
"female" perspective, but when we start to view feminism
not just as a valid point of view but as the decisive one that
supersedes all others, we cross over the line into fanaticism.

I fervently believe women and men are going to find
their way back to one another, that relations between the

sexes are going to improve. I believe that, by the time the new century arrives, we may be ready to make a fresh start. Partly this is because I'm an optimist at heart, but it's also because I've already witnessed a miracle.

In 1986, my husband and I billeted a feminist who'd come to town to deliver a speech. Her name was Tatyana Mamonova and, seven years earlier, she and three others had been exiled from the Soviet Union for their work on an underground women's publication. Mamonova is also a painter. During the few days she spent with us, she put the finishing touches on a watercolour that will always have a proud place in our home. The painting is of two larger-than-life people, a man and woman, with their hands inter-twined. The woman represents the East and the man the West, and they have each planted one of their feet on the opposite side of the Berlin Wall.

When Mamonova completed this work in 1986, the thought that the wall might come tumbling down, that the great city might be whole again, that people might be able to cross from East to West without being machine-gunned to death by their own government, was an impossible dream. Not in our wildest fantasies did we imagine that, three short years later, it would actually happen.

But it did. Unbelievably, practically overnight, the Cold War was no more.

Now it's time to put an end to the hostilities between men and women. It's time to restore reason, compassion and tolerance to gender relations.

Notes

Introduction

1 "Best cure for violence could be self-defence," *Toronto Star*, 6 Dec. 1993, p. A17; "Schools should teach girls to stop being passive," *Toronto Star*, 12 May 1992, p. A19; "Female self-defence training in Canadian schools," *Canadian Woman Studies*, Spring 1992, pp. 103-105 and "Lines of defence: the martial art for women has arrived in high schools to show teen-agers they're far from helpless," *Globe and Mail*, 7 March 1992, p. D3.

2 Private telephone conversation with the Canadian Centre for Justice Statistics, Ottawa. Numbers from the Revised Uniform Crime Reporting Survey, based on 111 Canadian police forces in 1994 (representing one-third of the police caseload in the country). Men under the age of twenty-six represent one-third of those accused of sexual assault, while those between the ages twenty-six and forty account for approximately another third, for a total of about 70 percent. This pattern is even more pronounced with respect to violent crime in general. Males up to age forty are accused in 80 percent of all violent crime.

3 David W. Moore and Alec Gallup, "Are Women More Sexist Than Men?" *The Gallup Poll Monthly*, Sept. 1993, pp. 20-21.

4 Lindsy Van Gelder, "The Truth About Bra-Burners," *Ms.*, Sept.-Oct. 1992, p. 81.

5 Associated Press, "Prom 'queen' joke gets student arrested," *Toronto Star*, 3 May 1993, p. A2.

6 D. Laframboise, "Real men don't have to wear a suit and tie," *Toronto Star*, 14 Nov. 1994, p. A21; Julie MacLellan, "Students don't skirt issue: offer support for beaten teen," *Barrie Examiner*, 4 Nov. 1994; "Two arrested after attack on teen taunted over kilt," *Toronto Star*, 25 Oct.

1994, p. A24; John Ryan, "Beaten teen an innocent victim, friends say," *Barrie Examiner*, 25 Oct. 1994; John Ryan, "Youth beaten for wearing kilt," *Barrie Examiner*, 24 Oct. 1994.

Chapter One

1 Doris Lessing, *Prisons We Choose to Live Inside* (Toronto: CBC Enterprises, 1986), p. 45.

2 Ann Landers, appearing in *The Toronto Star*. ST. LOUIS: 19 Jan. 1995, p. C8. SYD: 24 Dec. 1994, p. H9. CHINO: 5 Sept. 1994, p. E2. PEGGY and LOVE: 9 Sept. 1994.

3 Ann Landers, appearing in *The Toronto Star*. Alcoholic and philandering: 10 Nov. 1994, p. F2. Golf: 17 Mar. 1995, p. D3. Timid 39-year-old: 4 July 1994, p. C2. Wife batterers: 4 Sept. 1994, p. B3 and 16 Oct. 1994, p. F2. Acquaintance rape: 14 Aug. 1994, p. B3.

4 Ann Landers, appearing in *The Toronto Star*. Random kindness: 29 May 1995, p. D2. Teacher: 24 May 1995, p. E8. Loving mothers: 8 May 1994, p. B4. Ex-wife: 10 May 1995, p. C6. Grandmother: 16 Sept. 1995, p. C2. Soap operas: 15 Aug. 1994, p. E2. Credit cards: 13 Oct. 1994, p. C2. Snoops: 7 Apr. 1995, p. B2.

5 Ann Landers, appearing in *The Montreal Gazette*. Skinny dipping: 31 Aug. 1994, p. C6 and 1 Sept. 1994, p. C7. Ann Landers, appearing in *The Toronto Star*. GAINESVILLE: 24 Jan. 1995, p. C2. TOO MUCH: 20 May 1994, p. D3.

6 Laura Hamilton, "Making feminism's message clear," *Globe and Mail*, 12 Feb. 1992, p. A14.

7 Marilyn French, *The War Against Women* (New York: Ballantine Books, 1992), pp. 19 and 118.

8 Ibid., pp. 21, 26 and 136.

9 Ibid., p. 175.

10 Ibid., pp. 14, 21-22, 105, 182-83.

11 Ibid., p. 182.

12 Ibid., pp. 35 and 75.

13 Ibid., pp. 44, 181 and 199.

14 Ibid., pp. 139-40 and 175-76.

15 Ibid., pp. 113-14.

16 Ibid., p. 86.

17 Ibid., p. 197.

18 "Bookwatch," *Ms.*, May-June 1992, p. 73 and "Where do we stand on pornography?" (cover story), *Ms.*, Jan.-Feb. 1994, pp. 32-45. See also *Ms.*, Jan.-Feb. 1993, p. 24 and Jan.-Feb. 1994, p. 73.

19 Nancy Pollak, "Business as Usual," *Ms.*, May-June 1995, pp. 11 and 15.

20 Nadine Strossen, *Defending Pornography: Free Speech, Sex, and the Fight for Women's Rights* (New York: Scribner, 1995), p. 77.

21 Fred Strebeigh, "Defining Law on the Feminist Frontier," *New York Times Magazine* (cover story), 6 Oct. 1991.

22 Rene Denfeld, *The New Victorians: A Young Woman's Response to the Old Feminist Order* (New York: Warner Books, 1995), pp. 8, 101 and 104. Warren Farrell, *The Myth of Male Power: Why men are the disposable sex* (New York: Simon & Schuster, 1993), p. 316. Harry Stein, Interview with Christina Hoff Sommers, *Penthouse*, Jan. 1995, p. 74.

23 Rene Denfeld, *The New Victorians* (New York: Warner Books, 1995), pp. 12, 78, 100 and 238.

24 Ibid., pp. 9-10 and Karen Lehrman, "Off Course" (cover story), *Mother Jones*, Sept.-Oct. 1993.

25 For instance, see: *Ms.*, Jan.-Feb. 1992, pp. 70 and 86; July-Aug. 1992, pp. 29 and 64; May-June 1993, p. 10; Jan.-Feb. 1994, pp. 32-45; and Nov.-Dec. 1994, p. 75.

26 Kathleen Barry, "Deconstructing Deconstructionism," *Ms.*, Jan.-Feb. 1991, p. 84.

27 Naomi Wolf, *The Beauty Myth* (Toronto: Vintage Books, 1990), pp. 50, 57, 137 and 302.

28 Rene Denfeld, *The New Victorians* (New York: Warner Books, 1995), p. 241. See also pp. 91, 97-98, 106-07, 110, 115 and 120-21.

29 Catharine A. MacKinnon, *Toward a Feminist Theory of the State* (Cambridge, Massachusetts: Harvard University Press, 1989), p. 146.

30 Catharine A. MacKinnon, "Feminism, Marxism, Method, and the State: Toward feminist jurisprudence," *Feminism and Methodology*, Sandra Harding, ed. (Bloomington, Indiana: Indiana University Press, 1987), p. 142.

31 Catharine A. MacKinnon, "Liberalism and the Death of Feminism," *The Sexual Liberals and the Attack on Feminism*, Dorchen Leidholdt and Janice G. Raymond, eds. (New York: Pergamon Press, 1990), p. 4.

32 Ibid., pp. 13, 9, 4 and 10.

33 Ibid., p. 5.

34 Catharine A. MacKinnon, "Standards of Sisterhood," *Broadside*, Dec. 1985-Jan. 1986, p. 6 and Fred Strebeigh, "Defining Law on the Feminist Frontier," *New York Times Magazine*, 6 Oct. 1991, p. 56.

35 Catharine A. MacKinnon, "Liberalism and the Death of Feminism," *The Sexual Liberals and the Attack on Feminism*, Dorchen Leidholdt and Janice G. Raymond, eds. (New York: Pergamon Press, 1990), p. 12.

36 Catharine A. MacKinnon, "Turning Rape into Pornography: Postmodern Genocide," *Ms.*, July-Aug. 1993, pp. 24-26.

37 Catharine A. MacKinnon, *Toward a Feminist Theory of the State* (Cambridge, Massachusetts: Harvard University Press, 1989), p. 138.

38 James R. Petersen, "Catharine MacKinnon: Again," *Playboy*, Aug. 1992, p. 39.

39 Catharine A. MacKinnon, "Liberalism and the Death of Feminism," *The Sexual Liberals and the Attack on Feminism*, Dorchen Leidholdt and Janice G. Raymond, eds. (New York: Pergamon Press, 1990), p. 11. See also Nadine Strossen, *Defending Pornography* (New York: Scribner, 1995), pp. 179-98.

40 Letter to the editor, *Ms.*, Jan.-Feb. 1992, p. 5.

41 Kay Leigh Hagan, "Orchids in the Arctic: The predicament of women who love men," *Ms.*, Nov.-Dec. 1991, pp. 31-33.

42 Betty Friedan, "Why men die young...and why you'll live longer," *Playboy*, Apr. 1995. On p. 66, she writes: "Freud may have been wrong about women, but he wasn't wrong about everything."

43 Robin Morgan, "Whose Free Press Is It, Anyway?" (editorial), *Ms.*, July-Aug. 1991, p. 1 and Jane Caputi and Diana E.H. Russell, "'Femicide': Speaking the Unspeakable," *Ms.*, Sept.-Oct. 1990, p. 34.

44 Marcia Ann Gillespie, "Delusions of Safety: a personal story," *Ms.*, Sept.-Oct. 1990, p. 51 and "Where Do We Go From Here: An interview with Ann Jones," *Ms.*, Sept.-Oct. 1994, pp. 60-61.

45 Robert L. Allen and Paul Kivel, "Men Changing Men," *Ms.*, Sept.-Oct. 1994, p. 50.

46 Jane Caputi and Diana E.H. Russell, "'Femicide': Speaking the Unspeakable," *Ms.*, Sept.-Oct. 1990, pp. 36-37.

47 Kathleen Hirsch, "Fraternities of Fear: Gang rape, male bonding, and the silencing of women," *Ms.*, Sept.-Oct. 1990, p. 53 and Shere Hite, "Bringing Democracy Home: Shere Hite reports on the family" (cover story), *Ms.*, Mar.-Apr. 1995, pp. 57-58.

48 Phyllis Chesler, "Mothers on Trial," *Ms.*, May-June 1991, p. 47.

49 Lisa Maria Hogeland, "Fear of Feminism: Why young women get the willies," *Ms.*, Nov.-Dec. 1994, p. 20.

50 Andrea Dworkin, "The Unremembered: Searching for women at the Holocaust Memorial Museum," *Ms.*, Nov.-Dec. 1994, p. 58.

51 Jennifer Baumgardner, "Bold Type: Witchy Woman," *Ms.*, Mar.-Apr. 1995, p. 73.

52 See Ann Landers, *Toronto Star*, 30 July 1993, p. E2 and 23 Sept. 1993, p. E5.

53 "Majority oppose adult magazines Gallup poll shows," *Toronto Star*, 25 Apr. 1995, p. A13.

54 Tony Wong, "Panel to make national study of violence against women," *Toronto Star*, 16 Aug. 1991, p. A5. Sean Fine, "Panel takes aim at abuse of women," *Globe and Mail*, 17 Jan. 1992, p. A4. David Vienneau, "Abuse of women at crisis level, panel says," *Toronto Star*, 30 July 1993, p. A22. See also Canadian Panel on Violence Against Women, *Changing the Landscape: Ending Violence—Achieving Equality*, Final Report, Minister of Supply and Services Canada, 1993, pp. v-vii.

55 Status of Women Canada News Release No. 006, "Minister Collins Calls Panel's Report 'Historic,'" 29 July 1993. Barbara Aarsteinsen, "NAC's Rebick bows out, knocking 'Tory agenda,'" *Toronto Star*, 5 June 1993, p. A14. Barbara Aarsteinsen, "New feminist leader attacks 'Tory agenda,'" *Toronto Star*, 7 June 1993, p. A2. Kirk Makin, "NAC takes aim at the Tories," *Globe and Mail*, 11 Sept. 1993, p. A7.

56 Canadian Panel on Violence Against Women, *Changing the Landscape*, Minister of Supply and Services Canada, 1993, pp. 3, 4, 13, etc.

57 Ibid., pp. 32 and 39.

58 Ibid., p. 6.

59 Lisa Tuttle, *Encyclopedia of Feminism* (New York: Facts on File Publications, 1986), p. 242.

60 Canadian Panel on Violence Against Women, *Changing the Landscape*, Minister of Supply and Services Canada, 1993, p. 14.

61 Ibid., p. 19.

62 Ibid., pp. 6-7.

63 Ibid., pp. 4, 6, 10, 12, 14, etc.

64 In fairness to *Ms.*, amid the dozens of pages of coverage it has devoted to violence against women in recent years, it has also included two short pieces (approximately half a page in length each) to the issue of lesbian battering. *Ms.*, Oct.-Nov. 1990, p. 48 and Sept.-Oct. 1994, p. 53. See

also chapter three of this book.

65 Theresa Boyle, "'House slave' suffered year of brutality, police say," *Toronto Star*, 27 July 1993, p. A6. Wendy Darroch, "Woman guilty of enslaving roommate," *Toronto Star*, 12 Mar. 1994, p. A17. Wendy Darroch, "Woman gets 18 months for abuse of roommate," *Toronto Star*, 15 Apr. 1994, p. A28.

66 Roger Catlin, "Slain Selena's crossover dream comes true too late," *Toronto Star*, 22 July 1995, p. K12. Associated Press, "Selena trial ends in conviction," *Globe and Mail*, 24 Oct. 1995, p. C2.

67 Canadian Panel on Violence Against Women, *Changing the Landscape*, Minister of Supply and Services Canada, 1993, p. 25.

68 See Donna Laframboise, "Province funds studies of non-existent abuse," *Toronto Star*, 9 Jan. 1995, p. A15 and "Let public hear about conference," 16 Jan. 1995, p. A17. Spokespersons from the Ontario Women's Directorate and the Ministry of Northern Development and Mines provided this justification in private telephone conversations.

69 Status of Women Canada News Release No. 006, "Minister Collins Calls Panel's Report 'Historic,'" 29 July 1993.

Chapter Two

1 Janet Radcliffe Richards, *The Sceptical Feminist* (London: Penguin Books, 1980), 2nd edition, p. 48.

2 Harold Mersky, "Multiple Personality Disorder and False Memory Syndrome" (editorial), *British Journal of Psychiatry* (1995), p. 281. Debbie Nathan, "Dividing to Conquer? Women, men, and the making of multiple personality disorder," *Social Text*, Fall 1994, pp. 79-82. Mark Pendergrast, *Victims of Memory* (Hinesberg, Vermont: Upper Access, Inc., 1995), pp. 77 and 166-68.

3 G.K. Ganaway, "Historical Versus Narrative Truth: Clarifying the role of exogenous trauma in the etiology of MPD and its variants," *Dissociation* 2, No. 4, 1989, p. 209.

4 Debbie Nathan, "Dividing to Conquer?" *Social Text*, Fall 1994, p. 79. Harold Mersky, "Multiple Personality Disorder and False Memory Syndrome" (editorial), *British Journal of Psychiatry* (1995), p. 281. Mark Pendergrast, *Victims of Memory* (Hinesberg, Vermont: Upper Access, Inc., 1995), pp. 76-77 and 157.

5 Mark Pendergrast, *Victims of Memory* (Hinesberg, Vermont: Upper Access, Inc., 1995), p. 157 note *. Debbie Nathan, "Dividing to Conquer?" *Social Text*, Fall 1994, p. 101.

Notes

6 August Piper, Jr., "'Truth Serum' and 'Recovered Memories' of Sexual Abuse: A review of the evidence," *Journal of Psychiatry and Law*, Winter 1993.

7 Debbie Nathan, "Dividing to Conquer?" *Social Text*, Fall 1994, p. 79.

8 Marilyn French, *The War Against Women* (New York: Ballantine Books, 1992), p. 196.

9 Sylvia Fraser, "Freud's Final Seduction," *Saturday Night*, Mar. 1994, pp. 57 and 59.

10 Debbie Nathan, "Dividing to Conquer?" *Social Text*, Fall 1994, p. 100 refers to pediatrician Richard Kempe's "Battered Child Syndrome," in the *Journal of the American Medical Association*'s Vol. 181, 1962, as a "landmark."

11 Canadian Panel on Violence Against Women, *Changing the Landscape: Ending Violence—Achieving Equality*, Final Report, Minister of Supply and Services Canada, 1993, p. 14.

12 Debbie Nathan, "Dividing to Conquer?" *Social Text*, Fall 1994, p. 79.

13 In fairness, the new version of the Association's Diagnostic and Statistical Manual, DSM-IV, released in 1994, removed the word "full" from part B. Accordingly, John would now be considered a true MPD. However, this does not change the fact that, despite his failure to meet the then-official criteria, he was presented as a bona fide MPD sufferer. See Harold Mersky, "Multiple Personality Disorder and False Memory Syndrome" (editorial), *British Journal of Psychiatry* (1995), p. 281.

14 Debbie Nathan, "Dividing to Conquer?" *Social Text*, Fall 1994, p. 79.

15 August Piper, Jr., "'Truth Serum' and 'Recovered Memories' of Sexual Abuse: A review of the evidence," *Journal of Psychiatry and Law*, Winter 1993, p. 465.

16 Transcript #1402, Frontline. Copyright 1995, WGBH Educational Foundation.

17 Private telephone conversation with Gretchen's mother, Nancy, in Nov. 1995. For the sake of her grandchildren, Nancy requested that her surname not be published.

18 Elizabeth S. Rose, "Surviving the Unbelievable: A first-person account of cult ritual abuse," *Ms.*, Jan.-Feb. 1993, pp. 40-41 and 43.

19 Ibid., p. 44.

20 Ibid., p. 42.

21 Ibid., pp. 41 and 43.

22 Ibid., pp. 41, 43 and 45.

23 Ibid., p. 45.

24 Kenneth V. Lanning, *Investigator's Guide to Allegations of "Ritual" Child Abuse*, Federal Bureau of Investigation, January 1992.

25 Chi Chi Sileo, "Multiple Personalities: The Experts are Split," *Insight*, 25 Oct. 1993, p. 22.

26 Kenneth V. Lanning, *Investigator's Guide to Allegations of "Ritual" Child Abuse*, Federal Bureau of Investigation, January 1992.

27 National Center on Child Abuse and Neglect, *Ritual Abuse Allegations*, 1994. Report and/or Executive Summary available from the National Clearinghouse on Child Abuse and Neglect Information, Washington, D.C.

28 Daniel Goleman, "Proof lacking for ritual abuse by Satanists," *New York Times*, 31 Oct. 1994.

29 J.S. LaFontaine, *The Extent and Nature of Organized and Ritual Abuse*, (London: HMSO, 1994), p. 30.

30 Randy Emon, "SRA and evidence." Posted to witchhunt@mit.edu, 12 Jan. 1995. From sgtemon@aol.com.

31 Kenneth V. Lanning, *Investigator's Guide to Allegations of "Ritual" Child Abuse*, Federal Bureau of Investigation, January 1992.

32 Sherrill Mulhern, "Satanism, Ritual Abuse, and Multiple Personality Disorder: A sociohistorical perspective," *The International Journal of Clinical and Experimental Hypnosis*, Vol. XLII, No. 4, Oct. 1994, p. 280.

33 Judy Steed, "Ritual abuse does exist and must be combatted," *Toronto Star*, 18 Jan. 1995, p. A17. This piece was a direct rebuttal of two of my own columns: "Province funds studies of non-existent abuse," *Toronto Star*, 9 Jan. 1995, p. A15 and "Let public hear about conference," 16 Jan. 1995, p. A17.

34 Connie M. Kristiansen, "FMS, PMS...they're all the same if you are a sexist," *Ottawa Citizen*, 25 Aug. 1994. Michele Landsberg, "Let's clear up confusion over incest memories," *Toronto Star*, 6 May 1995, p. G1.

35 *Herizons*, Fall 1992, p. 19. R.J., "R.J.'s Story: A Survivor's Account," p. 22. Amethya, "Amethya's Story: A Survivor's Account," p. 23.

36 Marjaleena Repo, "'Ritual abuse,' my elbow!—a feminist critique of a hoax," unpublished, 1992.

37 Beckylane as told to Cathy Stonehouse, "Healing from Ritual Abuse: real memories, true courage," *Kinesis*, June 1995, p. 19.

38 Canadian Panel on Violence Against Women, *Changing the Landscape*, Minister of Supply and Services Canada, 1993, pp. 8, 27, 37, 45-57.

39 *Ms.*, Jan.-Feb. 1993, pp. 43-44.

40 Ibid., p. 44 and Jan.-Feb. 1995, p. 67. Other comments on recovered memories and/or ritual abuse can be found in *Ms.* at Nov.-Dec. 1993, p. 96, in an editorial May-June 1994, p. 1, July-Aug. 1994, p. 91, and Sept.-Oct. 1994, p. 78.

41 Ellen Bass and Laura Davis, *The Courage to Heal* (New York: Harper & Row Publishers, 1988), p. 41.

42 Ibid., p. 122. Subsequent page references in text.

43 Frederick Crews, Letters to the editor, *New York Review of Books*, 16 Feb. 1995.

44 E. Sue Blume, *Secret Survivors: Uncovering incest and its aftereffects in women* (New York: Ballantine Books, 1990). Steinem's quote on the front cover reads: "Explores the constellation of symptoms that result from a crime too cruel for mind and memory to face. This book, like the truth it helps uncover, can set millions free." The first five pages are devoted to a 34-point check-list which purportedly identifies people who "could be" survivors of incest. Among the conditions listed are: fear of the dark, gynecological disorders, wearing baggy clothing, depression, drug or alcohol abuse, compulsive behaviours, etc.

45 Carol Tavris, "Beware the Incest-Survivor Machine," *New York Times Book Review*, 3 Jan. 1993, p. 17.

46 Beverly Engel, *The Right to Innocence: Healing the Trauma of Childhood Sexual Abuse* (New York: Ivy Books, 1989), p. 9.

47 Carol Tavris, "Beware the Incest-Survivor Machine," *New York Times Book Review*, 3 Jan. 1993, p. 16.

48 Editors' Note, *Herizons*, Fall 1992, p. 19.

49 Peter Hellman, "Crying Rape: The politics of date rape on campus," *New York*, 8 Mar. 1993, pp. 32, 34 and 36.

50 Some of the relevant articles appearing in the *Hamilton Spectator* are as follows: 3 Feb. 1993, p. B1; 4 Feb. 1993, p. D3; 12 Feb. 1993, p. B2; 16 June 1993, p. A1; and 21 June 1993, p. B1. The report, by Avebury Research & Consulting Ltd., is titled *Independent Client Service Review of the Sexual Assault Centre (Hamilton and Area)*, 17 June 1993.

51 Avebury Research & Consulting Ltd., *Independent Client Service Review of the Sexual Assault Centre (Hamilton and Area)*, 17 June 1993, pp. ii, 7 and 9-10.

52 Ibid., pp. 12-13, 26, 32 and 46.

53 Ann Landers, appearing in *The Toronto Star*, 17 Sept. 1993, p. D4.

54 Ann Landers, appearing in *The Toronto Star*, 12 Dec. 1993, p. F3 and 18 Nov. 1993, p. D2.

55 Laura Pasley, "Misplaced Trust: A first-person account of how my therapist created false memories," *Skeptic*, Vol. 2, No. 3, 1994, pp. 62-67.

56 Gail Fisher-Taylor, "Ritual Abuse: Towards a feminist understanding," *Herizons*, Fall 1992, p. 21.

Chapter Three

1 Christie Blatchford, "Innocence lost," *Toronto Sun*, 7 Apr. 1994, pp. 16-18. Philip Mascoll, "Café killers linked to another robbery," *Toronto Star*, 8 Apr. 1994, p. A1.

2 "What's your reaction to these faces?" (editorial), *Toronto Star*, 9 Apr. 1994, p. B2. Julie Smyth, "Search for shooting suspects widens," *Globe and Mail*, 11 Apr. 1994, p. A6. Kirk Makin, "Young blacks brace for crime's aftermath," *Globe and Mail*, 9 Apr. 1994, p. A6. Rosie DiManno, "Sharing guilt 'appalling,' blacks told," *Toronto Star*, 18 Apr. 1994, p. A6.

3 John Barber, "Assertions on racism unfounded, outrageous," *Globe and Mail*, 14 June 1994, p. A7.

4 Amy Friedman, *Nothing Sacred: A conversation with feminism* (Ottawa: Oberon Press, 1992), p. 74.

5 "'Abducted' boys died strapped to car seats," *Toronto Star*, 5 Nov. 1994, p. A3. Associated Press, "Jury gives Susan Smith life in prison," *Toronto Star*, 29 July 1995, p. A2.

6 Henry Gale, "Not collective guilt, but collective responsibility," *Globe and Mail*, 23 Nov. 1994, p. A24 and Ted White, Letter to the editor, *Globe and Mail*, 6 Dec. 1994, p. A24.

7 Canadian Panel on Violence Against Women, *Changing the Landscape: Ending Violence—Achieving Equality*, Final Report, Minister of Supply and Services Canada, 1993, pp. 6 and 274.

8 Ibid., p. 4.

9 Camille Paglia, *Sex, Art, and American Culture* (New York: Vintage Books, 1992), pp. 56-57.

10 Canadian Panel on Violence Against Women, *Changing the Landscape*, Minister of Supply and Services Canada, 1993, p. 6.

11 Ibid., p. 74.

12 Claire M. Renzetti, *Violent Betrayal: Partner Abuse in Lesbian Relationships* (Newbury Park, California: Sage Publications, 1992), pp. 17-24. See also "Lesbian Battery," *Ms.*, Sept.-Oct. 1990, p. 48 and Achy Obejas, "Women Who Batter Women," *Ms.*, Sept.-Oct. 1994, p. 53.

13 Canadian Panel on Violence Against Women, *Changing the Landscape*, Minister of Supply and Services Canada, 1993, p. 161.

14 Ibid., p. 169.

15 John Fekete, *Moral Panic: Biopolitics rising* (Montreal: Robert Davies Publishing, 1994), p. 117.

16 Ibid., p. 224.

17 Marilyn French, *The War Against Women* (New York: Ballantine Books, 1992), pp. 24 and 112.

18 Ibid., pp. 114, 146-47 and 175-76.

19 Wendy Dennis, *Hot and Bothered: Sex and Love in the Nineties* (Toronto: Seal Books, 1992), pp. 59-60.

20 Canadian Panel on Violence Against Women, *Changing the Landscape*, Minister of Supply and Services Canada, 1993, Part 5, p. 70.

21 Naomi Wolf, *The Beauty Myth* (Toronto: Vintage Books, 1990), p. 47.

22 Ibid., pp. 47-48.

23 Philip Van Niekerk, in *The Globe and Mail*, "Winnie Mandela convicted of kidnapping," 14 May 1991, p. A1 and "Women's group bounces Mandela," 26 May 1992, p. A16. Bill Schiller in *The Toronto Star*, "Mandela's marriage over paper reports," 5 Apr. 1992, p. A3 and "Is ANC making another mistake?" 16 Apr. 1992, p. A31. See also Jonathan Manthorpe, "Getting the story on Winnie Mandela," *Toronto Star*, 14 Apr. 1992, p. A17 and Ellen Bartlett, "Mandela divorce turns messy," *Globe and Mail*, 19 Sept. 1995, pp. A1 and A13.

24 *Ms.*, Jan.-Feb. 1992, p. 12 and Sept.-Oct. 1990, p. 6.

25 See Christina Hoff Sommers, *Who Stole Feminism? How Women Have Betrayed Women* (New York: Simon & Schuster, 1994), p. 161.

26 (US) National Center for Health Statistics, *Monthly Vital Statistics Report*, Vol. 43, No. 6, 22 Mar. 1995, pp. 24-25. Statistics Canada, *Causes of Death 1993*, 1995.

27 Warren Farrell, *The Myth of Male Power: Why men are the disposable sex* (New York: Simon & Schuster, 1993), p. 100.

28 Canadian Centre for Justice Statistics, *Homicide Survey, Policing Services Program*, 1995 and Statistics Canada, *Causes of Death 1993*, 1995.

29 Betty Friedan, "Why men die young...and why you'll live longer," *Playboy*, Apr. 1995, p. 65. Statistics Canada, *Life Tables: Canada and the Provinces 1990-1992*, May 1995.

30 Marilyn French, *The War Against Women* (New York: Ballantine Books, 1992), p. 20.

31 (US) National Center for Health Statistics, *Monthly Vital Statistics Report*, Vol. 43, No. 6, 22 Mar. 1995, p. 8.

32 Ibid., p. 45. Canadian Centre for Justice Statistics, *Homicide Survey, Policing Services Program*, 1995. Canadian Centre for Justice Statistics, *Juristat*, Vol. 15, No. 2, Jan. 1995, p. 8.

33 John Fekete, *Moral Panic* (Montreal: Robert Davies Publishing, 1994), p. 68.

34 Canadian Centre for Justice Statistics, *Juristat*, Vol. 15, No. 2, Jan. 1995, p. 1.

35 Christina Hoff Sommers, *Who Stole Feminism? How Women Have Betrayed Women* (New York: Simon & Schuster, 1994), pp. 137-87. D. Laframboise, "Do we care if boys fall back?" *Toronto Star*, 27 Feb. 1995, p. A17. Charles Hymas and Julie Cohen, "The trouble with boys," *The London Sunday Times*, 19 June 1994, p. 14.

36 Andrew Duffy, "School system fails blacks, Portuguese," *Toronto Star*, 11 Feb. 1995, p. A1 and Margaret Philp, "Dropout rate high for Portuguese, black students," *Globe and Mail*, 14 Feb. 1995, p. A6.

37 (US) National Institute for Occupational Safety and Health, *Fatal Injuries to Workers in the US 1980-1989: A decade of surveillance*, Aug. 1993, p. 4. Statistics Canada, *Work Injuries: 1991-1993*, Dec. 1994, p. 13. Gender breakdown regarding 1993 fatalities secured through a private telephone conversation with Statistics Canada's Labour Division.

38 Warren Farrell, *The Myth of Male Power* (New York: Simon & Schuster, 1993), pp. 110 and 118.

39 Ibid., p. 105.

40 David Vienneau, "3 women reluctant to join top court PM told," *Toronto Star*, 20 Aug. 1992, p. A3, and Canadian Press, "Few women willing to join top court, Campbell says," *Globe and Mail*, 17 Nov. 1992, p. A6.

41 Letty Cottin Pogrebin, "The Stolen Spotlight Syndrome," *Ms.*, Nov.-Dec. 1993, p. 96.

42 Marilyn French, *The War Against Women* (New York: Ballantine Books, 1992), pp. 19, 69-72, 75, 84 and 99.

43 Leslie Scrivener, "Bare-breasts debate simmers in wake of topless

protests," *Toronto Star*, 26 July 1992, pp. A1 and A6. Susan Allan, "Women protest indecency laws," *Globe and Mail*, 20 July 1992, pp. A1 and A8.

44 Margo Roston, "MPs seeing lots of red in the House of Commons," *Toronto Star*, 8 Dec. 1994, p. G5.

45 Nicholas Van Rijn, "Postal supervisor fights to keep long hair, beard," *Toronto Star*, 14 Dec. 1994, p. A3 and Alan Barnes, "Bearded mail worker to keep job—for now," *Toronto Star*, 15 Dec. 1994, p. A5.

46 Warren Farrell, *The Myth of Male Power* (New York: Simon & Schuster, 1993), p. 135.

47 Ibid., p. 130.

48 Naomi Wolf, *The Beauty Myth* (Toronto: Vintage Books, 1990), pp. 181-82.

49 Ibid., pp. 207-08 and 194-95.

50 Christina Hoff Sommers, *Who Stole Feminism?* (New York: Simon & Schuster, 1994), pp. 11-12.

51 Ibid., p. 12 and Ann Landers, appearing in *Toronto Star*, 29 Apr. 1992, p. D12.

52 Ibid., pp. 13-15.

53 Sarah Crichton, "Sexual correctness: has it gone too far?" *Newsweek*, 25 Oct. 1993, pp. 55-56. See also "US study says 1 in 8 women is raped," *Toronto Star*, 24 Apr. 1992, p. A3.

54 Ann Landers, appearing in *Toronto Star*, 4 Sept. 1994, p. B3; 14 Aug. 1994, p. B3; 16 Oct. 1994, p. F2; and 3 Dec. 1994, p. L14.

55 Alanna Mitchell, "50% of women report assaults," *Globe and Mail*, 19 Nov. 1993, pp. A1 and A4.

56 Theresa Boyle, "98% of Metro women suffer sexual violation, panel says," *Toronto Star*, 30 July 1993, p. A23.

57 Ontario Women's Directorate, *Sexual Assault: Dispelling the myths*, Apr. 1994.

58 See John Fekete, *Moral Panic* (Montreal: Robert Davies Publishing, 1994), pp. 134-45, esp. p. 144. David Lees, "The War Against Men," *Toronto Life*, Dec. 1992, pp. 98-99.

59 David Lees, "The War Against Men," *Toronto Life*, Dec. 1992, pp. 47, 99-100. See also Eugene Lupri, "Male Violence in the Home," *Canadian Social Trends*, Statistics Canada 1989, pp. 19-21.

60 Lees, "The War Against Men," *Toronto Life*, Dec. 1992, pp. 47, 99-100.

61 Michele Landsberg, "The male myth of 'battered husbands,'" *Toronto Star*, 18 Dec. 1993, p. J1.

62 Reena Sommer, Gordon E. Barnes and Robert P. Murray, "Alcohol Consumption, Alcohol Abuse, Personality and Female Perpetrated Spouse Abuse," *Personality and Individual Differences*, Vol. 13, No. 12, 1992, pp. 1315-23. Reena Sommer, "Male and Female Perpetrated Partner Abuse: Testing a Diathesis-Stress Model," University of Manitoba Ph.D. Thesis, unpublished, 1994. See also John Fekete, *Moral Panic* (Montreal: Robert Davies Publishing, 1994), pp. 89-90.

63 Larry Saidman, Letter to the editor, "Some people still just don't get it," *Toronto Star*, 31 Oct. 1992, p. D3.

64 David Lees, "The War Against Men," *Toronto Life*, Dec. 1992, p. 100.

65 Canadian Panel on Violence Against Women, *Changing the Landscape*, Minister of Supply and Services Canada, 1993, p. 7. "Where Do We Go From Here: An interview with Ann Jones," *Ms.*, Sept.-Oct. 1994, p. 56.

66 Maria Augimer, Woman Abuse Protocol Project, Letter to the editor, *Toronto Star*, 31 Oct. 1992, p. D3. David Greenberg, "The myth of abusive wives is laughable...almost," *Globe and Mail*, 16 Nov. 1993, p. A28. Michele Landsberg, "The male myth of 'battered husbands,'" *Toronto Star*, 18 Dec. 1993, p. J1.

67 Ron Csillag, "When the wife is the primary breadwinner," *Globe and Mail*, 12 Apr. 1995, p. A26.

68 Warren Farrell, *The Myth of Male Power* (New York: Simon & Schuster, 1993), p. 19.

69 Ann Landers, appearing in *The Toronto Star*. MICHIGAN: 9 Nov. 1993, p. B2. ST. LOUIS: 3 June 1994, p. D3.

70 Dear Abby, appearing in *The Ottawa Citizen*, 5 Dec. 1994, p. B4.

71 "Suicides of family of 3 tied to Lepine massacre," *Toronto Star*, 17 July 1991, p. A3.

Chapter Four

1 Janet Radcliffe Richards, *The Sceptical Feminist* (London: Penguin Books, 1980), 2nd edition, p. 112.

2 Susan Faludi, "'I'm Not a Feminist. But I Play One on TV,'" *Ms.*, Mar.-Apr. 1995, pp. 30-39.

3 Robin Morgan, "Bearing Witness" (editorial), *Ms.*, Jan.-Feb. 1992, p. 1.

4 Doris Lessing, *Prisons We Choose to Live Inside* (Toronto: CBC Enterprises, 1986), pp. 46 and 69.

5 John Allemang, "Why Isaiah Berlin Matters," *Globe and Mail*, 25 Nov. 1994, p. A18. See also partial transcript of Berlin's speech, "Beware the one true answer," same page.

6 Camille Paglia, *Sex, Art, and American Culture* (New York: Vintage Books, 1992), p. 47.

7 Katie Roiphe, *The Morning After: Sex, Fear and Feminism* (Boston: Bay Back Books, 1993), pp. 19-21.

8 Rene Denfeld, *The New Victorians: A Young Woman's Response to the Old Feminist Order* (New York: Warner Books, 1995), p. 133.

9 Christina Hoff Sommers, *Who Stole Feminism? How Women Have Betrayed Women* (New York: Simon & Schuster, 1994), pp. 220-21.

10 *Ms.*, Jan.-Feb. 1992.

11 Robin Morgan, *Going Too Far: The Personal Chronicle of a Feminist* (New York: Random House, 1977), p. 169.

12 Some other *Ms.* references to porn in recent years: May-June 1991 (editorial), p. 1 and p. 32; Sept.-Oct. 1992 (editorial), p. 1; Nov.-Dec. 1994, pp. 19, 52 and 54.

13 Catharine A. MacKinnon, "Liberalism and the Death of Feminism," *The Sexual Liberals and the Attack on Feminism*, Dorchen Leidholdt and Janice G. Raymond, eds. (New York: Pergamon Press, 1990), p. 12. Pete Hamill, "Women on the Verge of a Legal Breakdown," *Playboy*, Jan. 1993, p. 186. Wendy Kaminer, "Exposing the new authoritarians," *San Francisco Examiner*, 29 Nov. 1992.

14 Robin Morgan, "On the Road" (editorial), *Ms.*, May-June 1993, p.1.

15 Rene Denfeld, *The New Victorians* (New York: Warner Books, 1995), p. 260.

16 Donna Minkowitz, "The Newsroom Becomes a Battleground: Is the media siege on lesbians in the women's movement a desperate attempt to undermine feminism?" (cover story), *The Advocate*, 19 May 1992, p. 34.

17 Camille Paglia, *Sex, Art, and American Culture* (New York: Vintage Books, 1992), pp. xii and 120. *Playboy* Interview: Camille Paglia, *Playboy*, May 1995, p. 64.

18 Harry Stein, interview with Christina Hoff Sommers, *Penthouse*, Jan. 1995, p. 70. Camille Paglia, *Sex, Art, and American Culture* (New York: Vintage Books, 1992), p.56.

19 Camille Paglia, *Sex, Art, and American Culture* (New York: Vintage Books, 1992), pp. 49-50. See also p. 67.

20 Ibid., pp. 57 and 74.

21 Katie Roiphe, *The Morning After* (Boston: Back Bay Books, 1993), p. xix. See also *Ms.*, May-June 1991, p. 61.

22 Headline on front cover of the Sept.-Oct. 1993 issue of *Ms.*: "No, Feminists *Don't* All Think Alike (Who Says We Have To?)." Inside, Steinem admits to the name-calling, p. 41, but doesn't apologize. Rene Denfeld, *The New Victorians* (New York: Warner Books, 1995), pp. 198-99.

23 Sally Quinn, "Who killed feminism?" *Washington Post*, 19 Jan. 1992, p. C1. Donna Minkowitz, "The Newsroom Becomes a Battleground" (cover story), *The Advocate*, 19 May 1992, p. 35.

24 Harry Stein, interview with Christina Hoff Sommers, *Penthouse*, Jan. 1995, p. 67. See also the reference to "feminist-basher Christina Hoff Sommers," in *Ms.*, July-Aug. 1995, p. 92.

25 Betty Friedan, "Why men die young…and why you'll live longer," *Playboy*, Apr. 1995, p. 152.

26 Sarah Crichton, "Sexual Correctness: has it gone too far?" *Newsweek*, 25 Oct. 1993. See also *Ms.* editorial, May-June 1994, p. 1 and Jan.-Feb. 1994, p. 47.

27 Katie Roiphe, *The Morning After* (Boston: Back Bay Books, 1993), pp. 5-6.

28 Amy Friedman, *Nothing Sacred: A conversation with feminism* (Ottawa: Oberon Press, 1992), pp. 41, 45-46, 59 and 86.

29 Danielle Crittenden, "New stereotypes replace the old," *Globe and Mail*, 27 Dec. 1990, p. A 20.

30 Margaret Atwood, "If You Can't Say Something Nice, Don't Say Anything At All," *Language in Her Eye: Writing and Gender*, Libby Scheier, Sarah Sheard and Eleanor Wachtel, eds. (Toronto: Coach House Press, 1990), p. 24.

31 Rene Denfeld, *The New Victorians* (New York: Warner Books, 1995), p. 43.

32 D. Laframboise, "Women's Day doesn't have much to do with women," *Globe and Mail*, 8 Mar. 1991, p. A13. Carmencita R. Hernandez and Jane Walsh, "Moving toward a new emancipation," *Globe and Mail*, 19 Mar. 1991, p. A21.

33 Salome Lucas, *et. al.*, "Gender isn't everything—*all* issues are women's issues," *Globe and Mail*, 14 May 1991, p. A17. See also Catharine A. MacKinnon, "Liberalism and the Death of Feminism," *The Sexual Liberals and the Attack on Feminism*, Dorchen Leidholdt and Janice G. Raymond, eds. (New York: Pergamon Press, 1990), p. 4.

34 Dianne Allen, Letter to the editor, *Globe and Mail*, 9 Feb. 1995, p. A22.

35 Michelle Shephard and Vicki White, "Gay Pride draws 500,000 people," *Toronto Star*, 3 July 1995, pp. A1 and A3.

36 Mark Zwolinski, "Women mark 'historic year,'" *Toronto Star*, 6 Mar. 1994, p. A4.

37 Ingrid MacDonald, "Conditions of Coalition," *Broadside*, Apr. 1986, p. 6.

38 Isabella Bardoel, "Women's rally stresses day care, deportations," *Globe and Mail*, 13 Mar. 1978, p. 29.

39 Dave Norris, "'Sisters' on parade," *Toronto Star*, 11 Mar. 1979, p. A6.

40 Faith Nolan, "Angela Davis: Making Connections," *Broadside*, Apr. 1985, p. 6.

41 Alfred Holden, "Cheers great Sophia Cook's speech at rally denouncing racism, violence," *Toronto Star*, 4 Mar. 1990, p. A1. Eric Skelton, "Attempted murder charge sought in Cook shooting," *Globe and Mail*, 18 Dec. 1989, p. A12. Bonnie M. Meyer, Letter to the editor, "Women's Day divisive," *NOW*, 15-21 Mar. 1990, p. 9.

42 Naomi Klein, "Politics of booze dampens annual Women's Day dance," *NOW*, 12-18 Mar. 1992, p. 17.

43 Sunera Thobani, "Why I am a feminist," *Toronto Star*, 3 June 1993, p. A21. See also Salome Lucas, *et. al.*, "Gender isn't everything—*all* issues are women's issues," *Globe and Mail*, 14 May 1991, p. A17.

44 "Women threaten to boycott violence hearings," *Toronto Star*, 8 June 1992, p. A1 and "Feuding in the family," (editorial), *Toronto Star*, 8 Aug. 1992, p. C2.

45 David Vienneau, "Feminists boycotting panel on violence," *Toronto Star*, 1 Aug. 1992, p. A10. See also "$10 million study a 'cheap' ploy critics charge," *Toronto Star*, 30 July 1993, p. A23 and Vivian Smith, "Equality called key to ending violence," *Globe and Mail*, 30 July 1993, pp. A1 and A4.

46 Margaret Wente, "Success stories: Which ones really count?" *Globe and Mail*, 23 July 1994, p. A2.

47 Michelle Shephard, "Callwood tribute helps homes," *Toronto Star*, 28 Sept. 1995, p. A28.

48 Adele Freedman, "White Woman's Burden," *Saturday Night*, Apr. 1993, p. 74.

49 Elaine Dewar, "Wrongful Dismissal," *Toronto Life*, Mar. 1993, p. 37.

50 June Callwood, "The Nellie's furor: June Callwood tells her side," *Toronto Star*, 23 July 1992, p. F1.

51 I was hand-delivering a story proposal to *Toronto Life* the day of the protest, and was given a photocopied flyer which had this message super-imposed over the magazine's cover: "TORONTO LIFE MAGAZINE'S: RACIST ATTACKS AGAINST WOMEN OF COLOUR."

52 Jean Kavanagh, "Racism charge 'the worst thing ever in my life,'" *Toronto Star*, 15 June 1992, p. A1.

53 Rene Denfeld, *The New Victorians* (New York: Warner Books, 1995), pp. 40 and 264.

54 Tiya Miles, "On the Rag," *Ms.*, May-June 1995, pp. 35-36.

55 Christina Hoff Sommers, *Who Stole Feminism?* (New York: Simon & Schuster, 1994), pp. 29-31.

56 Rene Denfeld, *The New Victorians* (New York: Warner Books, 1995), p. 203 and Camille Paglia, *Sex, Art, and American Culture* (New York: Vintage Books, 1992), p. 90.

57 Daphne Patai and Noretta Koertge, *Professing Feminism: Cautionary tales from the strange world of women's studies* (New York: Basic Books, 1994), pp. xvi-xvii.

58 Ibid., pp. 67 and 204.

59 See Karen Lehrman, "Off Course," *Mother Jones*, Sept.-Oct. 1993, p. 64.

60 Daphne Patai and Noretta Koertge, *Professing Feminism* (New York: Basic Books, 1994), pp. 101-102 and 105.

61 Karen Lehrman, "Off Course," *Mother Jones*, Sept.-Oct. 1993, pp. 48, 66 and 68.

62 Ibid., pp. 47, 51 and 64.

63 Backtalk, *Mother Jones*, Nov.-Dec. 1993, pp. 4-5 and 7. See also *Ms.*, Jan.-Feb. 1994, p. 47.

64 Daphne Patai and Noretta Koertge, *Professing Feminism* (New York: Basic Books, 1994), p. 176.

Chapter Five

1 Janet Radcliffe Richards, *The Sceptical Feminist* (London: Penguin Books, 1980), 2nd edition, p. 31.

2 bell hooks, "Men in Feminist Struggle—The Necessary Movement," *Women Respond to the Men's Movement*, Kay Leigh Hagan, ed. (San Francisco: Pandora, 1992), pp. 113 and 117.

3 Gloria Steinem, "Foreword," *Women Respond to the Men's Movement*, Kay Leigh Hagan, ed. (San Francisco: Pandora, 1992), pp. v-vii.

4 Kay Leigh Hagan, "Introduction," *Women Respond to the Men's Movement*, Kay Leigh Hagan, ed. (San Francisco: Pandora, 1992), p. viii.

5 Starhawk, "A Men's Movement I Can Trust," *Women Respond to the Men's Movement*, Kay Leigh Hagan, ed. (San Francisco: Pandora, 1992) p. 29.

6 Rosemary Radford Ruether, "Patriarchy and the Men's Movement," p. 16; Jane Caputi and Gordene O. MacKenzie, "Pumping Iron John," p. 71; and Elizabeth Dodson Gray, "Beauty and the Beast: A Parable for Our Time," p. 166 in *Women Respond to the Men's Movement*, Kay Leigh Hagan, ed. (San Francisco: Pandora, 1992).

7 Gloria Steinem, "Foreword," *Women Respond to the Men's Movement*, Kay Leigh Hagan, ed. (San Francisco: Pandora, 1992), p. ix.

8 Kay Leigh Hagan, "Introduction," *Women Respond to the Men's Movement*, Kay Leigh Hagan, ed. (San Francisco: Pandora, 1992), p. xii.

9 hattie gossett, "mins movement??? a page drama," *Women Respond to the Men's Movement*, Kay Leigh Hagan, ed. (San Francisco: Pandora, 1992), pp. 19-21.

10 Starhawk, "A Men's Movement I Can Trust," *Women Respond to the Men's Movement*, Kay Leigh Hagan, ed. (San Francisco: Pandora, 1992), p. 27.

11 Judy Steed, "Breaking the cycle of violence against women," *Toronto Star*, 4 Dec. 1994, pp. A1 and A18.

12 John Gray, Letter to the editor, "Which men are in trouble?" and Richard H. Velvart, Letter to the editor, "Violent beasts are unfamiliar," *Toronto Star*, 11 Jan. 1995, p. E2. Wayne Jones, Letter to the editor,"Men and housework," *Globe and Mail*, 23 Sept. 1992, p. A25.

13 *New York Times Review of Books*, 5 July 1992, p. 8.

14 Gloria Steinem, "Foreword," p. v; Kathleen Carlin, "The Men's Movement of Choice," p. 120; and Phyllis Chesler, "The Men's Auxiliary: Protecting the Rule of the Fathers," p. 139 in *Women Respond to the Men's Movement*, Kay Leigh Hagan, ed. (San Francisco: Pandora, 1992).

15 Laura S. Brown, "Essential Lies: A Dystopian Vision of the Mythopoetic Men's Movement," *Women Respond to the Men's Movement*, Kay Leigh Hagan, ed. (San Francisco: Pandora, 1992), pp. 93-94 and 98.

16 Vicki Noble, "A Helping Hand from the Guys," *Women Respond to the Men's Movement*, Kay Leigh Hagan, ed. (San Francisco: Pandora, 1992), pp. 104-105.

17 Starhawk, "A Men's Movement I Can Trust," *Women Respond to the Men's Movement*, Kay Leigh Hagan, ed. (San Francisco: Pandora, 1992), p. 34.

18 See "Return of the Gender Gap—Just in Time for November," *Ms.*, Jan.-Feb. 1992, p. 88.

19 bell hooks, "Men in Feminist Struggle—The Necessary Movement," p. 114 and Elizabeth Dodson Gray, "Beauty and the Beast: A Parable for Our Time," p. 167 in *Women Respond to the Men's Movement*, Kay Leigh Hagan, ed. (San Francisco: Pandora, 1992).

20 Margo Adair, "Will the Real Men's Movement Please Stand Up?" p. 55 and Margaret Randall, "'And So She Walked Over and Kissed Him...' Robert Bly's Men's Movement," p. 143 in *Women Respond to the Men's Movement*, Kay Leigh Hagan, ed. (San Francisco: Pandora, 1992).

21 Jane Caputi and Gordene O. MacKenzie, "Pumping Iron John," *Women Respond to the Men's Movement*, Kay Leigh Hagan, ed. (San Francisco: Pandora, 1992), p. 75. See also Robert Bly, *Iron John* (New York: Vintage Books, 1990), pp. 93-94.

22 Starhawk, "A Men's Movement I Can Trust," p. 31 and Laura S. Brown, "Essential Lies: A Dystopian Vision of the Mythopoetic Men's Movement," p. 98 in *Women Respond to the Men's Movement*, Kay Leigh Hagan, ed. (San Francisco: Pandora, 1992).

23 Lindsay Van Gelder, "The Truth About Bra-Burners," *Ms.*, Sept.-Oct. 1992, p. 80.

24 Wendy Dennis, *Hot and Bothered: Sex and Love in the Nineties* (Toronto: Seal Books, 1992), p. 62.

25 Riane Eisler, "What Do Men Really Want? The Men's Movement, Partnership, and Domination," *Women Respond to the Men's Movement*, Kay Leigh Hagan, ed. (San Francisco: Pandora, 1992), pp. 50 and 52.

26 "Like a Hole in the Head," *Ms.*, Jan.-Feb. 1995, p. 94 and "Worldwide," *Ms.*, May-June 1995, p. 17. See also Sharon Donbiago, "'Enemy of the mother': A feminist response to the men's movement," *Ms.*, Mar.-Apr. 1992, pp. 82-85.

27 Warren Farrell, *The Myth of Male Power: Why men are the disposable sex* (New York: Simon & Schuster, 1993), pp. 12-13.

28 Ibid., p. 174.

29 Ibid., pp. 164, 172-74, 210, and 259-60.

30 Ibid., pp. 15 and 42.

31 Ibid., p. 46. Wendy Dennis, *Hot and Bothered* (Toronto: Seal Books, 1992), pp. 22-23.

32 Warren Farrell, *The Myth of Male Power* (New York: Simon & Schuster, 1993), pp. 14-15.

33 *Sexual Assault: Dispelling the Myths*, Ontario Women's Directorate, Apr. 1994, p. 2. Iris S. Gorfinkel, Letter to the editor, *Globe and Mail*, 20 June 1995, p. A14.

34 Warren Farrell, *The Myth of Male Power* (New York: Simon & Schuster, 1993), p. 310.

35 Camille Paglia, "Challenging the Masculine Mystique," *Washington Post Book World*, 25 July 1993, pp. 1 and 8.

36 Susan Faludi, *Backlash* (New York: Anchor Books, 1991), pp. 300-304.

37 Liane Faulder, "Male power is no myth, but pain is real," *Toronto Star*, 22 Feb. 1994, p. C1 and Tom Wayman, "Who suffers more?" *Toronto Star*, 13 Nov. 1993, p. J15.

38 David Thomas, *Not Guilty: In Defence of the Modern Man* (London: Weidenfeld & Nicolson, 1993), pp. 11-12.

39 Ibid., pp. 1-3, 7 and 9.

40 Ibid., pp. 54-55.

41 Ibid., pp. 57-58.

42 Ibid., pp. 58 and 60.

43 Ann Landers, appearing in *The Toronto Star*, 19 July 1994, p. C2.

44 David Thomas, *Not Guilty* (London: Weidenfeld & Nicolson, 1993), pp. 75-78.

45 Ibid., pp. 79-80.

46 Ibid., pp. 75-78.

47 Statistics Canada, *Juristat*, Vol. 15, No. 11, Aug. 1995, p. 14.

48 *Police Response to Wife Assault*, Policing Standards Manual 0217.00, 13 Jan. 1994, pp. 3 and 7.

49 David Thomas, *Not Guilty* (London: Weidenfeld & Nicolson, 1993), p. 145.

50 Ibid., p. 147.

51 Ibid., p. 13.

52 Wendy Dennis, *Hot and Bothered* (Toronto: Seal Books, 1992), pp. 10 and 271.

53 Tom Harpur, "Beginning again this new year with the courage to forgive others," *Toronto Star*, 1 Jan. 1995, p. A16.

Chapter Six

1 Michele Barrett, ed., *Virginia Woolf: Women and Writing* (Dunvegan, Ontario: Quadrant Editions, 1984), p. 152. Woolf's article on George Eliot originally appeared in *The Times Literary Supplement*, 20 Nov. 1919.

2 George Eliot, *Middlemarch* (Harmondsworth, England: Penguin Books, 1984), p. 807. See also the bottom of p. 800.

3 John Fekete, *Moral Panic: Biopolitics rising* (Montreal: Robert Davies Publishing, 1994), pp. 83-84.

4 George Eliot, *Middlemarch* (Harmondsworth, England: Penguin Books, 1984), pp. 119-22.

5 Ibid., pp. 145-46 and 474-75.

6 Ibid., pp. 301, 380, 629 and 634.

7 Ibid., pp. 702, 710-11 and 718-19. See also the top of p. 815.

8 Ibid., pp. 825, 827-28, 834 and 892-93. See also the bottom of p. 858.

9 Ibid., pp. 790 and 894.

10 Ibid., pp. 182-83.

11 Ibid., p. 198.

12 hattie gossett, "mins movement??? a page drama," *Women Respond to the Men's Movement*, Kay Leigh Hagan, ed. (San Francisco: Pandora, 1992), pp. 21 and 24.

13 Margaret Atwood, "If You Can't Say Something Nice, Don't Say Anything At All," *Language in Her Eye: Writing and Gender*, Libby Sheier, Sarah Sheard and Eleanor Wachtel, eds. (Toronto: Coach House Press, 1990), p. 15.

14 Betty Friedan, "Why men die young...and why you'll live longer," *Playboy*, Apr. 1995, p. 151.

15 Warren Farrell, *The Myth of Male Power: Why men are the disposable sex* (New York: Simon & Schuster, 1993), pp. 35-36.

16 David Thomas, *Not Guilty: In Defence of the Modern Man* (London: Weidenfeld & Nicolson, 1993), pp. 80-84. Warren Farrell, *The Myth of Male Power* (New York: Simon & Schuster, 1993), pp. 33 and 374.

17 Anastasia Higginbotham, "Chicks going at it," *Ms.*, May-June 1995, p. 30.

18 Susan Faludi, *Backlash* (New York: Anchor Books, 1991), p. 65. See also David Thomas, *Not Guilty* (London: Weidenfeld & Nicolson, 1993), pp. 63-64.

19 Stephen Hawking, ed., *Stephen Hawking's A Brief History of Time: A Reader's Companion* (New York: Bantam Books, 1992), pp. 53-54.

20 Kurt Vonnegut, *Fates Worse Than Death: An autobiographical collage of the 1980s* (New York: G.P. Putnam's Sons, 1991), pp. 22-23.

21 Ibid., p. 28.

22 Warren Farrell, *The Myth of Male Power* (New York: Simon & Schuster, 1993), p. 52.

23 Ann Landers, appearing in *The Toronto Star*. UNEASY: 10 Mar. 1994, p. E7 and 23 May 1994, p. D3.

24 Ibid., 1 Mar. 1995, p. C7; 19 May 1995, p. B2; and 31 May 1995, p. C6. See also 8 Aug. 1993, p. D6.

25 Marilyn French, *The War Against Women* (New York: Ballantine Books, 1992), pp. 139-40.

26 Letty Cottin Pogrebin, "The Stolen Spotlight Syndrome," *Ms.*, Nov.-Dec. 1993, p. 96.

27 Phyllis Chesler, "The Men's Auxiliary: Protecting the Rule of the Fathers," *Women Respond to the Men's Movement*, Kay Leigh Hagan, ed. (San Francisco: Pandora, 1992), pp. 137-38.

Chapter Seven

1 Erica Jong, "Is Sex Sexy Without Power?" *Penthouse*, Apr. 1995, p. 56. Original italics.

2 Johanna Lindsey, *Prisoner of My Desire* (New York: Avon Books, 1991), p. 136.

3 Ibid., p. 141.

4 Ibid., pp. 151 and 174.

5 Ibid., pp. 182 and 185.

6 Ibid., p. 243.

7 Johanna Lindsey, *Surrender My Love* (New York: Avon Books, 1994).

8 Johanna Lindsey, *Captive Bride* (New York: Avon Books, 1977), p. 46.

9 Ibid., p. 62.

10 Ibid., p. 69.

11 Ibid., p. 87.

12 Ibid., pp. 124-25.

13 Johanna Lindsey, *Secret Fire* (New York: Avon Books, 1987), pp. 67 and 71.

14 Ibid., p. 248.

15 Amanda Quick, *Mistress* (New York: Bantam Books, 1994).

16 Mary Lou Rich, *Bandit's Kiss* (New York: Diamond Books, 1993).

17 Karen Robards, *To Love a Man* (New York: Warner Books, 1985). "Portrait: Karen Robards," *Romantic Times Magazine*, Oct. 1995, p. 76.

18 Heather Graham, *A Pirate's Pleasure* (New York: Dell, 1989) and Ann Lynn, *Slave of My Heart* (New York: Zebra Books, 1990).

19 Catherine Hart, *Silken Savage* (New York: Leisure Books, 1993), p. 53.

20 Ibid., p. 113.

21 Caroline Bourne, *Allegheny Captive* (New York: Zebra Books, 1990), p. 245.

22 Ann Lynn, *Slave of My Heart* (New York: Zebra Books, 1990), p. 245.

23 Susan Johnson, *Pure Sin* (New York: Bantam Books, 1994), pp. 155-56.

24 Ibid., p. 162.

25 Ibid., pp. 162 and 170.

26 Canadian Panel on Violence Against Women, *Changing the Landscape: Ending Violence—Achieving Equality*, Final Report, Minister of Supply and Services Canada, 1993, p. 50.

27 Catharine MacKinnon, "Not a Moral Issue," *Yale Law & Policy Review*, 2, 1984, p. 325.

28 Canadian Panel on Violence Against Women, *Changing the Landscape*, Minister of Supply and Services Canada, 1993, pp. 45 and 49. The writings of many women who consider themselves feminists and yet oppose censorship can be found in: Ann Snitow, Christine Stansell and Sharon Thompson, eds., *Powers of Desire: The Politics of Sexuality* (New York: Monthly Review Press, 1983); Carole S. Vance, ed., *Pleasure and Danger: Exploring Female Sexuality* (Boston: Routledge & Kegan Paul, 1984); and Varda Burstyn, ed., *Women Against Censorship* (Vancouver: Douglas & McIntyre, 1985). See also Sallie Tisdale, *Talk Dirty to Me* (New York: Doubleday, 1994).

29 Rene Denfeld, *The New Victorians: A Young Woman's Response to the Old Feminist Order* (New York: Warner Books, 1995), pp. 105-106. See also Marcia Pally, *Sex and Sensibility: Reflections on Forbidden Mirrors and the Will to Censor* (Hopewell, N.J.: Ecco Press, 1994) and Nadine Strossen,

Defending Pornography: Free Speech, Sex, and the Fight for Women's Rights (New York: Scribner, 1995), especially pp. 247-64.

30 Ibid., Denfeld: p. 108, Pally: pp. 99-108 and Strossen: pp. 258-59. See also Michael S. Kimmel, "Does Pornography Cause Rape?" *Violence Update*, Vol. 3, No. 10, June 1993.

31 Canadian Panel on Violence Against Women, *Changing the Landscape*, Minister of Supply and Services Canada, 1993, pp. 45 and 49.

32 Catharine A. MacKinnon, *Only Words* (Cambridge, Massachusetts: Harvard University Press, 1993), p. 12.

33 *R. v. Butler*, Canada Supreme Court Reports, 1992, Vol. 1 (Ottawa: Queen's Printer for Canada, 1992), p. 479.

34 Ibid., p. 479.

35 Michele Landsberg, "Canada: Antipornography Breakthrough in the Law," *Ms.*, May-June 1992, p. 14 and "Porn mutilates women's fight for equality," *Toronto Star*, 11 June 1991, p. F1. Jeff Sallot, "Legal victory bittersweet," *Globe and Mail*, 29 Feb. 1992, p. A6. In "Supreme Court porn ruling is ignored," *Toronto Star*, 14 Dec. 1993, p. D1, Michele Landsberg writes that "MacKinnon triumphed by having her views embedded in the language of the Butler decision."

36 John Duffy, "Masturbation and Clitoridectomy: A Nineteenth Century View," *Journal of the American Medical Association*, 19 Oct. 1963, pp. 166-68 and Alex Comfort, *The Anxiety Makers: Some Curious Preoccupations of the Medical Profession* (London: Thomas Nelson and Sons Ltd., 1967), pp. 98-104.

37 *Time* article reported in Wendy Dennis, *Hot and Bothered: Sex and Love in the Nineties* (Toronto: Seal Books, 1992), p. 227.

38 Mark Edwards, "Sex in the 90s," *Arena*, Spring 1993, p. 64. (Survey was conducted jointly with *New Woman*). *Details/Mademoiselle* survey reported in Rene Denfeld, *The New Victorians* (New York: Warner Books, 1995), pp. 258-59.

39 Val Ross, "Labours of love," *Globe and Mail*, 11 Feb. 1995, p. C1.

40 Gloria Steinem, "Women in the Dark: of Sex Goddesses, Abuse, and Dreams," *Ms.*, Jan.-Feb. 1991, p. 35.

41 Ibid., p. 35.

42 Kathleen Morgan, *Heart's Surrender* (New York: Pinnacle Books, 1994), p. 94.

43 Heather Graham, *A Pirate's Pleasure* (New York: Dell, 1989), pp. 20 and 22.

44 Katharine Kincaid, *Beloved Bondage* (New York: Zebra Books, 1993), pp. 5, 28, 63 and 129.

45 Susan Johnson, *Pure Sin* (New York: Bantam Books, 1994), p. 233.

46 Gloria Steinem, *Revolution from Within: A Book of Self-Esteem* (Boston: Little, Brown, 1992), p. 260.

47 Catharine A. MacKinnon, "Feminism, Marxism, Method, and the State: Toward feminist jurisprudence," *Feminism and Methodology*, Sandra Harding, ed. (Bloomington, Indiana: Indiana University Press, 1987), p. 144.

48 See Ann Landers, *Toronto Star*, 7 Sept. 1995, p. C2. Michelle Shephard, "30% of Canadians tell poll chocolate better than sex," *Toronto Star*, 30 Sept. 1995, p. L3.

49 Canadian Panel on Violence Against Women, *Changing the Landscape*, Minister of Supply and Services Canada, 1993, p. 51. See also Catharine A. MacKinnon, *Toward a Feminist Theory of the State* (Cambridge, Massachusetts: Harvard University Press, 1989), p. 138 and Ms., Jan.-Feb. 1994, pp. 37 and 42.

50 John de St. Jorry, "The unmasking of O," *New Yorker*, 1 Aug. 1994, pp. 42-50.

51 Carole S. Vance, "Epilogue," *Pleasure and Danger: Exploring Female Sexuality*, Carol S. Vance, ed. (Boston: Routledge & Kegan Paul, 1984), p. 433.

52 Wendy Dennis, *Hot and Bothered* (Toronto: Seal Books, 1992), p. 187.

53 Ibid., pp. 15-16 and 225.

54 Ibid., p. 190.

55 Diana E.H. Russell, *Rape in Marriage* (New York: Macmillan Publishing Co., 1982), pp. 156-66. See also Robin Warshaw, *I Never Called It Rape* (New York: Harper & Row, 1988), p. 44.

56 Sarah Crichton, "Sexual correctness: has it gone too far?" *Newsweek*, 25 Oct. 1993, p. 54.

57 Catharine A. MacKinnon, "Liberalism and the Death of Feminism," *The Sexual Liberals and the Attack on Feminism*, Dorchen Leidholdt and Janice G. Raymond, eds. (New York: Pergamon Press, 1990), p. 9.

58 Catharine A. MacKinnon, *Toward a Feminist Theory of the State* (Cambridge, Massachusetts: Harvard University Press, 1989), p. 202 and "Where Do We Stand on Pornography?" Ms., Jan.-Feb. 1994, p. 34.

59 Nadine Strossen, *Defending Pornography* (New York: Scribner, 1995), pp. 149-51 and 168.

60 Ibid., p. 104.

61 See D. Laframboise, "Another look at Playboy," *Toronto Star*, 27 Mar. 1995, p. A19.

Chapter Eight

1 "The Perils of Touching" (editorial), *Globe and Mail*, 18 Aug. 1995, p. A14.

2 Ontario Human Rights Complaints 60-926M, 60-9267M, 60-028M. See also D. Laframboise, "Anti-porn crusade victimizes 3 stores," *Toronto Star*, 5 July 1993, p. A17 and James Wallace, Christie Blatchford and Tracy Nesdoly, "Skin Deep: Human Rights porno fiasco," *Toronto Sun*, 18 Apr. 1993, pp. 7, 46-47.

3 Lynda Ackroyd, "Case Summary" (first), Human Rights Commission, undated, p. 4.

4 Ontario Human Rights Complaints 60-926M, 60-9267M, 60-028M.

5 James Wallace, Christie Blatchford and Tracy Nesdoly, "Skin Deep: Human Rights porno fiasco," *Toronto Sun*, 18 Apr. 1993, pp. 7 and 47.

6 Lynda Ackroyd, "Case Summary" (first), Human Rights Commission, undated and Owen Mahoney, Case Analysis, 15 Aug. 1995.

7 Letter to Four Star Variety, from Daniel E. Pascoe, Registrar, Ontario Human Rights Commission, 12 Jan. 1993, p. 1.

8 "In the matter of the Complaints of P. Findlay dated April 15, 1988 and M. McKay dated April 13, 1988, alleging discrimination against women against Mike's Smoke and Gifts and Mr. Soon Hwan Kim, Jug Mart and Four Star Variety," (official transcript), Vol. 3, p. 24.

9 James Wallace, Christie Blatchford and Tracy Nesdoly, "Skin Deep: Human Rights porno fiasco," *Toronto Sun*, 18 Apr. 1993, p. 7.

10 "Board dismisses magazine complaint," *Toronto Star*, 26 Oct. 1993, p. C1 and "Inquiry halts probe of explicit magazines," *Toronto Star*, 24 Oct. 1993, p. A16.

11 Written decision by Loretta Mikus, 22 Oct. 1993, pp. 16 and 25.

12 See Howard Levitt, "Human Rights Commission failing to attack workplace discrimination," *Toronto Star*, 6 Nov. 1995, p. C3.

13 Lynda Ackroyd, "Case Summary" (first), Human Rights Commission, undated, p. 2 and James Wallace, Christie Blatchford and Tracy Nesdoly, "Skin Deep: Human Rights porno fiasco," *Toronto Sun*, 18 Apr. 1993, p. 46.

14 Letter to Peter Israel, legal representative of Four Star Variety, from Fern Gaspar, Ontario Human Rights Commission, 20 Mar. 1995. Letter to Ontario Human Rights Commission from Peter Israel, 17 Feb. 1995. Owen Mahoney, Case Analysis, 15 Aug. 1995, p. 1. Letter to Peter Israel, from the Ontario Human Rights Commission, 16 Aug. 1995.

15 Ontario Human Rights Commission Respondent Questionnaire, completed by Peter Kwon, 28 July 1988.

16 *Human Rights Code*, Revised Statutes of Ontario, 1990, Chapter H.19, Section 41, article 1 (b).

17 "In the matter of the Complaints of P. Findlay dated April 15, 1988 and M. McKay dated April 13, 1988, alleging discrimination against women against Mike's Smoke and Gifts and Mr. Soon Hwan Kim, Jug Mart and Four Star Variety" (official transcript), Vol. 3, pp. 27 and 59. On p. 22, Geri Sanson, representing the Human Rights Commission, says: "The Commission requests that both complainants' names not be published, nor any other identifying circumstances which would enable a member of the public to identify the claimants."

18 Lynda Ackroyd, "Case Summary" (first), Human Rights Commission, undated, p. 4. Reva Landau, "Bread, milk and pornography," *Toronto Star*, 22 Feb. 1994, p. A21.

19 Owen Mahoney, Case Analysis, 15 Aug. 1995, p. 6.

20 Andrea Dworkin, *Woman Hating* (New York: E.P. Dutton, 1974), p. 184.

21 Andrea Dworkin, *Intercourse* (New York: Free Press, 1987), p. 137.

22 Peter Hamill, "Women on the Verge of a Legal Breakdown," *Playboy*, Jan. 1993, p. 187.

23 Andrea Dworkin, *Letters from a War Zone* (New York: E.P. Dutton, 1988), pp. 119 and 176.

24 Andrea Dworkin, "The Unremembered: Searching for women at the Holocaust Memorial Museum," Ms., Nov.-Dec. 1994, p. 52. Andrea Dworkin, "Israel: Whose Country is it Anyway?" Ms., Sept.-Oct. 1990, p. 2. "What Writers are Reading," Ms., Sept.-Oct. 1991, p. 76 and July-Aug. 1991, p. 82. See also Ms., July-Aug. 1994, p. 9 and Sept.-Oct. 1994, p. 75.

25 Michele Landsberg, "Real story behind call by feminist to 'kill men,'" *Toronto Star*, 21 May 1991, p. C1. Canadian Press, "Activist wants wife-beaters jailed—'or killed,'" *Toronto Star*, 13 May 1991, p. A1.

26 Andrea Dworkin, *Pornography: Men Possessing Women* (New York: Pedigree Books, 1981), p. 222-23.

27 Ann Jones, "Books: backlash and beyond," *Ms.*, Jan.-Feb. 1992, p. 58.

28 Sheila Jeffreys, "Sexology and Antifeminism," *The Sexual Liberals and the Attack on Feminism*, Dorchen Leidholdt and Janice G. Raymond, eds. (New York: Pergamon Press, 1990), pp. 21-22. See also Ellen Carol DuBois and Linda Gordon, "Seeking Ecstasy on the Battlefield: Danger and Pleasure in Nineteenth-century Feminist Sexual Thought," *Pleasure and Danger*, Carole S. Vance, ed. (Boston: Routledge & Kegan Paul, 1984), pp. 31-49.

29 Nadine Strossen, *Defending Pornography: Free Speech, Sex, and the Fight for Women's Rights* (New York: Scribner, 1995), p. 127.

30 Ibid., pp. 26-27.

31 Ibid., p. 28.

32 Ruth Shalil, "Sexual harassment hits the sandbox," *Globe and Mail*, 10 Apr. 1993, p. D1. (Reprinted from *The New Republic*.)

33 Nadine Strossen, *Defending Pornography* (New York: Scribner, 1995), p. 22.

34 Ibid., p. 134.

35 *Employers Guide: A Time for Action on Sexual Harassment in the Workplace*, Ontario Women's Directorate, Feb. 1993, p. 1.

36 Christina Hoff Sommers, *Who Stole Feminism? How Women Have Betrayed Women* (New York: Simon & Schuster, 1995), p. 186.

37 Quoted in Nadine Strossen, *Defending Pornography* (New York: Scribner, 1995), p. 122.

38 Camille Paglia, *Sex, Art, and American Culture* (New York: Vintage Books, 1992), p. 47.

39 Katie Roiphe, *The Morning After: Sex, Fear and Feminism* (Boston: Back Bay Books, 1993), p. 162. See also *Ms.*, Jan.-Feb. 1993, p. 89.

40 Canadian Panel on Violence Against Women, *Changing the Landscape: Ending Violence—Achieving Equality*, final report, Minister of Supply and Services Canada, 1993, p. 3. See also *Ms.*, Sept.-Oct. 1990, p. 34 and July-Aug. 1991, p. 1 (editorial).

41 John Fekete, *Moral Panic: Biopolitics rising* (Montreal: Robert Davies Publishing, 1994), p. 323.

42 Canadian Panel on Violence Against Women, *Changing the Landscape*, Minister of Supply and Services Canada, 1993, pp. xiii-xiv, etc.

43 Eric Schlosser, "Marijuana and the Law," *The Atlantic Monthly*, Sept. 1994, p. 90.

44 See Editorial, *New York Times*, 11 Oct. 1993, p. A16; George F. Will, "Sex Amidst Semicolons," *Newsweek*, 4 Oct. 1993, p. 92; Jeff Giles, "There's a Time for Talk, and a Time for Action," *Newsweek*, 7 Mar. 1994, p. 54.

45 Tracey Tyler, "US feminist applauds Canada's rape-law plan," *Toronto Star*, 17 Feb. 1992, p. A3.

46 Marlys Edwardh, quoted in Geoffrey York, "Lawyers oppose proposed rape law," *Globe and Mail*, 15 May 1992, p. A3.

47 Sean Fine, "No-means-no law still misunderstood," *Globe and Mail*, 31 May 1995, p. A1.

48 *Some important things for men to know about sex and dating*. Funded "by the Ministry of Colleges and Universities as part of the Government of Ontario interministerial initiative on sexual assault."

49 Katie Roiphe, *The Morning After* (Boston: Back Bay Books, 1993), pp. 59-60.

50 Robin Warshaw, *I Never Called It Rape* (New York: Harper & Row, 1988), p. 2.

51 Mary Koss, Letter to the editor, *Wall Street Journal*, 25 July 1991, p. A9.

52 Dale Brazao, "Lap dancing crosses line from striptease to sleaze," *Toronto Star*, 5 Aug. 1995, p. A16. Layton's wife and fellow Metro councillor, Olivia Chow, said of lap dancing a few days earlier, "I would call it rape; you can't call it anything else." Quoted in Gail Swinson, "Metro may ban lap dancing," *Toronto Star*, 1 Aug. 1995, first and last page of A section.

53 Camille Paglia, *Sex, Art, and American Culture* (New York: Vintage Books, 1992), p. 5. See also *Ms.*, May-June 1991, p. 61.

54 Deborah Wilson, "Judge's remarks raise storm," *Toronto Star*, 27 Apr. 1991, p. A4.

55 Robin Warshaw, *I Never Called It Rape* (New York: Harper & Row, 1988), p. 63.

56 Ibid., p. 154. See also p. 42.

57 *Some important things for men to know about sex and dating* and *Some important things for women to know about sex and dating*. Funded "by the Ministry of Colleges and Universities as part of the Government of Ontario interministerial initiative on sexual assault."

58 Robin Warshaw, *I Never Called It Rape* (New York: Harper & Row, 1988), p. 140.

59 Michele Landsberg, "Rape shield law offered protection," *Toronto Star*, 10 Sept. 1991, p. D1.

60 Jack Kammer, "The Other Kind of Rape: An interview with rape-trial lawyer Rikki Klieman," *Balance*, Fall 1994, pp. 18-21.

61 Canadian Centre for Justice Statistics, *Juristat*, Vol. 14, No. 7, March 1994, p. 10.

62 Eugene J. Kanin, "False Rape Allegations," *Archives of Sexual Behaviour*, Vol. 23, No. 1, 1994, p. 88.

63 Ibid., pp. 85-87.

64 D. Laframboise, "Schools should teach girls to stop being passive," *Toronto Star*, 12 May 1992, p. A19. Mary Lui, Letter to the editor, "Women tired of taking the blame," *Toronto Star*, 20 May 1992, p. A18.

65 Katie Roiphe, *The Morning After* (Boston: Back Bay Books, 1993), p. 101.

66 Camille Paglia, *Sex, Art, and American Culture* (New York: Vintage Books, 1992), p. 53.

Epilogue

1 Louis Menand, "The war of all against all," *New Yorker*, 14 Mar. 1994, p. 85.

2 Doris Lessing, *Prisons We Choose to Live Inside* (Toronto: CBC Enterprises, 1986), p. 34.

3 Susan Crean, "Writing along Gender Lines," *Language in Her Eye: Writing and Gender*, Libby Scheier, Sarah Sheard and Eleanor Wachtel, eds. (Toronto: Coach House Press, 1990), p. 83.

4 Dates from "A Selected Chronology of Women and Work in Canada," *Women's History Month*, Canadian Committee on Women's History, Government of Canada, Oct. 1993, pp. 8-12 and *Towards Equality for Women*, Status of Women Canada, 1983.

5 Nadine Crenshaw, *Edin's Embrace* (New York: Zebra Books, 1989), p. 221.

6 Catharine A. MacKinnon, "Liberalism and the Death of Feminism," *The Sexual Liberals and the Attack on Feminism*, Dorchen Leidholdt and Janice G. Raymond, eds. (New York: Pergamon Press, 1990), p. 5.

7 Ibid., pp. 5-6.

8 Ibid., p. 13.

9 Ibid., p. 7.

10 Vaclav Havel, "On Evasive Thinking," *Open Letters* (London: Faber and Faber, 1991), pp. 10-11.

11 Ibid., p. 12.

Index

aboriginal peoples 4, 95-96, 146, 152, 170-171, 264

abortion 5, 33, 44, 60, 136, 148, 152-153, 183, 233-234, 275, 283, 293, 298-299, 317

abuse, child *see* child abuse

abuse, psychological 64

abuse, verbal 43

Advocate, The 139

AIDS/HIV 138, 155

alcohol 16, 18, 53, 93-94, 97, 151, 170-171, 237, 272-273, 298

Alcott, Louisa May 218

American Anorexia and Bulimia Association 115

American Civil Liberties Union 293

American Civil War 113-114, 316

American Psychiatric Association 51, 58, 59

amytal, sodium 49, 53, 61-63

anger/rage as a political virtue 74-75, 132-134

anorexia and bulimia 84, 101, 111, 115-116

Anticlimax: A Feminist Perspective on the Sexual Revolution 290

Antioch College, Ohio 299

apartheid 170

Aquinas, Thomas 5

Aristotle 5

Association of American Colleges 163

Atwood, Margaret 144-145, 213

Aury, Dominique 267

automobiles and men 99, 224

backlash 7-9, 39, 73, 86, 91, 137, 142-143, 178, 182, 236

Backlash: The Undeclared War Against American Women 128, 189, 225

Bart, Pauline 163

Bass, Ellen 73

battered women's shelters *see* crisis centres

Beauty Myth, The 26, 99, 111, 115, 262

Berkeley 162

Berlin Wall 324

Berlin, Isaiah 133, 274-275

Bible, the 35, 252

birth control 101, 204, 271, 309, 314-315, 320

birth defects and domestic violence 116-117

Blue Sky 213-214, 219

Bly, Robert 178-179

Bolsheviks 319

bondage, sexual 240-244, 248, 253-255, 265, 267

Bosnia-Herzegovina 30

Boston University School of Law, 181

Boston Women's Health Collective 33, 274

Bourne, Caroline 249

Boyd, Marion 120

Brief History of Time, A 226

British Broadcasting Corporation (BBC) 203

Broadside 151

Brown, Laura S. 179

Budapest, Zsuzsanna 37, 167

Buel, Sarah 117

Butler (pornography) decision 25, 253-255

Callwood, June 155-157

Canada Customs 243, 271-272, 278

Canadian Bar Association 299

Canadian Civil Liberties Association 5, 155, 279

Canadian Mental Health Association 288

Canadian Panel on Violence Against Women 41-47, 55-56, 72, 92-95, 98, 119, 122, 154, 196, 212, 251-253, 265, 266, 295-296

Canadian Woman Studies 5

Canadians for Decency 279

capital punishment 283, 317

Caputi, Jane 170

causes of death, leading 105, 110, 169

censorship 24, 73, 136-137, 268, 273-274, 295, 348 note 28

Chicago Theological Seminary 292

child abuse, physical 56, 90, 172, 197-199, 237-238, 316

child abuse, sexual 20, 50-60, 62-63, 74-75, 77-80, 82-83, 161-162, 165, 172, 257, 269, 275, 316

child access 238

child care 134, 149-150, 153

child custody 23, 36-37, 172, 181, 235-238

child support 20, 21, 238

children and men 44, 232-238

chocolate versus sex 265

Chung, Connie 141

civil liberties 5, 155, 252, 274, 279, 293

Civil War, American 113-114, 316

Claiming of Sleeping Beauty, The 267

Clinton, Bill 113

clothing and gender 9-11, 93, 98-99, 111-112, 193, 218, 221, 319-320

Coalition of Visible Minority Women 146-147

Color Purple, The 102

Columbia University 77, 142

Committee Against the Deportation of Jamaican Women 151

Communism 4, 132, 322

condoms 34, 167, 213, 309

continuum theory 66, 295-296

contraception *see* birth control

convenience stores 40, 277-287, 291, 293

Cosmopolitan 286-287

Courage to Heal, The 73-75, 79, 95

Crean, Susan 235

Crichton, Sarah 118, 340, note 26

crime and gender 95-96

crime and race 91-92

crime victimization rates 106-107, 169-171, 319

Criminal Code, Canada 299, 314

crisis centres 76-79, 134, 148, 153, 155-157, 313, 316

Crittenden, Danielle 144

cult ritual abuse *see* Satanic ritual abuse

date rape 26, 140, 272, 300-304

Davis, Angela 151

Davis, Laura 73

Dear Abby 126-127, 219

death penalty 283, 317

Defending Pornography: Free Speech, Sex, and the Fight for Women's Rights 274, 293

Denfeld, Rene 8, 129, 134-135, 138-139, 146, 159

Dennis, Wendy 98, 180, 186, 200, 269-270

Dines, Gail 141

disabled, the 24, 56, 119, 148, 159

dissident feminists 8, 71, 94, 128, 134-135, 311

divorce 181, 231, 236

Dodson Gray, Elizabeth 170

domination and submission, sexual 240-251, 253-261, 263-271

drugs, illicit 30, 97, 192, 238, 298

Dworkin, Andrea 26, 274, 288-291

eating disorders *see* anorexia and bulimia

Ecole Polytechnique de Montreal *see* Montreal Massacre

education 39, 98, 101, 107-108, 119, 158, 169, 171, 203-204, 218

Edwardh, Marlys 353, note 46

Eisler, Riane 181

Eliot, George 203-205, 207, 212, 238-239, 290

Emon, Sergeant Randy 68-69

Emory University 158

emotions and men 93, 124, 193-194

employment and men 108-110, 171, 184, 215-218, 225-232, 239, 320

employment and women 20-21, 38, 108-110, 215, 230-231, 314-316, 320

employment attitudes, women bosses 6

Encyclopedia of Feminism, The 43

Engel, Beverly 75

environmental issues 4, 148, 177, 184

equal pay for equal work 195-196

Equal Rights Amendment 142

erotica 251, 256, 267-268

establishment feminists 8, 287, 311

ethnic cleansing 29-30

Evans, Don 292

Evans, Mary Ann 203

exotic dancers 32, 304-305

Fairstein, Linda 272

false allegations of rape and sexual abuse 81-85, 132, 172, 305, 307-310

Faludi, Susan 128-132, 134-138, 141, 163, 189, 225

family, traditional 3, 36, 55-56

Farrakhan, Louis 31

Farrell, Warren 104, 108-109, 114, 124, 182-191, 217, 229

Federal Bureau of Investigation (FBI) 66-67, 76, 118

Fekete, John 96, 106, 296

female sexuality 45, 184, 213, 254-255, 263, 265, 290-291, 312

feminism, definition of 8, 19

Feminists Against Censorship Task Force 137

Feminists for Free Expression 295

feminists, dissident 8, 71, 128, 134-135, 311

feminists, establishment 8, 287, 311

Findlay, Pat 277-287, 294

Fox-Genovese, Elizabeth 163

Fraser, Sylvia 55

French, Marilyn 19-25, 32, 45, 48, 54-55, 97, 111, 135, 139, 175, 235, 315

Freud, Sigmund 305, 328, note 42

Friedan, Betty 35, 105, 141, 215-216

Friedman, Amy 8, 89, 142-144

Garson, Marc 299-300

gay and lesbian issues 24, 34, 40, 56, 94-95, 146, 148, 150, 155, 158-159, 162, 165, 179, 253-254, 268, 274, 290, 312

gender and military service 12, 23, 112-114, 169, 177, 190, 218

gender wage gap 101, 124, 126, 134

General Motors of Canada, Ltd. 154

genital mutilation 23, 97, 254

Gingrich, Newt 130, 136

Globe and Mail 91, 146, 175, 187, 277, 299

Goddess in the Office, The 38

goddess worship 38, 134, 148

Goodman, Dr. Gail 67-68

Graham, Heather 259

Great Britain 68, 107, 182, 192, 197-198, 203

Gulf War 146

Hagan, Kay Leigh 34, 167, 172, 180

Hamilton Sexual Assault Centre 77-78

Harpur, Tom 201

Hart, Catherine 248

Harvard 117, 141

Havel, Vaclav 322-323

Hawking, Stephen 226

Hefner, Christie 276

Herizons 70-72, 77, 85-86

Higginbotham, Anastasia 221-222

Hill, Anita 25

HIV/AIDS 138, 155

Hoff Sommers, Christina 129, 130, 134-135, 159

Hollywood 257-258, 262, 264, 286

Holocaust Memorial Museum 37

Holocaust/Nazi analogy and gender issues 36-37, 70, 115-116, 139, 170, 177, 190-191

Home Box Office (HBO) 50, 63

homeless, the 56, 170-171, 319

homicide *see* murder

hooks, bell 168

Hostile Environment Sexual Harassment Program 292

Hot and Bothered: Sex and Love in the Nineties 98, 180, 269

House of Commons, Canada 88, 112

Human Right Commission, Ontario 278-287

I Never Called it Rape: The Ms. Report on Recognizing, Fighting and Surviving Date and Acquaintance Rape 301, 306-307

illicit drugs 30, 97, 192, 238, 298

Illinois Coalition Against Sexual Assault 65-66

incest *see* child abuse, sexual

Incest and Sexuality 75

income and gender 101, 124, 126, 134

infanticide 12, 197

infertility 149, 201

International Men's Day 181

International Society for the Study of Multiple Personality and Dissociation 63

International Women's Day 5, 146-147, 149-152

Internet 68, 161, 271

Invasion of the Body Snatchers 129

Iron John: A Book About Men 178

Jeffreys, Sheila 290-291

Jews 24, 37, 159, 173, 176

Jobs Related Almanac, The 109

Johnson, Joan 155-156

Johnson, Susan 249

Jong, Erica 240

Kanin, Eugene 308

Kempston Darkes, Maureen 154

Kennedy Smith, William 131

Kincaid, Katharine 260

Kinesis 332, note 37

Klieman, Rikki 308

Koertge, Noretta 8, 160-161, 164

Koss, Mary 303

Kristiansen, Connie M. 332, note 34

Krop, Dr. Harry 80

Kwon, Peter 282

Landau, Reva 283, 285

Landers, Ann 15-18, 40, 47, 81-83, 116, 118, 124-125, 194, 228-229, 233, 265

Landsberg, Michele 4, 288-289, 307-308, 332, note 34, 338, note 66, 349, note 35

Lanning, Supervisory Special Agent Kenneth 66-67, 69

lap-dancing 304-305

law schools 117, 143, 181, 319

Layton, Jack 304

Le Guin, Ursula 167

leading causes of death 105, 110, 169

Lees, David 120, 123

Legal Education Action Fund (LEAF) 254

legal system and sexism 181, 204, 235, 237-238

Lehrman, Karen 162-164

Leimonis, Georgina 87

Lepine, Marc 41, 88-89, 127

lesbian and gay issues 24, 34, 40, 56, 94-95, 146, 148, 150, 155, 158-159, 162, 165, 179, 253-254, 268, 273-274, 290, 312

Lessing, Doris 15, 132-133, 313

life spans and gender/race 105, 169-171, 192, 312, 319

Lindsey, Johanna 244, 247

Little Women 218, 225-226

Los Angeles County Commission for Women 65

Lupri, Eugene 120

MacKenzie, Gordene O. 170

MacKinnon, Catharine A. 25-33, 40, 45, 48, 56, 61, 99, 135, 139, 251, 253-254, 263, 273-274, 288, 290-291, 299, 315, 317-319

MacKinnon, Catharine A. and feminist intolerance 32-33, 137-138

MacKinnon, Catharine A. and Ms. 26, 29, 31

MacKinnon, Catharine A. and sexual assault 26-29, 31-32, 287

MacKinnon, Catharine A., degree of influence 25-26, 254, 291, 299

Madonna 138-139, 290

male sexuality 287, 290-291, 294

Mamonova, Tatyana 324

Mandela, Nelson, 102

Mandela, Winnie 102

March of Dimes 116-117

marriage 185-186, 212, 288

McKay, Marty 277-287, 294

McManiman, John 174

McNeill, Elizabeth 267

media, the 39, 144, 180, 235, 280, 283, 304, 310, 322

medicine and alleged gender bias 105-106

Meese Pornography Commission 253

men and automobiles 99, 224

men and children 44, 232-238

men and emotions 93, 124, 193-194

men and employment 108-110, 171, 184, 215-218, 225-232, 239, 320

men and power 46-47, 92, 203-239

men, Afghani 22

men, Kenyan 22

men's movement 167-172, 176-177, 179-181

Menand, Louis 313

mental health care 50, 52-54, 59, 61-62, 79, 86, 165

Middlemarch 203-212, 219, 290

Miles, Tiya 158

military service and gender 12, 23, 112-114, 169, 177, 190, 218

Minneapolis Hostile Environment Sexual Harassment Program 292

Montreal Massacre 41, 88, 126, 127, 174

Moral Panic: Biopolitics Rising 96

Morgan, Kathleen 258

Morgan, Robin 137-140

Morning After: Sex, Fear and Feminism, The 129

Mother Jones 162-163

MPD: The Search for Deadly Memories 52

Ms. 33-38, 45, 73, 102, 111, 123, 145, 158, 169, 181, 189, 221, 256, 302-304

Ms. and feminist extremists 25-26, 29-31, 34, 36-37, 288, 290

Ms. and feminist intolerance 128-132, 134-138

Ms. and pornography 136-140

Ms. and Satanic ritual abuse 64-65

Ms. Foundation 111, 301

Mulhern, Sherrill 69

multiple personality disorder 50-52, 54, 57-62, 70, 73, 76-78, 85, 165, 257, 258

murder 46, 106, 177, 197

murder mysteries 269, 276

Myth of Male Power, The 108-109, 181-191

National Action Committee on the Status of Women 3, 147, 149-150, 154

National Association for the Advancement of Colored People 146

National Association for the Advancement of White People 170

National Center on Child Abuse and Neglect 67

National Film Board of Canada 272

National Organization for Women 3, 26, 182, 293

National Rifle Association 117

National Victim Center 118

National Women's Studies Association 158-160

native issues 4, 95-96, 152, 170-171, 264

Nazi/Holocaust analogy and gender issues 36-37, 70, 115-116, 139, 170, 177, 190-191

Nellies Women's Shelter 155-157

New Victorians: A Young Woman's Response to the Old Feminist Order, The 129

New York City 87, 94, 140, 142, 157, 182

New York Times 25, 175, 192, 247

New York University Law School 319

Newsweek 118, 141

9 1/2 Weeks: A Memoir of a Love Affair 267-268

"No" Means "No" slogan 305-307

North American Indians 4, 95-96, 152, 170-171, 264

Not a Love Story 4, 272

Not Guilty: In Defence of the Modern Man 182, 191-200

Nothing Sacred: A Conversation with Feminism 142

occupational injuries and fatalities 108, 169, 190

occupational role models, female 111

Oka Crisis 146

Only Words 253

Ontario Criminal Lawyers' Association 80

Ontario government 119, 187, 277, 353, note 35

Ontario Human Rights Code 293

Ontario Human Rights Commission 278-287

Our Bodies, Ourselves 4, 34, 274

Outrageous Acts and Everyday Rebellions 4

Overeaters Anonymous 126

Paglia, Camille 8, 94, 129, 134, 139-140, 160, 163, 188, 290, 295, 305-306, 311

Panel on Violence Against Women *see* Canadian Panel on Violence Against Women

Parliament, Canadian 88, 112

Pasley, Laura 83-85

Patai, Daphne 8, 160-161, 164

peace activism 5, 183

Pennsylvania State University 292

Penthouse 255, 266, 271-272, 277, 286

Philippines 25, 30

Planned Parenthood 293

Playboy 39-40, 215, 255, 265-266, 277, 286, 293

Playboy Enterprises Inc. 276

Playgirl 286

Pogrebin, Letty Cottin 110-111, 169, 236

police 39, 57, 62, 76, 197-198, 282, 299, 308, 314

popular culture 7, 20, 39, 130

pornographic models 32-33, 61

pornography 25, 28, 30-32, 39-40, 73, 136-138, 178, 251-252, 255, 265-266, 271-287, 289, 293, 295

pornography and Islamic countries 28

pornography and racism 265-266

pornography and violence 28-32, 136-137, 251-253, 272-273, 289

pornography in convenience stores 40, 277-287, 291-293

pornography, Vance's One Third Rule 268, 275

Pornography: Men Possessing Women 289

power and men 46-47, 92, 203-239

power and women 23, 46-47, 205-206, 208-209, 212-213, 215-217, 219-224, 239, 264-265, 307

power, sexual 218-224, 307

pregnancy 200-201, 204, 230, 232-233, 263, 275, 289

Premenstrual Syndrome (PMS) 184

Princeton 141

prisons 30, 170-171, 298, 318-319

Prisons We Choose to Live Inside 132

privacy 55-56

pro-choice activism 44, 148, 152-153, 183, 275, 283

Professing Feminism: Cautionary Tales from the Strange World of Women's Studies 160

Prohibition 272-273
pro-lifers 33, 283
prostate cancer funding 190
prostitution 12, 30-33, 137, 155, 238
psychiatric patients 155
psychological abuse 64
Public Broadcasting Service (PBS) 113, 203
public opinion 3, 6, 40, 253
publication bans, media 280, 283
Quayle, Dan 113, 130
Quick, Amanda 247
Quinn, Sally 340, note 23
race analogy and gender 169-171, 173-174
race and crime 87-89
race and pornography 265-266
racial issues 5, 56, 91, 119, 142-162, 171, 220, 264
Radcliffe Richards, Janet 49, 128, 167
Radford Ruether, Rosemary 170
rage/anger as a political virtue 35-36, 74-75, 132-134
rape see sexual assault
rape crisis centres see crisis centres
rape fantasies 241-245, 247-249, 255, 265, 269-270
Reagan, Ronald 130, 298
Reage, Pauline 267
recovered/repressed memories 50, 63-65, 73, 76-78, 165
religion 4, 5, 39, 138, 262, 269-270, 293
Repo, Marjaleena 71-72
Report of the Royal Commission on the Status of Women 57
repressed/recovered memories 50, 63-65, 73, 76-78, 165
reproductive technologies 149
Revolution from Within 115, 263
Rice, Anne 267
Rich, Adrienne 35
Rich, Mary Lou 247
Richards, Janet Radcliffe 49
Right to Innocence, The 75
right wing thought 5, 128, 130-131, 165, 191, 312
rights versus responsibilities 98, 114
ritual abuse see Satanic ritual abuse

Robards, Karen 247

Roiphe, Katie 8, 129, 130, 134-135, 141-142, 163, 251, 295, 301, 311

Rolling Stones 223

romance novels 240-251, 255-256, 258-267, 276

Romantic Times 247

Roquelaure, A.N. 267

Royal Commission on the Status of Women, Report of 57

RU 486 (abortion pill) 136

Ruether, Rosemary Radford 170

Russell, Diana 272

San Francisco Family Violence Prevention Fund 117

Satanic ritual abuse 63-72, 76-77, 82, 165, 312

Saudi Arabia 5, 102

Schlafly, Phyllis 130, 139

Secret Survivors 75

self mutilation 52, 62, 70

self-defence instruction 5, 301, 310

self-esteem and girls 107, 111

Sex, Art, and American Culture 129

sexism in the courtroom 204, 235, 237-238

sexual abuse *see* child abuse, sexual

sexual assault 6, 12, 140-141, 177, 296-305, 310-312, 316, 323

sexual assault and alcohol 272

sexual assault and Catharine A. MacKinnon 26-29, 31-32, 287

sexual assault and Ms. 36-37, 134, 137, 140, 302, 304

sexual assault and power 187-188

sexual assault *see also* crisis centres

sexual assault *see also* false allegations

sexual assault *see also* pornography and violence

sexual domination and submission 240-251, 253-261, 263-271

sexual harassment 3, 25-26, 107, 119, 134, 137, 141, 199, 280-281, 291-296, 310-311

Sexual Personae 129

sexual power 219-224, 307

sexuality, female 45, 184, 213, 254-255, 263, 265, 290-291, 312

sexuality, male 287, 290-291, 294

sexually transmitted disease 138, 155, 270

shelters *see* crisis centres

single motherhood 101, 155

Skeptic 83

Smith, Susan 90, 176
social assistance programs 101, 177, 219, 317
sodium amytal 49, 53, 61-63
Sommer, Reena 122
Sommers, Christina Hoff 8, 116-118, 139-141
South Africa 170, 175-176
Soviet Union 324
Star Wars 35
Starhawk 170, 173, 177, 179
Statistics Canada 107, 119, 152, 308
Status of Women Canada 42
Steed, Judy 70, 343, note 11
Steinem, Gloria 4, 115, 135, 167-169, 171-172, 180, 189, 190, 263
Steinem, Gloria and feminist extremists 24-25, 167-168
Steinem, Gloria and feminist intolerance 139-141
Steinem, Gloria and repressed memories/multiple personality disorder 52, 54,
    57-62, 75, 79, 85, 333, note 44
Steinem, Gloria and sexual fantasies/abuse 256-258
stereotypes and men 44, 88-90, 201
Story of O 267
strippers 32, 304-305
Strossen, Nadine 274, 293
suffrage 203, 239, 313-316
suicide 62, 103-105, 127, 169-171, 184, 192, 312, 319
Supreme Court of Canada 25, 110, 253-255, 313-314
Supreme Court, U.S. 34
Sweden 25, 102
Sybil 51
Take Our Daughters to Work Day 111
Talmud, the 292
Tavris, Carol 75, 76
tennis 195-196
Thailand 30
therapy 50-53, 59-70, 82, 84-85, 312
Thobani, Sunera 152-154
Thomas, Clarence 25, 38, 130, 141
Thomas, David 182, 191-200, 218
Three Faces of Eve, The 51-52
Time 116-117, 255, 308
Toronto 80, 87, 107, 181, 277, 304, 308, 321

Toronto Board of Education 107-108

Toronto Life 156

Toronto Star 5, 152, 174, 190, 201

Toronto Sun 281

Toward a Feminist Theory of the State 26

traditional family 3, 36, 55-56

truth serum 49, 53, 62-63, 79

TVOntario 50

U.S. Navy 199

United Way 77

University of Calgary 120

University of Iowa 162

University of Nebraska 292

University of Toronto 4, 133

Vamps and Tramps 129

Van Buren, Abigail 125-126, 219

Vance, Carole 268

Vancouver 91, 306

Vanderbilt University 292

verbal abuse 43

videotapes, explicit 29-30, 40, 50, 136, 243, 252-253, 255, 266, 268, 270-271

Vietnam war 112-114

violence against men, 18, 22, 45-46, 94-95, 106, 121-127, 172, 184, 212

violence against women 5, 16, 20-22, 28-31, 41-48, 77, 93-95, 99-100, 104, 118-127, 252, 257, 310

violence against women *see also* Canadian Panel on Violence Against Women

violence against women *see also* sexual assault

violence committed by women 45-46, 94-95, 121-127, 172, 184, 212

violence *see also* pornography and violence

violence statistics 106-107, 118-119, 168-171, 302, 319

violence victimization rates by gender 106-107

violence, domestic - lesbian battering 94-95

violence, domestic 3, 36-37, 43, 45-46, 57, 94-95, 101, 116-117, 119-126, 134, 137, 172, 177, 181, 184, 197-198, 212, 219, 272, 315-316

violence, domestic and birth defects 116-117

violence, domestic and children 43

Vonnegut, Kurt 226-228

voting rights 203, 239, 313-316

wage gap, *see* gender wage gap

Walker, Alice 102, 142

Wall Street Journal 303
War Against Women, The 19-25, 97, 175, 235
Washington Post 141, 188
Wayman, Tom 190-191
White, Eve 51
Whitehead, Caroline 117
Who Stole Feminism? How Women Have Betrayed Women 116, 129
Why Men are the Way they Are 188
Wife Assault Prevention Month 120
Wilde, Jane 226
witches 36, 38
Wolf, Naomi 26, 99-100, 111, 115, 134-135, 262
women and employment 20-21, 38, 108-110, 215, 230-231, 314-316, 320
women and power 23, 46-47, 205-206, 208-209, 212-213, 215-217, 219-224,
   239, 264-265, 307
women as a majority of the electorate 41, 178
Women in the Media conference 144
Women of Colour Caucus 155-156
Women Respond to the Men's Movement 167-168, 180, 188, 201, 213, 236
women, African 23
women, immigrant and refugee 43, 80
women, Iranian 151
women, Saudi Arabian 5
Women's Action Committee (WAC) 157-158
Women's Room, The 19
women's studies 4-5, 26, 47, 142, 160-165, 183, 186-187
Woolf, Virginia 203
World Health Organization 51
World War I 114
World War II 114-115, 185, 313
Young Offenders Act, Canada 296
young women and feminism 37
Yugoslavia 29
zero tolerance 296-299